ST. LOUIS

BROOKE S. FOSTER

Contents

Maps

DR. MARTIN LUTHER KING JR DR

DELMAR BLVD

City Museum

LINDEN ST

LUCAS AVE

ST. CHARLES ST

LOCUST ST

WASHINGTON AVE

OLIVE ST

Lucas Gardens

SEE MAP 2

OLIVE ST

Campbell House Museum

PINE ST

CHESTNUT ST

MARKET ST

Union Station

Memorial

EUGENIA ST

Plaza

DOWNTOWN

Union Station

CLARK AVE

Scottrade Center

WALNUT ST

Civic Center

CLARK AVE

SPRUCE ST

64

CERRE ST

GRATIOT ST

CHOUTEAU AVE

LEBANON DR

LASALLE ST

HICKORY ST

DILLON DR

© AVALON TRAVEL

SIGHTS
1 CITY MUSEUM
8 CAMPBELL HOUSE MUSEUM
25 EADS BRIDGE
28 UNION STATION

33 OLD POST OFFICE
37 OLD COURTHOUSE
39 GATEWAY ARCH
42 EUGENE FIELD HOUSE & TOY MUSEUM

RESTAURANTS
6 WASABI
9 SEN THAI ASIAN BISTRO
12 CIELO
15 ROOSTER
17 KITCHEN K

34 THE EDIBLE DIFFERENCE
35 MIKE SHANNON'S STEAKS & SEAFOOD
45 THE CEDARS AT ST. RAYMOND'S MARONITE CATHEDRAL

NIGHTLIFE
5 RUE 13
22 SKYBOX SPORTS BAR AND GRILL
24 MORGAN STREET BREWERY

43 B.B.'S JAZZ, BLUES, & SOUPS
44 BROADWAY OYSTER BAR

ARTS AND LEISURE
2 ST. LOUIS WALKING TOURS
4 PHILIP SLEIN GALLERY
7 ST. LOUIS BLACK REP
11 ST. LOUIS RAMS

20 ROBERTS ORPHEUM
26 UPPER LIMITS ROCK CLIMBING GYM
29 BIKE ST. LOUIS
30 ST. LOUIS BLUES
41 ST. LOUIS CARDINALS

SHOPS
3 MARTE SHOES
10 PAPER DOLLS

16 URBAN MATERIALS + ACCESSORIES (UMA)
18 THE TIME

HOTELS
13 FOUR SEASONS ST. LOUIS
14 HOTELUMIÈRE
19 THE ROBERTS MAYFAIR
21 RENAISSANCE GRAND
23 HAMPTON INN
27 HYATT REGENCY

31 SHERATON ST. LOUIS CITY CENTER
32 OMNI MAJESTIC
36 HILTON ST. LOUIS AT THE BALLPARK
38 DRURY PLAZA HOTEL
40 WESTIN ST. LOUIS

COLE ST

CONVENTION PLAZA

Edward
Jones
Dome
11 Ⓐ

70

CARR ST

12 Ⓡ 13
Ⓗ 14

N WHARF ST

VETERANS
MEMORIAL
BRIDGE

CONVENTION PLAZA

LUCAS AVE

DR. MARTIN LUTHER KING JR DR
Ⓝ 22

MARTIN
LUTHER
KING
BRIDGE

LUCAS AVE

17

18 Ⓖ
Ⓐ 20
19 Ⓗ

21 Ⓡ

LACLEDE'S
LANDING

DELMAR BLVD

Ⓝ 24

WASHINGTON AVE

LUCAS AVE

Ⓜ
Convention
Center

Ⓗ 23

Eads
Bridge

Old Post
Office
33 Ⓐ

OLIVE ST

LOCUST ST

Ⓜ
Arch-
Laclede's
Landing

WASHINGTON AVE

25

PINE ST

Ⓜ
8th &
Pine

Ⓡ 34

N LEONOR K SULLIVAN BLVD

CHESTNUT ST

Kiener

Ⓗ 38

Old Courthouse
37 Ⓐ

Ⓡ 35

36 Ⓗ

Plaza

MARKET ST

STADIUM PLAZA

WALNUT ST

Gateway
Arch
39 ✪

M I S S O U R I

I L L I N O I S

M i s s i s s i p p i

R i v e r

Stadium

41 Ⓐ
Busch
Stadium

CLARK AVE

70

Jefferson
National
Expansion
Memorial

SPRUCE ST

Eugene Field
House & Toy
Museum
Ⓐ 42

64

Ⓝ 43

POPLAR ST

Ⓝ 44

CEDAR ST

POPLAR
STREET
BRIDGE

55

55 64 70

TOMBARD ST

SEE MAP 3

0   200 yds

0   200 m

DISTANCE ACROSS MAP
Approximate: 1.7 mi or 2.8 km

0   500 yds
0   500 m
DISTANCE ACROSS MAP
Approximate: 3.5 mi or 5.6 km

Pickett Playground

ENRIGHT AVE
DELMAR BLVD
WASHINGTON PL
WESTMINSTER PL
WATERMAN BLVD

DEBALIVIERE PLACE

SEE MAP 6

PORTLAND PL
WESTMORELAND PL
LINDELL BLVD

UNION BLVD
LAKE AVE
ENRIGHT AVE
EUCLID AVE
AUBERT AVE
N EUCLID AVE
BAYARD AVE
WALTON AVE

D. BANKS AVE
W BELLE PL
ENRIGHT AVE

WASHINGTON BLVD

DELMAR BLVD
WASHINGTON BLVD

OLIVE ST

31 H

WESTMINSTER PL
McPHERSON AVE

N KINGSHIGHWAY BLVD
LENOX PL

1 R
5 S 2 N
S   3 R
S 6 S 4
S 8
PERSHING PL
S 9
N 10 14 N
11 S N 12
M A R R 13
15 16 17 S 18

MARYLAND PLAZA
MARYLAND AVE

19 S

20 R N 21
24 N
25 R 26

Barnes-Jewish Hospital North

St. Louis Children's Hospital

FOREST PARK PKWY

Forest Park

22 A

A 23

JEFFERSON DR
FAULKNER DR

S KINGSHIGHWAY BLVD

Barnes-Jewish Hospital South

M Central West End

McKINLEY AVE

28 ⊛
Cathedral Basilica

W PINE BLVD

W PINE BLVD
LACLEDE AVE

FOREST PARK AVE

N 27

29 30
R N

32 R

CENTRAL WEST END

N 33

TAYLOR AVE
NEWSTEAD AVE
BOYLE AVE
WHITTIER ST
SARAH ST

DUNCAN AVE

SARPY AVE

CLAYTON AVE

CLAYTON AVE

64

OAKLAND AVE

BERTHOLD AVE

WISE AVE

KINGS OAK

WISE AVE

SEE MAP 5

A 58

SWAN AVE

MACKLIND AVE
EAST RD
TAWN ST

OAKLAND AVE
WICHITA AVE
ARCO AVE
GIBSON AVE
CHOUTEAU AVE

FOREST PARK SOUTHEAST

MANCHESTER AVE

59 R

R 60

61 62 64
N N R
N 65
N 63

67

SWAN AVE
NORFOLK AVE
VISTA AVE
HUNT AVE

PAPIN ST
GRATIOT ST

S VANDEVENTER AVE

CENTRAL INDUSTRIAL AVE

BOTANICAL HEIGHTS

PARK AVE

THE HILL

FOLSOM AVE

PATTISON AVE
NORTHRUP AVE

MCREE AVE

44

S KINGSHIGHWAY BLVD

S VANDEVENTER AVE

SEE MAP 4

BLAINE AVE
MCREE AVE

SIGHTS
- 28 CATHEDRAL BASILICA
- 53 SCOTT JOPLIN HOUSE
- 57 ERNEST TROVA AT SAINT LOUIS UNIVERSITY

RESTAURANTS
- 1 DRESSEL'S PUB
- 3 LLYWELYN'S
- 13 COFFEE CARTEL
- 20 RASOI
- 25 CHEZ LEON
- 26 MOXY CONTEMPORARY BISTRO
- 29 THE GRIND
- 32 TERRENE
- 34 NADOZ
- 44 THE BEST STEAK HOUSE
- 46 VITO'S
- 50 PAPPY'S SMOKEHOUSE
- 51 THE U
- 54 SCHLAFLY TAP ROOM
- 59 FIVE
- 60 SWEETIE PIE'S
- 64 EVEREST CAFÉ AND BAR
- 67 REVIVAL

NIGHTLIFE
- 2 VIVA
- 10 SUB ZERO VODKA BAR
- 12 MANDARIN LOUNGE
- 14 BRENNAN'S WINE BAR AND CIGAR SHOP
- 15 CAFÉ EAU
- 21 34 CLUB
- 24 ROSIE'S PLACE
- 30 SOL
- 33 THE SCOTTISH ARMS
- 43 JAZZ AT THE BISTRO
- 47 CREEPY CRAWL
- 49 DANTE'S
- 52 SPRUILL'S
- 55 THE PEPPER LOUNGE
- 56 THE BILLIKEN CLUB
- 61 NOVAK'S
- 62 THE CHURCH KEY
- 63 ATOMIC COWBOY
- 65 ATTITUDES
- 66 JJ'S CLUBHOUSE
- 68 THE COMPLEX

ARTS AND LEISURE
- 16 CHASE PARK PLAZA THEATER
- 22 FOREST PARK
- 23 STEINBERG SKATING RINK
- 35 MOOLAH THEATRE & LOUNGE
- 36 CONTEMPORARY ART MUSEUM ST. LOUIS
- 37 BRUNO DAVID GALLERY
- 38 PULITZER CENTER FOR THE ARTS
- 39 SHELDON ART GALLERIES
- 39 SHELDON CONCERT HALL
- 40 FOX THEATRE
- 41 HOTCITY
- 42 POWELL SYMPHONY HALL
- 45 MUSEUM OF CONTEMPORARY RELIGIOUS ART
- 48 THE MOTO MUSEUM
- 58 WHITE FLAG PROJECTS

SHOPS
- 4 CENTRO MODERN FURNISHINGS
- 5 LEFT BANK BOOKS
- 6 ROTHSCHILD'S ANTIQUES AND HOME FURNISHINGS
- 7 MEZZANINE
- 8 WOLFGANG'S PET STOP
- 9 CASSIE'S FRAGRANCE BOUTIQUE AND SCENT BAR
- 11 MORIS FASHIONS
- 18 BIG SLEEP BOOKS
- 19 CENTRAL WEST END

HOTELS
- 17 CHASE PARK PLAZA
- 27 THE PARKWAY HOTEL
- 31 CENTRAL WEST END BED & BREAKFAST
- 69 MARRIOTT RESIDENCE INN

● SIGHTS
- 10 **C** SOULARD FARMERS MARKET
- 19 ANHEUSER-BUSCH BREWERY
- 26 **C** LEMP MANSION

● RESTAURANTS
- 3 ARCELIA'S MEXICANA RESTAURANT
- 4 **C** BAILEYS' CHOCOLATE BAR
- 9 FRANCO
- 13 NORTON'S CAFÉ
- 14 JOANIE'S PIZZERIA
- 16 **C** NICHE
- 20 LA VALLESANA
- 21 TAQUERÍA EL BRONCO
- 23 THE SHANGRI-LA DINER

● NIGHTLIFE
- 5 **C** 33 WINE SHOP & TASTING BAR
- 8 **C** OLD ROCK HOUSE
- 11 JOHN D. MCGURK'S
- 12 CLEMENTINE'S
- 15 THE WAY OUT CLUB
- 17 YEMANJA BRASIL
- 18 THE VENICE CAFÉ
- 27 **C** OFF BROADWAY

● ARTS AND LEISURE
- 1 LAFAYETTE PARK

● SHOPS
- 22 CHERRY BOMB VINTAGE
- 24 CHEROKEE STREET

● HOTELS
- 2 PARK AVENUE MANSION BED & BREAKFAST
- 6 NAPOLEON'S RETREAT
- 7 **C** DWELL 912
- 25 LEMP MANSION RESTAURANT & INN

SEE MAP 5

⭘ SIGHTS

2	MISSOURI BOTANICAL GARDEN	5	COMPTON HILL WATER TOWER
3	THE "ANCIENT RUINS" IN TOWER GROVE PARK	32	INTERNATIONAL INSTITUTE OF METROPOLITAN ST. LOUIS

⭘ RESTAURANTS

9	COURTESY DINER	33	GRBIC
14	THE SHAVED DUCK	35	STELLINA PASTA CAFÉ
19	CITY DINER	37	MOM'S DELI
20	MANGIA ITALIANO	41	MURDOCH PERK
22	KING & I	43	ONESTO
23	LEMONGRASS	47	EL BURRITO LOCO
25	BLACKTHORN PIZZA & PUB	48	IRON BARLEY
26	PHO GRAND	49	SCHLAFLY BOTTLEWORKS
30	MESKEREM ETHIOPIAN RESTAURANT	51	FU MANCHU

⭘ NIGHTLIFE

7	VAN GOGHZ	27	ABSOLUTLI GOOSED
8	SANDRINA'S	31	URBAN
10	TIN CAN TAVERN & GRILL	39	THE FAMOUS BAR
15	RILEY'S PUB	40	THE MACK
16	ERATO	44	LEMMONS
18	THE UPSTAIRS LOUNGE	45	PEPPER'S BAR AND GRILL
21	MANGIA ITALIANO		

⭘ ARTS AND LEISURE

12	PRIDEFEST	50	ARTOUTSIDE
12	FESTIVAL OF NATIONS	52	SARATOGA LANES
34	EPIPHANY LANES	53	FOCAL POINT
46	CARONDELET PARK	55	BLACK CAT REPERTORY THEATRE COMPANY

⭘ SHOPS

1	GRINGO JONES IMPORTS	28	CHEAP TRX
11	GROVE HOME FURNISHINGS	29	T.F.A.
13	BOTANICALS DESIGN STUDIO	36	GROOMINGDALE'S
17	DUNAWAY BOOKS	38	CATHOLIC SUPPLY
24	GRAND SOUTH GRAND	42	RECORD EXCHANGE
		54	O'MALLEY'S IRISH GIFT SHOP

⭘ HOTELS

4	CASA MAGNOLIA BED AND BREAKFAST	6	FLEUR-DE-LYS MANSION

0   500 yds

0   500 m

DISTANCE ACROSS MAP
Approximate: 5.3 mi or 8.5 km

SIGHTS
1 TURTLE PARK
7 ST. LOUIS SCIENCE CENTER
13 BOYHOOD HOMES OF YOGI BERRA AND JOE GARAGIOLA

RESTAURANTS
2 PAT'S BAR & GRILL
3 FELIX'S
4 SEAMUS MCDANIEL'S
9 OLYMPIA KEBOB HOUSE & TAVERNA
10 MICHAEL'S BAR & GRILL
14 GIOIA'S DELI
15 MODESTO
18 AMIGHETTI'S BAKERY AND CAFÉ
19 GUIDO'S PIZZERIA AND TAPAS
21 PIZZA-A-GO-GO

NIGHTLIFE
5 THE ARENA BAR AND GRILL
8 NICK'S PUB
20 LA ONDA
22 THE HIDE AWAY
23 MR. B'S

ARTS AND LEISURE
6 TRIPLE A GOLF AND TENNIS CLUB IN FOREST PARK

SHOPS
16 BERTARELLI CUTLERY INC.
17 JOHN VIVIANO & SONS GROCER

HOTELS
11 DRURY INN & SUITES
12 RED ROOF INN ST. LOUIS-HAMPTON

© AVALON TRAVEL

SEE MAP 6

SEE MAP 2

CLAYTON AVE

CLAYTON AVE

64

Forest Park

6 A

64

GIBSON AVE

ARCO AVE

OAKLAND AVE

Forest Park
Community
College

7 ✪
St. Louis
Science Center

OAKLAND AVE

BERTHOLD AVE

WICHITA AVE

WISE AVE

SOUTH DR

EAST RD

KINGS
OAK

CHELTENHAM

WISE AVE

WISE AVE

MACKLIND AVE

LAWN PL

SWAN AVE

SEE MAP 2

5 N 5
W PARK PL

HUGHES PL

MANCHESTER AVE

S KINGSHIGHWAY BLVD

MCREE AVE

SUBLETTE AVE

MACKLIND AVE

NORTHRUP AVE

PATTISON AVE

20 N

44

44

SHAW AVE

12 H
WILSON AVE

Vigo
Park

LILLY AVE

15 R
SHAW AVE

17 S

R 19

SHAW AVE

R 14

16 S

THE HILL

DAGGETT AVE

S VANDEVENTER AVE

BISCHOFF AVE

WILSON AVE

EDWARDS ST

R 18

MARCONI AVE

HEREFORD ST

MAURY AVE

Boyhood Homes of
Yogi Berra and
Joe Garagiola
13 A

59TH ST

BISCHOFF AVE

ELIZABETH AVE

ELIZABETH AVE

ELIZABETH AVE

SEE MAP 4

JANUARY AVE

DUGAN AVE

BOTANICAL AVE

BOTANICAL AVE

SHENANDOAH AVE

ALFRED AVE

COLUMBIA AVE

DALTON AVE

JANUARY AVE

COLUMBIA AVE

TOWER GROVE PL

HEGER CT

HEGER CT

Missouri

Botanical

Garden

MAGNOLIA AVE

MAGNOLIA AVE

BRANNON AVE

HEREFORD ST

MAGNOLIA AVE

REBER PL

REBER PL

REBER PL

REBER PL

SOUTHWEST AVE

Tower Grove Park

23

Sublette
Park

SUBLETTE AVE

ODELL ST

SOUTHWEST
GARDEN

0   300 yds

0   300 m

DISTANCE ACROSS MAP
Approximate: 2.6 mi or 4.3 km

✪ SIGHTS

1   CITY HALL, LION GATES, AND THE WALK OF FAME
48 THE CARMELITE MONASTERY
57 CONCORDIA SEMINARY AND PARK

61 FOREST PARK
63 C SAINT LOUIS ZOO
64 JEWEL BOX
65 MISSOURI HISTORY MUSEUM
68 THIRD DEGREE GLASS FACTORY

ⓡ RESTAURANTS

5   RACANELLI'S
10 ST. LOUIS PIZZA HAUS
11 GYRO HOUSE
12 FITZ'S AMERICAN GRILL & BOTTLING WORKS
13 C BLUEBERRY HILL
15 AL-TARBOUSH

21 RIDDLE'S PENULTIMATE CAFE & WINE BAR
29 THAI PIZZA CO.
37 IL VICINO
38 REARN THAI
39 THE FATTED CALF
56 HARVEST
67 C ATLAS

ⓝ NIGHTLIFE

2   CICERO'S
14 THE DUCK ROOM
27 DELMAR RESTAURANT & LOUNGE
28 THE U LOUNGE

33 THE PAGEANT
42 REMY'S KITCHEN & WINE BAR
45 THE RITZ-CARLTON LOBBY LOUNGE
58 SASHA'S WINE BAR & MARKET

ⓐ ARTS AND LEISURE

3   BIG SHARK
22 TIVOLI THEATER
30 PIN-UP BOWL
34 HEMAN PARK

50 TROPICANA LANES
60 HI-POINTE THEATER
62 SAINT LOUIS ART MUSEUM

ⓢ SHOPS

4   R. SOLE
6   CRAFT ALLIANCE
7   TANTRUM
8   PITAYA
9 C VINTAGE VINYL
16 PHOENIX RISING
17 C GOOD WORKS
18 C ZIEZO
19 RAG-O-RAMA
20 C CITY SPROUTS
23 SUBTERRANEAN BOOKS
24 TAG (TIMELESS AUTHENTIC GARMENTS)
25 C PLOWSHARING CRAFTS
26 DELMAR LOOP

32 FIFI'S
35 CLAYTON
40 C LOLA AND PENELOPE'S
44 EXTRA VIRGIN, AN OLIVE OVATION
47 THE WINE & CHEESE PLACE
49 C KITCHEN CONSERVATORY
51 THE BUILD-A-BEAR WORKSHOP
51 SAINT LOUIS GALLERIA
52 THE BOULEVARD
55 INTAGLIA
66 THE LOUISIANA PURCHASE

ⓗ HOTELS

31 MOONRISE HOTEL
36 C SEVEN GABLES INN
41 CROWNE PLAZA ST. LOUIS-CLAYTON
43 SHERATON CLAYTON PLAZA HOTEL

46 RITZ-CARLTON ST. LOUIS
53 MARRIOTT RESIDENCE INN
54 SPRINGHILL SUITES
59 C CHESHIRE LODGE

DELMAR BLVD

Jackson Park

PRINCETON AVE

University City

Flynn Park

PERSHING AVE

LADUE RD

St. Louis Country Club

WESTMORELAND DR

Forsyth

FORSYTH BLVD

Shaw Park

DELMAR LOOP

FOREST PARK PKWY

Clayton

WYDOWN BLVD

CLAYTON RD

The Carmelite Monastery
48 ✪

Laude

OXFORD DR

Clayton

Bogey Golf Course

Richmond Heights

51 ⓢ
Saint Louis Galleria

50 ⓐ

52

EAGER RD

EAGER RD

Brentwood I-64

DALE AVE

ELLSWORTH LN

STRASSNER DR

54 55
ⓗ ⓗ

W BRUNO AVE

ELINORE AVE

Tilles Park

© AVALON TRAVEL

City Hall, Lion Gates, and the Walk of Fame

PAGEDALE

WEST END

Wellston

Oleman Park

University City–Big Bend

Washington University

Skinker

SKINKER DEBALIVIERE

DEBALIVIERE PLACE

WYDOWN SKINKER

Concordia Seminary and Park

Fontbonne College

Oak Knoll Park

HI-POINTE

Forest Park

Forest Park Hospital

CLAYTON TAMM

Visitation Park

Third Degree Glass Factory
68

Forest Park–DeBaliviere

Missouri History Museum
65   66

67

Saint Louis Zoo
63   Zoo

Jewel Box
64

Forest Park Community College

CHELTENHAM

See Detail

SEE MAP 2

SEE MAP 5

DISTANCE ACROSS MAP
Approximate: 6.1 mi or 9.8 km

0   500 yds

0   500 m

🅐 SIGHTS
3	BUTTERFLY HOUSE	17	OLD WEBSTER HISTORIC DISTRICT
16	MAGIC HOUSE CHILDREN'S MUSEUM	34	GRANT'S FARM

🅡 RESTAURANTS
10	NACHOMAMA'S	25	BIG SKY
19	NATURAL FACT DELI	32	GROWLER'S PUB

🅝 NIGHTLIFE
15	ICE AND FUEL	36	IRON HORSE SALOON

🅢 SHOPS
4	MISTER GUY CLOTHIERS	11	THE FACE & THE BODY
5	TESTIMO BOUTIQUE	12	K. HALL DESIGNS
7	WEST COUNTY MALL	14	BLUSH BOUTIQUE
8	KANGAROO KIDS	18	OLD WEBSTER
9	THE BOOK HOUSE	20	YUCANDO
		21	NATURALLY PURE
		24	EUCLID RECORDS

🅐 ARTS AND LEISURE
1	NORMANDIE GOLF CLUB	27	SHAW NATURE RESERVE
2	FAUST PARK	28	MERAMEC STATE PARK CAVE TOUR
6	AMERICAN KENNEL CLUB MUSEUM OF THE DOG	29	HIDDEN VALLEY
13	STAGES ST. LOUIS	30	POWDER VALLEY CONSERVATION NATURE CENTER
22	OPERA THEATER ST. LOUIS	31	LAUMEIER SCULPTURE PARK
23	ST. LOUIS REPERTORY THEATER	33	TAPAWINGO NATIONAL GOLF COURSE
26	LONE ELK PARK AND WORLD BIRD SANCTUARY	35	QUAIL CREEK GOLF CLUB

© AVALON TRAVEL

Greendale

Uplands
Park

Calvary
Cemetery

St. Peters
Cemetery

70

Bellefontaine
Cemetery

HALL ST

180

Hillsdale

115

Penrose
Park

O'Fallon
Park

PAGE BLVD

GOODFELLOW BLVD

UNION BLVD

NATURAL BRIDGE AVE

CARTER AVE

FLORISSANT AVE

SKINKER PKWY

KINGSHIGHWAY BLVD

DR. MARTIN LUTHER KING JR DR

PAGE BLVD

VANDEVENTER AVE

GRAND BLVD

Fairgrounds
Park

FLORISSANT AVE

3RD ST

70

Washington
University

FOREST PARK PKWY

DELMAR BLVD

CENTRAL
WEST
END

LINDELL BLVD

MIDTOWN

CASS AVE

DeSoto
Park

Fontbonne
College

Forest
Park

64

FOREST PARK AVE

Saint Louis
University

OLIVE ST

St. Louis

DOGTOWN

MANCHESTER AVE

100

VANDEVENTER AVE

CHOUTEAU AVE

GRAND BLVD

64

DOWNTOWN

Jefferson
National
Expansion
Memorial

PARK AVE

LAFAYETTE
SQUARE

Lafayette
Park

100

70

64

55

44

THE
HILL

HAMPTON AVE

Missouri
Botanical
Garden

Compton
Hill Park

ARSENAL ST

Tower Grove
Park

30

SOULARD

SOUTH CITY

MORGANFELD RD

GRAND BLVD

GRAVOIS AVE

ARSENAL ST

JEFFERSON AVE

MISSOURI

366

CHIPPEWA ST

ILLINOIS

3

Francis
Park

JAMIESON AVE

WATSON RD

HAMPTON AVE

55

Mississippi River

Willmore
Park

BATES ST

St.
Matthew
Cemetery

GRAND BLVD

VIRGINIA AVE

157

Canokia

Saints Peter
and Paul
Cemetery

HOLLY HILLS BLVD

Carondelet
Park

MISSISSIPPI AVE

Wilbur
Park

MORGANFELD RD

MICHIGAN AVE

231

3

North
Dupo

55

Bella
Villa

S BROADWAY

N 36

255

50

267

To A 35 Quail Creek
Golf Club

0   1 mi

0   1 km

DISTANCE ACROSS MAP
Approximate: 15.5 mi or 25 km

© METRO ST. LOUIS

Discover St. Louis

St. Louis is a remarkable city, full of strange and beautiful secrets. Old stories die hard in this red-brick town on the Mississippi River; the triumphs and follies of the past are visible everywhere. This is where Lewis and Clark began their journey, and it's where Charles Lindbergh first took flight. In Forest Park – one of the largest urban green spaces in the nation – the pavilion from the 1904 World's Fair still stands. There's the incredible soaring majesty of Eero Saarinen's Gateway Arch, and the otherworldly beauty of the Cathedral Basilica. On the city's south side sits the eerie home of the Lemp brewing family, who took their own lives after being pushed into insolvency by the Anheuser-Busch empire. There's the saloon on the river where Stagger Lee shot Billy Lyons, inspiring dozens of stories and songs. The clubs and bars are filled with living blues legends – and with the memories of those who have come before. Just across the river, in East St. Louis, a young man named Miles Davis revolutionized jazz.

Visitors will discover dozens of unique neighborhoods, from Grand South Grand, where you can find a halal meat market and a raucous Italian-restaurant-slash-rock-club within one city block, to the Central West End, where charming bistros and haute-couture boutiques occupy some of St. Louis's most architecturally stunning buildings, to Soulard, where you can stop in real-deal Irish pubs and dance-all-night clubs, all in the impressively looming shadow of the Anheuser-Busch brewery complex.

And because St. Louis is not widely heralded by glossy travel magazines and guidebooks, to discover the real St. Louis is to discover what feels like your very own secret.

Planning Your Trip

▶ WHERE TO GO

Downtown

Visitors to downtown will find plenty to see and do—from the iconic **Gateway Arch** to shopping in one of the city's most cosmopolitan retail districts. After the bankers and lawyers head home at day's end, Downtown's many restaurants and bars come alive. Whether you're looking for a sports bar packed with Cardinals fans or a chic martini lounge, you'll find it here.

Midtown and Central West End

Midtown is fast becoming the fine-arts hub of St. Louis, thanks largely to the reopening of the historic **Fox Theatre** and the development of Grand Center. In the Central West End, stately mansions nestle against modernist art galleries, which in turn neighbor high-end boutiques and rave-worthy restaurants.

Fox Theatre

Soulard and Lafayette Square

Soulard is home to pretty red-brick rowhouses and friendly bars serving Anheuser-Busch beverages. In adjacent Lafayette Square, the Victorian-era mansions make this one of the most architecturally dazzling neighborhoods in the city. The many shops and restaurants hum with energy, and the bars and cafés that face historic **Lafayette Park** are particularly popular.

South City

The neighborhoods of South City are perhaps the most ethnically diverse in St. Louis. Within five city blocks of **Grand South Grand,** you can find three Vietnamese restaurants, a sushi restaurant, two Chinese restaurants, an Afghan restaurant, a Middle Eastern restaurant, and a halal meat market. At the **Missouri Botanical Garden,** visitors can explore the nation's oldest private botanical park and the first geodesic-dome greenhouse, the Climatron.

Dogtown and the Hill

The Hill is St. Louis's **Italian neighborhood** and a restaurant destination for visitors and native St. Louisans alike. On warm nights, it's not uncommon to see bocce tournaments unfolding on the neighborhood's lawns. Dogtown, to the north, is St. Louis's historically **Irish neighborhood,** and visitors won't be disappointed by the area's authentic Irish food and generous Guinness pours.

Delmar Loop and University City

The Delmar Loop spans both St. Louis and University City, and the area is constantly bustling with life. A visitor could spend an entire day in the Loop, **shopping** in boutiques and record stores, catching a movie at the art-house **Tivoli Theater,** attending a sold-out concert at **The Pageant,** and bowling till 3 A.M. at the **Pin-Up Bowl.**

Greater St. Louis

While some city-dwellers grumble about the homogenous nature of "the county," there are many suburbs with personalities all their own. There are stellar restaurants, hip boutiques, and great bars (including a micro-brewery) in **Ladue** and **Maplewood.** Main Street in **Webster Groves** hearkens back to the turn of the 20th century. Best of all, most of these suburbs can be reached via the recently expanded MetroLink system, meaning that visitors can check out Greater St. Louis easily and affordably.

Missouri Botanical Garden

▶ WHEN TO GO

As is true in many Midwestern cities, winter temperatures can dip into the single digits, while summer temperatures sometimes soar past 100 degrees. If extreme temperatures bother you, plan to visit St. Louis in April, May, September, or October. The city's vibe is downright joyous in **spring** months, when people say goodbye to winter and make haste to St. Louis's many parks. In the **fall,** the tree-lined streets are awash in red and gold. If you don't mind some heat, pack plenty of shorts and sundresses and experience **summer** in St. Louis. The only time to avoid St. Louis is in the dead of **winter:** Freezing temperatures and icy roads can easily turn a fascinating city into a frustrating one.

The park near Concordia Seminary in Clayton is beautiful year-round.

Explore St. Louis

► THE TWO-DAY BEST OF ST. LOUIS

The Old Courthouse played a key role in several major civil rights cases.

Day 1

► Start your first day in St. Louis off right—with a strong cup of coffee and delicious crêpe at **Rooster.**

► After your appetite has been sated (and your caffeine needs met), head due east on Locust Street. The Jefferson Expansion Memorial Park and world-famous **Gateway Arch** are just eight blocks away.

► After a tram ride to the Arch's observation deck, stop by the **Old Courthouse** for a mini-St. Louis history lesson, and then head southwest toward **Busch Stadium** to see the **St. Louis Cardinals.** Even if you don't have game tickets, it's worth walking around Busch's perimeter to get a sense of St. Louis sports history.

► The 8th Street MetroLink station is directly across the street from the stadium, and from there you can take the train to the **Delmar Loop.** Walk three blocks west of the Delmar Boulevard MetroLink stop, and you will find myriad shops and lunch options, including the landmark **Blueberry Hill.**

► Take the MetroLink to the DeBaliviere stop, then hop on the 90 or 3 bus into **Forest Park.** From the stop at the top of Art Hill, the **Saint Louis Zoo** is less than a five-minute walk away.

► By day's end, a cocktail will be in order, and there is no finer place (or view!) than **Cielo** in the Four Seasons hotel. Kick back at this elegant bar and watch the sun set over the Mississippi River.

► After whetting the appetite with a few small plates, head to **Niche** for dinner via car or the hotel's limousine service. It's not every day that a *Food & Wine* Best New Chef makes you dinner.

▶ Finish the evening at **B.B.'s Jazz, Blues, & Soups** for more drinks and some live music.

Day 2

▶ Start off your day with a delicious, leisurely breakfast at one of the delightful coffeehouses in the Central West End, then head over to the **Cathedral Basilica** for a self-guided tour.

▶ From the cathedral, the **Contemporary Art Museum St. Louis** is only a short ride away.

▶ After taking in the latest exhibition at the Contemporary, head south down nearby Grand Boulevard. The **Grand South Grand** neighborhood, just past Tower Grove Park, offers some great shops and ethnic markets.

▶ Next, head over to the **Missouri Botanical Garden**. After a stroll around the grounds, head toward the intersection of Grand and **Cherokee Street**.

▶ A short jaunt down Cherokee puts you in the heart of the city's largest Latino neighborhood. **Taquería El Bronco** offers some great, fresh choices for an inexpensive dinner, and some good margaritas as well.

BEER, BLUES, AND BARBECUE

BEER

No tour of this beer, blues, and barbecue town is complete without a visit to the **Anheuser-Busch Brewery.** Take a narrated tour of the King of Beer's castle, and afterward, enjoy complimentary A-B products in the hospitality room.

Head toward downtown to check out the popular local microbrewery **Schlafly Tap Room** at 21st and Locust.

Sample a pint at **Morgan Street Brewery** on Laclede's Landing and get a taste of another great St. Louis microbrewery.

BLUES

Grab a table on the patio at the **Broadway Oyster Bar,** toss back a few chilled oyster shooters, and enjoy some great live blues. Live music plays pretty much every night at the Oyster Bar.

B.B.'s Jazz, Blues, & Soups is a legendary venue that serves up live tunes every night of the week alongside great Cajun classics like jambalaya and gumbo.

The **Old Rock House** is a fabulous refurbished saloon that serves up both blues *and* barbecue.

BARBECUE

When it comes to barbecue in St. Louis, the key word is pork. Lots and lots of pork. There are countless St. Louis restaurants that serve up their best pork steaks and country-style spare ribs every day. But to really satisfy your 'cue cravings, head to **Pappy's Smokehouse** in Midtown. Open for just over a year, this altar to smoked pig is the best barbecue restaurant in town.

The Schlafly Tap Room pairs great microbrews with tasty gastropub fare.

TOP 10 PLACES TO TAKE THE KIDS

- **Best Place to See an Animatronic T-Rex:** the fun, interactive St. Louis Science Center (page 37).

- **Best Place to Build Your Own Cuddly Companion:** the original Build-A-Bear Workshop at the Saint Louis Galleria (page 142).

- **Best Place to See Hundreds of Free-Flying Butterflies:** the Butterfly House at Faust Park (page 42).

- **Best Place to Fill Up on Popcorn and Hot Dogs:** a Cardinals game at Busch Stadium (page 123).

- **Best Place Solve a Math Problem on a Four-Foot Calculator:** the Magic House Children's Museum (page 43).

- **Best Place to Lunch with Lions:** near the sea lion's pond at the Saint Louis Zoo (page 40).

- **Best Place to Cool Off During the Summer Heat:** the fountain near the children's garden at the Missouri Botanical Garden (page 36).

- **Best Place to Climb Through a 20-Foot Slinky:** the enormous, whimsical City Museum (page 27).

- **Best Place for a Paddle-Boat Ride:** around the lagoon at Forest Park (page 118).

- **Best Place to Dream of Broadway:** at a show performed by the Center of Creative Arts' student acting company, where local kids hone big-time talent (page 102).

Say hello to residents of the Saint Louis Zoo – possibly the finest urban zoo in the nation.

SIGHTS

St. Louis is a city of iconic structures, from the soaring curve of the Gateway Arch to the shimmering dome of the Cathedral Basilica. A trip to St. Louis would not be complete without visiting such important sights—yet visitors also will not want to miss the smaller landmarks that make St. Louis the historical, beautiful, and downright quirky city that it is. Most of the region's architectural treasures are concentrated downtown, making it easy to walk from one stunning structure to the next. Every St. Louis neighborhood has its own special character, and this is reflected in the sights. Midtown is a thriving arts center, and sights include Baroque theaters and Art Deco buildings. Life in the Delmar Loop and Central West End revolves around the 1,293-acre Forest Park, where many of the city's cultural institutions are located. The sights of Soulard reflect the city's strong French history, while South City boasts a proud amalgam of businesses and institutions built by immigrants from all points of the globe. Throughout the entire region, visitors will find gorgeous old churches, historically significant homes, and you-have-to-see-it-to-believe-it structures.

HIGHLIGHTS

LOOK FOR 【 TO FIND
RECOMMENDED SIGHTS.

【 **Most Magical Museum:** There is no place in the world like **City Museum** – and that's not hyperbole. Spend an hour or a day in this artist-designed wonderland, and come away with experiences that include walking through an enchanted forest and clambering into a rooftop school bus that teeters over the city (page 27).

【 **Most Iconic Landmark:** At 630 feet, the **Gateway Arch** is the tallest national monument in the United States. Approximately one million visitors ride the tram to the top of the Arch each year (page 29).

【 **Best Escape to Europe:** The **Cathedral Basilica** rises like a gorgeous European landmark along historic Lindell Boulevard. Newer than most American cathedrals, yet imbued with the grandeur of centuries-old churches, the cathedral is well worth a tour for architecture and history buffs alike (page 33).

【 **Best Haunted Mansion:** The **Lemp Mansion** is beautiful and historic, to be sure – but it's also the home of dark local legends. Take a tour of Lemp Mansion and you're certain to acquire new St. Louis knowledge (along with a few goose bumps) (page 34).

【 **Best St. Louis Microcosm:** Bustling with life all year round, the **Soulard Farmers Market** is more than just a one-stop shop for fresh produce. The market also hosts live entertainment, sells St. Louis delicacies (like Gus' Pretzels), and offers some of the best people-watching in the city (page 35).

【 **Best Place for Green Thumbs:** The 79-acre **Missouri Botanical Garden** features some of the best horticultural displays in the nation. Don't miss the Climatron, the first geodesic-dome greenhouse ever built (page 36).

【 **Best Roadside Attraction:** Sculpted by Bob Cassilly (the same genius behind the City Museum), the giant snapping turtles of **Turtle Park** occupy a whimsical oasis off Highway 40. Visitors can stroll around these gigantic critters – and even climb on top of them (page 37).

【 **Best Free Attraction:** The City of St. Louis is wonderfully generous with its cultural institutions: The art museum, history museum, and many other attractions are free. But it's the world-renowned **Saint Louis Zoo** that has visitors and residents returning again and again to see the charismatic megafauna that call this place home (page 40).

Downtown

Map 1

CAMPBELL HOUSE MUSEUM

1508 Locust St., 314/421-0325

HOURS: Wed.-Sat. 10 A.M.-4 P.M., Sun. noon-4 P.M.

COST: $6 adult, free for children

Thanks to a set of interior photographs from the early 20th century, the rooms in this historic downtown landmark were restored precisely—right down to the placement of the original furnishings. This attention to detail is impressive, and the home is beautiful, yet visitors might also find their tour a bit disquieting. With just a glimpse out of the Campbell House's tall windows, one can see how much St. Louis has changed in the past two centuries.

Today, the meticulously restored Campbell House seems out of place where it stands: a lovely anachronism. There is nothing else like it for blocks. Campbell House is all that remains of the once-prestigious Lucas Place, a neighborhood of rowhouses for which this avenue was the main drag. At the time of its development, the neighborhood's boundaries lay just outside the city's limits. The Campbell House is all that remains of this, St. Louis's first suburb.

◖ CITY MUSEUM

701 N. 15th St., 314/231-2489, www.citymuseum.org

HOURS: Fall/winter Wed.-Thurs. 9 A.M.-5 P.M., Fri. 9 A.M.-1 A.M., Sat. 10 A.M.-1 A.M., Sun. 11 A.M.-5 P.M.; spring/summer Mon.-Thurs. 9 A.M.-5 P.M., Fri. 9 A.M.-1 A.M., Sat. 10 A.M.-1 A.M., Sun. 11 A.M.-5 P.M.

COST: $12 general admission, $10 after 5 P.M. on Fri. and Sat.

There is no other museum on earth like this one. Here, visitors can wander through

COURTESY OF CITY MUSEUM

City Museum's "MonstroCity" attraction combines playground classics with, well, aircraft fuselages.

© MICHAEL DEFILIPPO

Catch the Aerial Silks act at the City Museum's Circus Harmony Center.

a 13,500-square-foot aquarium, climb through a 20-foot Slinky, explore an eight-story tunnel system made from conveyor belts, walk into the belly of a whale, and peek inside a school bus (which just happens to be teetering on the top of the building).

What is City Museum? It's what might result if a magic spell turned a Kilimanjaro-sized mountain of steel, stone, metal, plastic, and glass (salvaged from the relentless demolition of St. Louis buildings) into an enchanted playground. The imagination behind this 600,000-square-foot urban funhouse belongs to artist Bob Cassilly. An urban revivalist in a city not known for its preservation, Cassilly has dedicated his life to saving St. Louis's history from the wrecking ball. Together with a team of 20 artisans, this revered urbanist is piecing together a never-ending puzzle, one abandoned city relic at a time.

EADS BRIDGE

Between Laclede's Landing and the Arch grounds (at the foot of Washington Ave.)

HOURS: Accessible 24 hours daily

COST: Free

Although not a frequent tourist destination, the Eads Bridge is both an impressive sight and a historically significant one. This 135-year-old dual-level, three-span steel-arch bridge, designed and built by Captain James Buchanan Eads, connects St. Louis to East St. Louis. It was the first to span the Mississippi River, and the first road-and-railway bridge. The Eads was built upon a caisson that descends more than 100 feet down into the bedrock below, and it represents a feat of engineering respected around the world.

The second level of Eads Bridge is open to foot traffic, but pedestrians share the 1,022-foot span with vehicles traveling at highway speeds. The view is spectacular, but those concerned with life and limb may find the walk anything but serene. The MetroLink (St. Louis's light-rail train), which travels smoothly along the deck below, offers a safer alternative.

EUGENE FIELD HOUSE & TOY MUSEUM

634 S. Broadway, 314/421-4689,
www.eugenefieldhouse.org
HOURS: Mar.-Dec. Wed.-Sat. 10 A.M.-4 P.M., Sun. noon-4 P.M., Mon.-Tues. by appointment; tours in Jan. and Feb. by appointment only
COST: $5 adult, $1 child

Roswell Martin Field occupies an important place in St. Louis—and U.S.—history. An attorney, Field defended the citizenship of Dred and Harriet Scott before the Supreme Court in the landmark Dred Scott case. His son, Eugene, was a writer best known for his children's poetry and humorous essays. Visitors can tour Eugene's boyhood home on Broadway, just outside the center of downtown. The home fell into disrepair during the Great Depression, but in 1936 children in the St. Louis Public Schools raised $2,000 to restore the home to its former Victorian elegance. Admission includes a visit to an antique toy museum, and to this day, all St. Louis schoolchildren are admitted free of charge.

🅲 GATEWAY ARCH

St. Louis Riverfront, 877/982-1410,
www.gatewayarch.com
HOURS: Labor Day-Memorial Day 9 A.M.-6 P.M. daily, Memorial Day-Labor Day 8 A.M.-10 P.M. daily
COST: $10 adult, $7 youth, $3 child

The Arch is to St. Louis what Lady Liberty is to New York: iconic. Reaching 630 feet at the apex, it is the tallest man-made monument in the United States. This stunning structure

© NATIONAL PARK SERVICE, JEFFERSON NATIONAL EXPANSION MEMORIAL

In the winter, the Arch cuts an impressive figure against the snowy landscape.

was designed by architect Eero Saarinen and structural engineer Hannskarl Bandelin in 1947, although construction did not begin until 1963. By the time the Arch opened to the public in 1967, it was already writ large on the national imagination. The Jefferson National Expansion Memorial, as the Arch and small national park on which it sits are officially called, symbolizes St. Louis's historic status as the "Gateway to the West," the jumping-off point for every Pacific-bound pioneer since Lewis and Clark.

Be sure to catch a screening of *Monument to the Dream*, a short documentary that chronicles the curve's construction, including how the left and right sides didn't exactly align at the top as work was nearly completed, forcing the St. Louis fire department to shrink the stainless steel plates a fraction of an inch by hosing them down with cold water. Finally, take a claustrophobic tram ride to the top (the elevator curves within the structure), feast your eyes on the fine view of the city, and think how much better the skyline would look with a giant, sleek, silver arch in the foreground.

OLD COURTHOUSE

11 N. 4th St., 314/655-1600,
www.gatewayarch.com

HOURS: Daily 8 A.M.-4:30 P.M.

COST: Free

The Old Courthouse plays an integral role in the history of American race relations. Unfortunately, that role wasn't always positive, as slaves were sold in estate sales on the courthouse steps. But then, the first trials of the Dred and Harriet Scott case—one of the main sparks that ignited the American Civil War—took place here.

Dred Scott, a slave who traveled with his owner to free territory, argued that he and his wife could no longer be enslaved after living in a free state. The Scotts even offered to purchase their freedom, but their master refused. The case was argued at the Old Courthouse, and in 1850 the jury ruled in favor of the Scotts. In 1857, the United States

---

RESURRECTING OLD NORTH

Few parts of St. Louis City have seen as much devastation as North St. Louis. Once a thriving industrial hub, North St. Louis lost much of its wealth – and much of its vitality – in the mid-20th century, as St. Louis suffered a breathtakingly sharp population decline. In the early 21st century, ruthless developers bought up huge swaths of land in North St. Louis, only to let the buildings rot with blight.

Fortunately, many St. Louisans are unwilling to sit by while a beautiful historic neighborhood falls victim to neglect and the wrecking ball. Civic leaders in this predominantly African American area are mobilizing residents to take back Old North, as the area just north of downtown is called, and bring it back to life. Quite a few visionary young city dwellers have joined the cause, leaving comfy middle-class neighborhoods to join the fight for Old North's survival. But make no mistake: The residents of Old North won't just stop at seeing their neighborhood survive; they're ready to see it flourish. Below are some can't-miss stops that provide a great introduction to Old North and its ongoing resurrection.

Crown Candy Kitchen: There's no better first stop in Old North St. Louis than Crown Candy Kitchen (1401 St. Louis Ave.). Every day, this old-fashioned diner teems with life. Business people, tourists, foodies, and cops all crowd into this legendary space. Open since 1913, Crown Candy has remained a constant in Old North St. Louis's rise and fall and rise. Maybe that's because there's always a need for great comfort food at super-low prices. Try the excellent BLT, the egg salad sandwich, or the giant gourmet hot dog (when's the last time you had lunch for $3.85?). Crown Candy also boasts an amazing ice-cream-sundae menu, plus old-time favorites like malteds and phosphates. Homemade candy is available by the pound. And when you eat at Crown Candy, you'll have a great view of Crown Square, the $32 million

Supreme Court ruled that Dred and Harriet Scott did not have the right to be free. But while it seemed inevitable that this decision would expand slavery, it in fact caused abolitionists to redouble their efforts to end slavery. Those fights were waged in newspapers, at town meetings, and ultimately on the battlefields of the Civil War.

The Old Courthouse is listed in the National Park Service's National Underground Railroad Network to Freedom, in recognition of the building's crucial place in abolitionist history. Many human- and civil-rights cases have been argued at the Old Courthouse; 30 years after the Dred Scott decision, in the very same courtroom, Virginia Minor fought for women's voting rights. One of the building's courtrooms has been remodeled to reflect this monumental era, and the lobby features regularly revolving exhibits that trace the history of justice in St. Louis.

OLD POST OFFICE
815 Olive St.

COST: Free

Put the history of a once-thriving downtown into perspective by exploring one of revitalization project that's bringing life back to this historic area.

Mullanphy Emigrant Home: After lunch at Crown Candy Kitchen, take a stroll or a quick drive up to the Mullanphy Emigrant Home (1609 14th St.). This building, once a triumph of late-19th-century masonry, is in dire need of saving. Owing to blight and natural disaster, Mullanphy has lost many of its extraordinary original details (including a round-topped cornice), but its beauty is still evident. Mullanphy Emigrant Home, as its name suggests, housed dozens of European immigrants in the waning days of the 19th century. In its 140-year existence, it has also served as everything from a schoolhouse to a motorcycle repair shop. But although St. Louis's alt-weekly gave Mullanphy the dubious "Best Lost Cause" award in 2007, its hope for survival is far from dim. The Old North Restoration Group, a hard-working neighborhood organization, purchased Mullanphy and plans to restore it to its former elegance.

New Roots Urban Farm: New Roots is a force for good in Old North St. Louis. While its ideals would no doubt be embraced by proponents of the Slow Food movement (and with all due respect to Slow Food), New Roots is not an organization devoted to making middle- and upper-class folks feel good about eating local. Rather, New Roots helps an impoverished area survive by sharing food — and food production methods — with its neighbors. New Roots describes its model as not just nonprofit but "antiprofit." Following the Catholic Worker ethos, New Roots' goals are to nourish the community and to teach others how to nourish themselves. Throw in a healthy dose of environmentalism and pacifism, and you have a group that's doing some pretty revolutionary things in this Midwestern city. Stop by the farm (1830 Hogan St.) or see New Roots' wares at the North City Farmers' Market (right across from Crown Candy Kitchen, 9 A.M.–1 P.M. Sat.).

the last remnants of its boom years. St. Louis's former Post Office and Custom House was dedicated in the optimistic years of the post–Civil War economy. Some urbanists say the demolition of the historic Century Building across the street irrevocably frayed the fabric of downtown St. Louis. Fortunately, the crown jewel of this historic square still survives. A massive renovation completed in 2006 preserved the Old Post Office's extravagant, Second Empire–style architecture and glass atrium for future generations of St. Louisans. This isn't a tourist attraction, per se, but visitors are welcome to explore the shared spaces of its first level. The Old Post Office is now home to the downtown branch of Webster University, offices of the Missouri Arts Council, a casual restaurant, and a branch of the St. Louis Public Library. Downtown St. Louis is currently making a thrilling comeback, and this gorgeous structure reminds natives and visitors alike of how vibrant the city can be.

UNION STATION

1820 Market St., 314/421-6655,
www.stlouisunionstation.com
HOURS: Mon.-Sat. 10 A.M.-9 P.M., Sun.
10 A.M.-6 P.M. (guided tours available by
appointment only; call in advance)
COST: Free

Union Station is the elegant transportation hub that began greeting visitors and returning residents in 1894. This national landmark now houses a luxury hotel and a less-than-stellar shopping mall, but it was once a full-scale train depot on the order of Chicago's Union Station. At St. Louis's height, it was the largest, busiest railway station in the country, servicing 100,000 people a day. Despite its retrofitting, the station's elegant grand lobby remains intact. Its 65-foot barrel-vaulted ceiling, Romanesque archways, and stained-glass windows provide a beautiful glimpse of Union Station's true glory days. This iconic structure is best viewed from the exterior, unless you want to ask yourself this depressing question: Why in the world would anyone turn such an important building into a third-rate tourist trap of a mall? Visitors looking to complete their Hard Rock Café T-shirt collection will, unfortunately, find an outpost of the international chain here.

Midtown and Central West End   Map 2

◖ CATHEDRAL BASILICA

4431 Lindell Blvd., 314/373-8240,
www.cathedralstl.org

HOURS: Daily 7 A.M.-5 P.M. (guided tours by
appointment; call in advance to schedule)

COST: Free

As in many cities in Europe, the most impressive work of art in St. Louis isn't housed in the local museum but rather in the cathedral. As far as cathedrals go, this one is in its infancy—ground was broken in 1907, and construction was not completed until the late '80s. Still, what the cathedral lacks in longevity, it makes up for in beauty. The 83,000-square-foot ceiling of the Cathedral Basilica, the emerald-domed jewel of the Central West End, is covered by a mosaic made of 41.5 million pieces of glass in more than 7,000 colors. The work took 20 different artists 76 years to complete. The cathedral's beauty and magnitude rival the grandeur of cathedrals that are centuries older, and yet some of the intricate mosaic work reflects modern themes. Here and there, priestly vestments are replaced by suits and skinny ties. Look closely, and you'll even see a computer or two. Docent-led tours are offered a couple of times each week and are highly recommended. Pope John Paul II honored the cathedral as a basilica in 1997.

ERNEST TROVA AT
SAINT LOUIS UNIVERSITY

221 N. Grand Blvd.

St. Louis's collection of public art is impressive. Among the artists responsible for these works-about-town is Ernest Trova, a renowned surrealist who was born here in 1927. A donation of 40 of his works led to the establishment of Laumeier Sculpture Park in Sunset Hills, and additional Trova sculptures can be found all over St. Louis. Enjoy works from Trova's *Profile Canto* series while taking a walking tour of the scenic Saint Louis University campus off Grand Boulevard in Midtown. Trova's dynamic works can also be seen in downtown Clayton; his *FM6 Walking Jackman,* at 98 Brentwood Boulevard, is particularly stunning. The 82-year-old artist still makes his home in St. Louis.

SCOTT JOPLIN HOUSE

2658A Delmar Blvd., 314/340-5790,
www.mostateparks.com/scottjoplin.htm

HOURS: Nov.-Feb. Tues.-Sat. 10 A.M.-4 P.M.,
Mar.-Oct. Mon.-Sat. 10 A.M.-4 P.M.
and Sun. noon-4 P.M.

COST: $2.50 adult, $1.50 child

Walk in the footsteps of the King of Ragtime by visiting his modest Delmar walk-up. A historical society has preserved the rooms where Joplin composed many of his most famous works, including the "Maple Leaf Rag." The musical history of St. Louis is rich, and Joplin's years here (between 1900 and 1907) coincided with the birth of the city's burgeoning jazz culture. Joplin lived near the honky-tonk dives of Chestnut Valley and Gaslight Square—cultural hotbeds that would later foster the talents of Miles Davis, Josephine Baker, and Ike and Tina Turner.

Soulard and Lafayette Square   Map 3

ANHEUSER-BUSCH BREWERY

12th and Lynch St., 314/577-2626,
www.budweisertours.com

HOURS: Mar.-May and Sept.-Oct. Mon.-Sat.
9 A.M.-4 P.M., Sun. 11:30 A.M.-4 P.M.; June-Aug.
Mon.-Sat. 9 A.M.-5 P.M., Sun. 11:30 A.M.-5 P.M.;
Nov.-Feb. Mon.-Sat. 10 A.M.-4 P.M., Sun.
11:30 A.M.-4 P.M.

COST: Free

St. Louis is a beer-making, beer-drinking, beer-loving town. Celebrate this heritage by touring the facilities of sudsy stalwart Anheuser-Busch (and be rewarded at the end of your tour with, you guessed it, a beer).

Before the invention of refrigeration, a vast network of natural caverns below St. Louis provided a consistent, cool temperature ideal for aging beer. By the mid-1800s, plenty of brewers wanted in on this sweet beer-cave deal, and St. Louis was home to nearly 50 breweries. But by 1950, thanks to factors like Prohibition, the Great Depression, and the wild success of the Anheuser-Busch family, only eight remained (including Griesedieck, Falstaff, and Lemp). Only A-B struck it rich and stood the test of time; it is now the largest brewer in the country and operates distributorships all over the world. (Please don't refer to it by the company's new name, Anheuser-Busch InBev, unless you want to get dirty looks from the locals; the company was recently sold to Belgian brewing giant InBev, and as a result many local jobs were lost.)

◖ LEMP MANSION

3322 DeMenil Pl., 314/664-8024,
www.lempmansion.com

HOURS: No regular hours; call ahead to schedule tour

COST: Free ("haunted" tours are $15)

This 33-room mansion was once the estate of William Lemp, an industrious German immigrant who brought the hearty beer of his homeland to St. Louis in the 1840s. Lemp began producing lager, and he sold it in the grocery stores his family owned. The popularity of the lager soon outpaced the popularity of the stores, so Lemp left the grocery business and devoted his attention entirely to beer-making. He eventually became one of the city's wealthiest residents.

Today the Lemp family is a part of local legend—but that legend is a dark one. The Lemps were eccentric and suicide-prone, and not one descendant remains. The brewery closed a couple of years ago, after a very brief resurrection. The mysterious death of son Frederick was only the beginning of a tumultuous, fiercely secretive, 70-year family saga that included three suicides. Creep yourself out with a haunted tour led by medium Betsy Belanger. These tours are typically given on Monday night, but it's recommended that you call ahead. Tours are given more frequently in the weeks leading up to Halloween, when guests are given a half-hour lecture about the fascinating family, then led throughout the rooms. During the tour, Belanger points out family heirlooms, spends extra time in rooms where a death occurred, and tries to communicate with beyond-the-grave Lemps. Depending on your viewpoint, these tours are either totally scary or hilariously kitschy. But either way, they're quite interesting.

◖ SOULARD FARMERS MARKET

730 Carroll St., 314/622-4180,
www.soulardmarket.com
HOURS: Year-round Wed.-Fri. 8 A.M.-5 P.M.,
Sat. 6 A.M.-5 P.M.
COST: Free

Peruse the colorful offerings of local vendors and enjoy the spectacle that is Soulard Market, the oldest market west of the Mississippi River. A vital source of inexpensive foodstuffs, this historic market has survived through two centuries of relocations and transformations. It was even once a Civil War encampment for the Union Army.

The structure that the market now occupies was built in the 1930s and was restored only recently, after a long period of decline. Stalls are open here Wednesday through Saturday, but the market sees most of its activity on Saturday. On this day only, every stall is open and stocked, and the thoroughfares are crowded with residents from all over the region. The Soulard Market offers something of a St. Louis microcosm, as people from all backgrounds gather to find good prices on fresh foods. The social aspect of a day at Soulard Market hearkens back to the ancient Greek ideal of an *agora*—a place where friendly conversation, political involvement, and cultural edification can coexist. To that end, Soulard Market allows everything from political canvassing (although it's rarely in-your-face) to strolling musicians. Soft pretzels, frozen custard, and cold beer are available for purchase, as are fresh flowers and numerous handicrafts.

South City   Map 4

THE "ANCIENT RUINS" IN TOWER GROVE PARK

Next to the Piper Palm House, on the upland north of Main Dr., 314/771-4424,
www.towergrovepark.org
HOURS: Sunrise-sunset
COST: Free (docent-led group tour available for minimum donation of $40; call to schedule)

The broken stone columns along the north edge of Tower Grove Park's fountain pond are not the ancient ruins they appear to be. Rather, these faux-Greco curiosities were hand-selected by park benefactor Henry Shaw. They were plucked from the remains of the old Lindell Hotel, which burned to the ground shortly before Shaw deeded the land for Tower Grove Park to the city. Inspired by the spooky aesthetics of the fire-damaged blocks, Shaw had a pile of them transported to the park and arranged according to his design. The stone balustrade at the pond's southern shore was rescued from the U.S. Custom House and Post Office, which was demolished in 1939.

COMPTON HILL WATER TOWER

Grand Blvd. and Russell Blvd., in Reservoir Park, 314/552-9000, www.watertowerfoundation.org
HOURS: Occasional tours; call or visit the website for dates and times
COST: $5 adult, $3 children 6-12, free for children 5 and under

The observation deck of this 100-foot-tall retired Romanesque water tower offers visitors a 360-degree view of the city and a glimpse into another era. The tower's staircase has 198 steps and seven landings. The water tower was built in 1898, when the population of St. Louis was just over half a million and quickly outgrowing its water-delivery system. It was renovated during the 1990s. The Compton Hill Water Tower is open for climbing just a few times per year, but visitors can stroll along the walks of the tower's beautifully landscaped 36-acre park, and around neighboring Stacy Park Reservoir, anytime.

INTERNATIONAL INSTITUTE OF METROPOLITAN ST. LOUIS

3654 S. Grand Blvd., 314/773-9090, www.iistl.org
HOURS: Tour available last Tues. of the month at 10 A.M.
COST: Donation requested

One of several international institutes in the United States, this center for civic development serves St. Louis City's burgeoning international population by providing new Americans with English classes and other important transition services. Tours are available to interested parties, but the classrooms and offices of this South City sight are not so much a tourist destination as a place that enriches the very fabric of St. Louis.

The vibrant population of new Americans in this city is infusing some of its decaying neighborhoods with new life. If you're not in St. Louis on the last Tuesday of the month, consider visiting some of the city's immigrant-owned businesses. Browse in the Central American markets and Mexican *taquerías* along Cherokee Street. Stop in one of Grand Boulevard's many Vietnamese restaurants for a steaming bowl of *pho ga*. The International Institute is perhaps best experienced at the Festival of Nations, a weekend-long celebration of ethnic foods, art, and dancing held in Tower Grove Park every August.

◖ MISSOURI BOTANICAL GARDEN

4344 Shaw Blvd., 314/577-9400, www.mobot.org
HOURS: Daily 9 A.M.-5 P.M., Memorial Day-Labor Day open Wed. until 9 P.M., closed Christmas Day
COST: $8 adult, free for children

Escape the din of the city for an afternoon and explore the setting of the nation's oldest private botanical park. Opened to the public in 1859 by botanist and civic leader Henry Shaw, the garden is internationally renowned for its botanical research and exploration. Tucked into the well-kept residential neighborhoods of South City, the garden's paved paths meander through 79 acres of some of the nation's greatest horticultural displays. Must-see attractions include the Climatron, the first geodesic-dome greenhouse ever constructed, and the sprawling traditional Japanese garden. Lesser-known but equally notable features include a six-million-specimen herbarium and an extensive historical library with volumes dating back to the garden's establishment.

© MISSOURI BOTANICAL GARDEN

The Missouri Botanical Garden's flora is spectacular.

Dogtown and the Hill
Map 5

BOYHOOD HOMES OF YOGI BERRA AND JOE GARAGIOLA

5400 block of Elizabeth Ave. on the Hill

St. Louis is a sports-loving town (to put it mildly), and so it's no great surprise that two of its most cherished heroes are baseball legends. Yogi Berra and Joe Garagiola were boyhood neighbors in the historically Italian, working-class Hill neighborhood, where one can imagine them playing baseball in the streets on 1940s summer afternoons. Berra and Garagiola lived across the street from one another on the 5400 block of Elizabeth Avenue (the late Jack Buck, a Hall of Fame baseball announcer and one of St. Louis's most beloved native sons, also lived on Elizabeth). Visitors can take a stroll through the baseball giants' old stomping grounds while also enjoying the array of Italian markets, delis, and restaurants for which the neighborhood is renowned.

ST. LOUIS SCIENCE CENTER

5050 Oakland Ave., 314/289-4400, www.slsc.org

SCIENCE CENTER HOURS: Mon.-Thurs. and Sat. 9:30 A.M.-4:30 P.M., Fri. 9:30 A.M.-9:30 P.M., Sun. 11:30 A.M.-4:30 P.M.

PLANETARIUM HOURS: Mon.-Sat. 9:30 A.M.-4:30 P.M., Sun. 11:30 A.M.-4:30 P.M.

COST: Free admission; parking $8

Although general admission to the St. Louis Science Center (SLSC) is free, an important distinction shared by many of the city's most popular attractions, no expense has been spared in its making. SLSC is one of the largest of its kind in the country, as well as one of the top five science centers in the nation. Two full stories, plus the neighboring James S. McDonnell Planetarium, boast hundreds of fun, interactive exhibits (many have admission charges) designed to teach visitors the basic principles of science. The state-of-the-art, four-story Omnimax theater (separate admission) screens everything from ocean documentaries to rock concerts, and the ExploraDome plays host to a year-round schedule of touring exhibits.

◖ TURTLE PARK

Oakland Ave. and Tamm Ave., south of Forest Park

HOURS: Dawn-10 P.M.

COST: Free

Bob Cassilly is the powerful visionary behind the awe-inspiring City Museum. But before he dreamed up the great whale that greets visitors there, he was envisioning gigantic snapping turtles, red-eared sliders, and a snake crawling along Highway 40. Concrete sculptures of these Missouri wildlife natives now decorate a small park directly across from the zoo and Forest Park, and they are difficult to miss. Wondering if it's okay to climb atop the humongous turtles? Not to worry—locals do it all the time. They provide the perfect vantage point for watching the traffic go whizzing by on the freeway, which is actually much more relaxing than it sounds. Lie under the sun on the broad back of a Missouri snapping turtle for a few hours and the roar of the cars blurs into an unbroken wall of white noise, the perfect soundtrack for letting your mind drift while watching the clouds. In addition to the big turtles, there's a sandpit with sculptures of enormous turtle eggs in various stages of cracking open—the robust child (or daring adult) can perch atop these as well, and try to leap from egg to egg around the circumference of the pit.

A nearby swing set offers more traditional recreation, but it's almost always empty (small wonder).

Delmar Loop and University City   Map 6

THE CARMELITE MONASTERY

9150 Clayton Rd., Ladue, 314/993-6899

HOURS: Always open

COST: Free

The spiritual focus of the Carmelites, a monastic order founded in the 12th century, is contemplative prayer. This Discalced Carmelite monastery, one of only 70 in the world, is intended for exactly that. The painstakingly maintained grounds offer visitors several settings for prayer and contemplation, including an inspiring chapel that is open to the public and holds a daily mass and benediction. No matter their beliefs, visitors are likely to find the quiet beauty of this place thoroughly moving.

CITY HALL, LION GATES, AND THE WALK OF FAME

6801 Delmar Blvd., University City, 314/862-6767, www.ucitymo.org

COST: Free

University City, one of St. Louis's oldest suburbs, is now widely considered one of its most liberal and diverse. Founded by publisher Edward Gardner Lewis in 1906, the city was a streetcar suburb in the late 19th and 20th centuries. The Beaux Arts architecture of the southern portion of the town, where the octagon-shaped City Hall and majestic Lion Gates stand, reflects this historic legacy and unique charm (and '80s-movie buffs might recognize the Lion Gates from *Back to the Future*; screenwriter

Bob Gale is a U. City native). Just down the street from these signature sights, you'll find one of St. Louis's most popular entertainment districts—the Delmar Loop—and its eclectic assembly of shops, restaurants, and clubs.

The wide sidewalks of the Loop in University City are perfect for leisurely strolling and alfresco dining. And while the window-shopping is tempting, be sure to look down every once in a while and see St. Louis's very own walk of fame. The brass stars and bronze plaques embedded in the pavement (there are now more than 115) commemorate the lives and achievements of the city's most well-known residents. Honorees include Ulysses S. Grant, T. S. Eliot, Josephine Baker, Joseph Pulitzer, Charles A. Lindbergh, Betty Grable, and many others. The Walk of Fame began as the project of civic good-guy Joe Edwards, the Loop's foremost developer and tireless champion. Fans of 1970s crooner Michael McDonald will be pleased to see that he, too, has a star on the boulevard.

CONCORDIA SEMINARY AND PARK

801 Seminary Pl., Clayton, 314/505-7000, www.csl.edu

COST: Free

Located in the inner-ring suburb of Clayton, this meditative seminary campus is one of the largest in the country. Concordia was built in 1926, but the beautiful carved stonework of its main buildings and

© BROOKE FOSTER

St. Louis is full of lovely parks, including this one adjacent to Concordia Seminary.

quadrangle has a mid-19th century feel. Visitors will enjoy the pretty park that tumbles down the hill upon which the seminary is built. This lush park often bustles with life: It's a favorite study spot for Washington University students, a great place to take the dog for a run, and a destination for yoga and tai chi practitioners. Concordia is home to a 245,000-volume library and 49-bell carillon.

FOREST PARK

Between Skinker and Kingshighway
HOURS: Sunrise-sunset
COST: Free

Bordered by Kingshighway to the east and Skinker Boulevard on the West, this 1,293-acre urban oasis is larger than New York's Central Park. On a warm day, the park attracts visitors in the thousands. Its rolling

grounds are home to the Saint Louis Art Museum, the Missouri History Museum, the Saint Louis Zoo, and an 18-hole golf course. The museums and zoo are free to visit, and a tee time will set you back just $30. At the recently renovated Boat House, guests can have a cocktail and a simple meal, then rent a paddleboat to tour the beautiful Grand Basin and canals. As part of a massive parkwide renovation project begun in the mid-'90s, this elegant water feature has been restored to its original state and recalls the glory days of the 1904 World's Fair.

If you need a break from sightseeing, head to **Art Hill** (just across the street from the Saint Louis Art Museum). On a warm afternoon, set up a picnic on this broad lawn and nap in the shadow of the monument to King Louis XIV. Lazily contemplate the paddleboats in the Grand Basin below, and perhaps the golfers off to the north. Enjoy the breeze. Fall back asleep. (Freshly fallen snow in the winter makes this a popular sledding destination for locals, so you may want to restrict your sleepy Art Hill reveries to the summer months.)

JEWEL BOX

Wells Dr. and McKinley Dr. in Forest Park, 314/531-0080
HOURS: Mon.-Fri. 9 A.M.-4 P.M., Sat. 9 A.M.-11 A.M., Sun. 9 A.M.-2 P.M.
COST: $1

The popularity of this Forest Park attraction has waned in the last 20 years, perhaps due to a renovation in which much of its display space and kitsch appeal were surrendered to the modern amenities of a full-scale event space. But the Jewel Box remains a compelling structure, and visitors to the park should not miss it. Resembling a Victorian terrarium, this elegant old world-style greenhouse was a WPA project. It was built in 1936, as the nation struggled through the first years of economic depression, and its beautiful, jewel-like floral displays beckon visitors through its doors year-round. It is a popular photo opportunity for local families—particularly during the holidays, when the house offers its traditional poinsettia display and a welcome reprieve from the dreary winter months.

MISSOURI HISTORY MUSEUM

Lindell Blvd. and DeBaliviere Ave. in Forest Park, 314/746-4599, www.mohistory.org
HOURS: Daily 10 A.M.-5 P.M., Tues. 10 A.M.-8 P.M.
COST: Free

This stately museum offers a rotating collection of themed exhibitions with a mainly regional focus. Well-attended events have included a Miles Davis retrospective and a 1904 World's Fair exhibit, and also a traveling exhibit from the Baseball Hall of Fame. Museum officials seem to have a healthy appetite for audio tours, and several are usually available, but it's the wealth of supplemental events to the main exhibits that make the museum an everyday possibility. From presenting 15-minute plays about famous abolitionists to opening up the auditorium for a screening of home movies donated (temporarily) by area families to hosting the Urban Stories series, which pairs interesting guest speakers with unusual topics (how about Andre Royo of HBO's *The Wire* discussing "How Art Reflects Life" with his character Bubbles as the prism?), the Missouri History Museum makes a strong case for history being very much alive and very entertaining. While the special exhibits require a modest fee for entry, most if not all

of the supporting programs are free; so once you've done the tour, you can stick around and make a full day of it—and maybe catch a meal at the on-site café, which serves an excellent brunch.

◖ SAINT LOUIS ZOO

1 Government Dr. in Forest Park, 314/781-0900, www.stlzoo.org
HOURS: Daily 9 A.M.-5 P.M. (closed Christmas Day and New Year's Day)
COST: Free

That's right, admission to the Saint Louis Zoo is free, by act of the Missouri state legislature. But don't let the budget-line admission fool you—this is a world-class zoo, with recently rehabbed natural enclosures for the great apes (with heavy-duty glass instead of bars), a state-of-the-art Penguin and Puffin Coast where the only thing between you and the flightless waterfowl is a few inches of frosty air, and the River's Edge, a lengthy trail that shows you how the hippopotamuses live above and below the waterline. But the zoo doesn't just focus on the charismatic megafauna—the Insectarium provides entry into the world of bugs and arachnids in horrifying, close-up detail (may not be suitable for the squeamish, but kids love it). There's also a zoo within the zoo: The Children's Zoo requires an admission fee of $4 per person, but it's free 8–9 A.M., and worth being the first stop. Here's where the baby animals are tended to and kept on limited display, and educational programs on various small animals (such as birds and reptiles) are presented throughout the day. And no trip to the zoo is complete without taking a ride on the Zooline Railroad, a small-scale train that circles the entire park; tickets for this family

© CHUCK DRESNER, SAINT LOUIS ZOO

The Asian elephant exhibit is a perennial favorite at the Saint Louis Zoo.

favorite are $5 per person, but hooting while going through the tunnels is free. Two well-stocked, sit-down cafés—the Lakeside Café and the Painted Giraffe—provide lunch options beyond burgers and fries.

THIRD DEGREE GLASS FACTORY

5200 Delmar Blvd., 314/367-4527, www.stlglass.com

HOURS: Mon.-Sat. 10 A.M.-5 P.M., Wed. until 10 P.M.

COST: Free to visit; classes and demonstrations available at varying rates

Third Degree Glass Factory is one of Delmar Boulevard's most interesting newcomers. The staff, volunteers, and team of instructors offer the city's only public-access glass-arts education center, in an 8,000-square-foot space converted from a dilapidated 1930s service station. In this now-inviting space, visitors can take classes in the craft, watch demonstrations, rent studio space, and purchase the work of local glass artists. In addition to offering normal visiting hours, the organization holds well-attended art events like the Wall Ball throughout the year. If you're in St. Louis on the third Friday of the month, be sure to check out Third Degree's free open house (6–10 P.M.).

Greater St. Louis Map 7

BUTTERFLY HOUSE

Faust Park, 15193 Olive Blvd., Chesterfield,
636/530-0076, www.butterflyhouse.org
HOURS: Tues.-Sun. 9 A.M.-4 P.M. (9 A.M.-5 P.M.
Memorial Day-Labor Day)
COST: $6 adult, $4.50 senior, $4 child

The Butterfly House is located on the elegant grounds of Faust Park in Chesterfield. A former home of Circus Flora, the grounds of this 8,000-square-foot garden feature a carousel, which only adds to the already whimsical nature of the place. Butterflies thrive in the glass house's humid environment; all told, the conservatory is home to 150 tropical plant species and more than a thousand tropical butterflies in free flight. Guests are free to walk among the fluttering creatures and can watch them emerge from their chrysalises in a fascinating "Miracle of Metamorphosis" display.

The Butterfly House was founded in 1998 to foster a better understanding of butterflies' life cycles and natural habitats. In addition to daily visiting hours, the facility offers educational programs, special events, and lectures. Be sure to check the full-length mirrors upon leaving the conservatory, or you might accidentally take a monarch home in your hat.

GRANT'S FARM

10501 Gravois Rd., 314/843-1700,
www.grantsfarm.com
HOURS: mid-Apr.-early May Sat.-Sun.
9 A.M.-3:30 P.M., early May-mid-Aug. Tues.-Fri.
9 A.M.-3:30 P.M. and Sat.-Sun. 9 A.M.-4 P.M.,
mid-Aug.-late Oct. Sat.-Sun. 9:30 A.M.-3:30 P.M.
COST: Free admission; parking $10

Free to all, thanks to funding by the community-outreach efforts of Anheuser-

Yes, you can get *this close* to the gorgeous creatures at the Butterfly House.

Busch, this popular summer destination's slogan is "Get closer to your family, courtesy of ours." At Grant's Farm, the equation for family fun includes picturesque views, German sausages, and cool encounters with critters. Visitors to the 281-acre farm can see educational elephant and bird shows, check out the nursery facilities of the famous A-B Clydesdales, and visit a petting zoo where kids can hand-feed a swarm of pygmy goats. The farm also boasts a well-kept wildlife refuge that can be toured via tram. Even better, the popular Bauernhof welcomes roadweary parents (and the rest of the drinking set) at tour's end with a Bavarian-style beer garden. Brood or no, anyone with an appreciation for beer and bratwurst will find happiness in the scenic surroundings of this re-created 19th-century farm. Just don't ask for a Coors.

MAGIC HOUSE CHILDREN'S MUSEUM

516 S. Kirkwood Rd., 314/822-8900, www.magichouse.org
SCHOOL YEAR HOURS: Tues.-Thurs. noon-5:30 P.M., Fri. noon-9 P.M., Sat. 9:30 A.M.-5:30 P.M., Sun. 11 A.M.-5:30 P.M.
SUMMER HOURS: Mon., Tues., Thurs., and Sat. 9:30 A.M.-5:30 P.M., Wed. and Fri. 9:30 A.M.-9 P.M., Sun. 11 A.M.-5:30 P.M.
COST: $7.50 admission
The Magic House gives kids (yes, of all ages) the chance to step into life-size science experiments. This huge Kirkwood house—more than double its original size thanks to a recent expansion—plays host to all manner of fun, educational activities. You can touch an electrically charged ball and make your hair stand on end, solve a math problem on a four-foot-tall calculator, create your own TV newscast, and walk into a giant soap bubble. While it's true that the exhibits at the Magic House are designed to captivate the younger set, parents will appreciate the inventiveness of the exhibits. For a minimal admission, you and your happy brood can partake in more than 100 activities, and top off the experience by zinging down a three-story slide.

OLD WEBSTER HISTORIC DISTRICT

Roughly bounded by Allen Ave., Elm Ave., W. Lockwood Ave., and the Missouri Pacific Railroad tracks, www.historicwebster.org, www.webstergroves.org
The shady lanes and craftsman-built homes of this prized St. Louis suburb have a cinematic quality that has not gone unnoticed. For decades, filmmakers and journalists have looked to Webster Groves for images of the quintessential middle-American town. Beginning with the 1965 CBS documentary *Sixteen in Webster Groves* and perhaps ending with photojournalist Laura Greenfield's portrayal in her best-selling book *Girl Culture*, Webster has always served as a microcosm of the Midwestern experience. Take it all in by joining the locals in a stroll down Lockwood Avenue. Enjoy this main drag's eclectic assortment of restaurants and shops, and then head south for a self-guided tour of the pristine residential neighborhoods. If the day is sunny and the air is warm, you may feel like the star of your very own Metro-Goldwyn Mayer film.

RESTAURANTS

Over the past decade, St. Louis has shaken off its reputation as a culinarily timid town. For years, visitors associated St. Louis with good-but-unadventurous fare, including plates heaped with meat and potatoes and bowls of pasta sauced with sweet marinara. Fast forward to today, when fine-dining options can be found in practically every neighborhood and the city boasts James Beard nominees, *Bon Appétit* award winners, and one of *Food & Wine* magazine's "Best New Chefs of 2008" (that would be Niche's Gerard Craft). Cozy bistros such as Atlas and Franco serve food inspired by the French countryside, and hip spots like Five and Moxy try adventurous pairings that always seem to work out just right.

Of course, it's not always about haute cuisine and molecular gastronomy in this Midwestern city. True to its strong immigrant roots, the food scene in St. Louis is a delightful assemblage of Italian sandwich shops, Vietnamese noodle cafés, and Bosnian smokehouses. International options are particularly abundant in South City, where immigrant groups from Sarajevo to Addis Ababa have settled. St. Louis's Thai and Vietnamese restaurants are great bets for hungry vegetarians, as these spots turn out consistently delicious dishes loaded with tofu and fresh veggies.

© AMY FERGUSON

HIGHLIGHTS

LOOK FOR 【 TO FIND
RECOMMENDED RESTAURANTS.

【 Most Eco-Friendly Restaurant: Terrene gets all of its food from local farmers, and the restaurant's eco-consciousness translates into some of the freshest, most delicious fare in town. Just how dedicated is Terrene to the environment? The chef gives the restaurant's used cooking oil to neighbors who power their motorbikes with the stuff (page 53).

【 Best Brewpub: The world may know St. Louis as the hometown of Anheuser-Busch, but folks in the know favor the **Schlafly Tap Room.** Pair Schlafly's excellent microbrews with homemade soft pretzels, a bratwurst sandwich, or the best fish-and-chips in town. If you're visiting St. Louis during the winter, don't miss the Coffee Stout (page 55).

【 Best Soul Food: A former backup singer for Ike Turner, Robbie Montgomery opened **Sweetie Pie's** in Forest Park Southeast in 2003. Offerings change daily and include pork steaks, okra, mac 'n' cheese, and an oxtail stew that would give any high-end joint a run for its money (page 55).

【 Best Gourmet Experience: Mention **Niche** to any St. Louis foodie, and brace yourself for rapturous descriptions of what very well might be the best restaurant in town. Gerard Craft isn't afraid to make dishes like pork cheeks with bacon ice cream – and *Food & Wine* didn't hesitate to name him one of the Best New Chefs of 2008 (page 56).

【 Best Place for a First Date: With its sultry lighting, abundant red roses, and decadent desserts, **Baileys' Chocolate Bar** is the perfect first-date spot. Indulge in dark-chocolate martinis, or nibble on a variety of truffles. Romance comes easy at this Lafayette Square gem (page 57).

【 Best Pizza: Fistfights have probably started over St. Louis pizza – that's how loyal St. Louisans are to their favorite pie. For perfectly crisp thin-crust pizza, try **Pizza-A-Go-Go,** a homey BYOB spot near the city's south side. If you crave a thicker crust, stop by the legendary **Blackthorn Pizza & Pub** (pages 67 and 65).

【 Best Burgers: Get your burger with a side of nostalgia at **Blueberry Hill,** where owner Joe Edwards's collection of Americana covers both levels of this Delmar Loop landmark. The burgers are perfectly seasoned (don't miss the onion rings). The burgers at super-friendly Irish pub **Seamus McDaniel's** rival those at Blueberry Hill, and in the summer you can enjoy your meal on Seamus's huge patio (pages 69 and 68).

【 Best Bistro: Bistros have popped all over town in the past five or six years, but **Atlas** does bistro fare best. The seasonally changing menu features classic dishes like gravlax, *steak frites,* and cassoulet. Be sure to save room for dessert – the *marjolaine* cake alone is worth a trip to this West End bistro (page 71).

RESTAURANTS

RESTAURANTS

There are plenty of gastronomic adventures to be had in the Gateway City. But make no mistake about it: St. Louisans also know their comfort food. After all, how better to withstand a harsh Missouri winter than with a heaping bowl of spaghetti or a blue-plate special? Visitors should not leave town without trying foods that are quintessentially St. Louis: We're talking toasted ravioli, thin-crust pizza topped with Provel, barbecued pork steaks, and gooey butter cake.

PRICE KEY

$	Entrées less than $10
$$	Entrées $10-20
$$$	Entrées more than $20

Downtown

Map 1

AMERICAN

THE EDIBLE DIFFERENCE $

615 Pine St., 314/588-8432,
http://theedibledifference.com
HOURS: Mon.-Fri. 7 A.M.-3 P.M.

From early in the morning, the towering high-rises surrounding The Edible Difference teem with businesspeople. For these downtown worker bees, this café is the ideal breakfast and lunch spot. The casual, serve-yourself efficiency and great home-style breakfasts draw crowds that sometimes spill out onto the sidewalk. Menu offerings include everything from a classic cold pastrami sandwich to a massive Cobb salad to a big slice of meatloaf served with a heap of mashed potatoes. Lunch specials change daily and are always inexpensive.

MIKE SHANNON'S STEAKS & SEAFOOD $$$

620 Market St., 314/421-1540,
www.shannonsteak.com
HOURS: Mon.-Fri. 11 A.M.-11 P.M., Sat. 5-11 P.M.,
Sun. 5-10 P.M. Bar open until 3 A.M. daily.

Mike Shannon is one of St. Louis's best-loved native sons. A former Cardinals slugger, Shannon switched to the broadcast booth in the early 1970s and continues to call each game with his trademark giddy fervor ("a hit up the middle right now would be like a nice ham sandwich and a cold, frosty one!"). His downtown restaurant is half sports bar, half upscale steakhouse, and wholly filled with baseball-loving bonhomie. On game days, fans pack the bar to take in Cardinals action on the plasma TVs, and those who stick around past the bottom of the ninth are often treated to a visit by the man himself. Even people who care little about Redbird Nation will likely be impressed by the food. The dry-aged steaks are extraordinarily good, and side-item options include some of the best mashed potatoes you'll ever eat.

ASIAN

SEN THAI ASIAN BISTRO $

1221 Locust St., 314/436-3456,
www.senthaibistro.com
HOURS: Mon.-Fri. 11 A.M.-2:30 P.M. and
5-9:30 P.M., Sat.-Sun. 5-9:30 P.M.

This section of Downtown could use a quick-and-cheap noodle shop, but the more upscale Sen fills residents' curry cravings perfectly well. The menu can best be described as "Asian eclectic": a little Chinese, a little Vietnamese, a *lot* of Thai. While some local Asian restaurants dial down the spice for Midwestern palates, Sen creates dishes that are full of delicious, peppery heat. Try the *kao pad kapao* (spicy fried rice flecked with fresh basil and chiles), or tuck into the *bamee* barbecued pork. Just don't be too proud to ask for a glass of water.

WASABI $$

1228 Washington Ave., 314/421-3500,
www.saucemagazine.com/wasabi

HOURS: Mon.-Thurs. 11 A.M.-2 P.M. and
5-9:30 P.M., Fri. 11 A.M.-2 P.M. and 5-10:30 P.M.,
Sat. 5-10:30 P.M.

Wasabi occupies an unassuming storefront on otherwise glitzy Washington Avenue. Visitors distracted by the strip's fashionable boutiques and trendy bars might walk right past the place, despite its red neon sign declaring the presence of "SUSHI." That, however, would be a mistake. The cavernous space behind Wasabi's door is far more impressive than its exterior, and the rolls and *nigiri* also draw raves. Signature non-sushi dishes include the beautifully presented *ishi yaki* (white tuna or salmon served on a hot stone).

BREAKFAST

ROOSTER $

1104 Locust St., 314/241-8818,
www.roosterstl.com

HOURS: Mon.-Fri. 7 A.M.-3 P.M., Sat.-Sun.
8 A.M.-3 P.M.

Rooster is one of the few breakfast options in downtown St. Louis, but it's worth seeking out on its own merits. Crepes are a house specialty, with both savory and sweet varieties available. Savory crepes range from simple combinations like brie-and-apple or cheddar-and-bacon to such fancier fare as baby arugula-and-goat cheese. Sweet crepes include everything from an indulgent pairing of figs and nuts to a simple and tasty lemon crepe with ricotta cheese. Sandwiches are available for lunch, and the brunch menu features excellent French toast and a classed-up version of that meat-tastic St. Louis staple, the slinger.

CONTEMPORARY AND NEW AMERICAN

CIELO $$$

999 N. 2nd St. (in the Four Seasons Hotel),
314/881-5800, www.fourseasons.com/stlouis

HOURS: Daily 6:30-10:30 A.M., 11 A.M.-2 P.M., and
6-10 P.M.

Like the Four Seasons Hotel in which it's located, Cielo is elegant and expensive. But this is *not* your typical overpriced hotel food. Chef Karen Hoffman turns out contemporary Italian fare that is both beautiful and delicious. Small plates shine brighter at Cielo than entrées (although if Hoffman's flawless scallops-on-butternut-squash-puree is on offer, by all means order it), and the appetizer portions of pasta are particularly good. Veal-cheek pappardelle is a favorite. Cielo offers one of the best—if not *the* best—views in the entire city. Snag a table by the floor-to-ceiling windows, and you'll spend your meal gazing out at the hotel's rooftop infinity pool and, beyond that, the Arch.

RESTAURANTS

KITCHEN K ⑤⑤
1000 Washington Ave., 314/241-9900,
www.kitchen-k.com
HOURS: Mon.-Thurs. 11 A.M.-10 P.M., Fri.
11 A.M.-11 P.M., Sat. noon.-11 P.M., Sun. 9 A.M.-2 P.M.

Kitchen K's elegant, ambitious design complements its equally ambitious menu: Jamaican jerk chicken, shrimp *pad thai*, vegetable tempura, and mango baby-back ribs all coexist on the same bill of fare. Decision-makingcan be overwhelming, and not every dish succeeds—but Kitchen K's glamorous bar is the perfect place to kick back with a cocktail and a snack (try the house-made sweet-potato fries). The floor-to-ceiling windows flood the space with sunlight and offer a great view of the Washington Avenue streetscape.

MIDDLE EASTERN
THE CEDARS AT ST. RAYMOND'S MARONITE CATHEDRAL ⑤
939 Lebanon Dr., 314/241-8248,
http://cedars.straymonds.net
HOURS: Wed. 11 A.M.-2 P.M.

Every Wednesday, volunteers from St. Raymond's congregation gather to prepare a lunch of delicious Lebanese favorites. This midweek meal is a 39-year-old tradition—and a secret known only by locals, including high-ranking government officials from nearby City Hall. Traditional spinach and meat pies, *dolmas* (minced meat, rice, and parsley steamed in grape leaves), and *kibbeh* (fried mini-footballs of seasoned meats and bulgur) are served cafeteria-style beneath the mirror balls of The Cedars' banquet facility. Nothing costs more than $4, and visitors are likely to see some of the city's most influential residents casually chatting over their baklava.

Midtown and Central West End   Map 2

AMERICAN
THE BEST STEAK HOUSE ⑤
516 N. Grand Blvd., 314/535-6033,
www.thebeststeakhousestl.com
HOURS: Mon.-Fri. 10 A.M.-10 P.M., Sat.
11 A.M.-9 P.M., Sun. 11 A.M.-8 P.M.

Across the street from the historic Fox Theatre, The Best Steak House offers a great lunch at a great price, and is arguably one of the city's best-kept secrets. Visitors in the mood for simple, satisfying fare (think grilled beef, fried fish, Texas toast, and baked or French-fried potatoes) will not be disappointed. This cafeteria-style restaurant is nearly always crowded, and for good reason: The Best Steak House's crave-worthy, no-nonsense food is grilled right in front of diners, then handed over efficiently on red plastic trays—and it never costs more than 10 bucks.

BARBECUE
PAPPY'S SMOKEHOUSE ⑤
3106 Olive St., 314/535-4340,
www.pappyssmokehouse.com
HOURS: Mon.-Fri. 11 A.M.-8 P.M., Sat.-Sun.
11 A.M.-4 P.M.

When Pappy's Smokehouse opened its doors in early 2008, you could practically hear the chorus of hallelujahs (well, except from the pigs—they weren't too happy). This is the best barbecue restaurant in St. Louis.

© MIKE EMERSON

The digs at Pappy's aren't fancy – but the barbecue is the best in town.

Mike Emerson, a barbecuing champ who got his start with local chain Super Smokers, serves meat so tender that knives are an afterthought. Ribs are absolutely perfect, whether you devour them dry or with one of Pappy's three sauces. Don't miss the sweet-potato fries; their salty-crunchy exterior gives way to a sweet-pillowy interior. This is also one of the few places where you can (and should) get Frito Pie: corn chips piled high with pulled pork, onions, baked beans, and melted cheddar. Just be sure to call before you go—when the day's supply of barbecue runs out, Pappy's closes.

THE U $

3108 Olive St., 314/371-1718, www.theustl.com

HOURS: Mon.-Sat. 11 A.M.-3:30 A.M.

Named for its proximity to Saint Louis University and Harris-Stowe State University, the U offers an education in the arts and science of sandwich making. The U's flat-top grill is the crucial element behind the eatery's hot, made-to-order sandwiches: The course-catalog-inspired menu offers chicken, beef, ham, and tofu concoctions, often paired with melted cheese and savory sauces. You may want to wear your expandable slacks when ordering the cheese fries, available with any combination of chili, bacon, and ranch dressing. Best of all, the U stays open until 3:30 A.M. each night, giving late-night revelers a chance to launch a preemptive strike against tomorrow's hangover.

COFFEEHOUSES

COFFEE CARTEL $

2 Maryland Plaza, 314/454-0000, www.cwecartel.com

HOURS: Daily 24 hours

Located at the busy corner of Euclid Avenue and Maryland Avenue, this popular neighborhood stop teems with life all hours of the

RESTAURANTS

day. Business is at its peak on sunny afternoons, when the café's enormous sidewalk patio welcomes a diverse crowd of coffee-lovers. The Cartel also draws a large crowd most weekend evenings, when it plays host to the under-21, non-drinking set. During the week, local professionals stop in for caffeine fixes and deli sandwiches, and late-night hours make the Cartel a preferred haunt for college students. Visitors are advised to save room for dessert, as the café's most popular items include Edy's hard-serve ice cream and an alluring selection of cheesecakes and tortes.

THE GRIND ⑤

4239 Lindell Blvd., 314/534-1300
HOURS: Tues.-Sun. noon-1:30 A.M.

St. Louisans have witnessed the evolution of The Grind over the years. Back in its early days, this urban coffee oasis was a dingy, smoky study spot for undergrads and med students. Today, the Grind is all grown up. It occupies the first floor of a stately Lindell Boulevard mansion (the mansion's lower level is home to fashionable nightspot Sol), and visitors can take advantage of free WiFi while lounging on designer furniture. The Grind may have received a chic makeover,

EAT LIKE A LOCAL

Spend enough time in St. Louis – and by "enough time" we mean "really just a couple days" – and you will find certain foods listed on practically every restaurant's menu, from hot spots to corner dives. There are a few foods that are so distinctively *St. Louis* that you'd be remiss not to try them at least once. Read the list below, and understand why Tums were invented in St. Louis, too.

ST. LOUIS-STYLE PIZZA

Politics. Religion. Pizza. If you're looking for a good argument in St. Louis, bring up one of the aforementioned topics. St. Louisans take their pizza very, very seriously – even when outsiders consider it strange (or, even worse, mediocre). True St. Louis-style pizza starts with a cracker-thin crust topped with Provel cheese. It's the Provel that really incites debate. Delicious, melty pizza topping or inferior "cheese food"? Decide for yourself by visiting any outpost of the beloved local chain Imo's. Just don't out yourself as a tourist by asking for a "slice" – St. Louis-style pizza is served by the square.

TOASTED RAVIOLI

The origin story of the toasted ravioli varies from teller to teller. Some claim that toasted ravioli is the result of a happy accident, when a St. Louis chef mistakenly dropped stuffed pasta into the deep fryer. Others say that toasted ravioli got its (intentional) start at Oldani's restaurant on the Hill. No matter where they came from, T-ravs (as the locals say) are a super-popular appetizer. You can order meat-filled or cheese-filled T-ravs (meat-filled are more traditional). The deep-fried delights have a structural integrity similar to that of a fried mozzarella stick, and are also served with marinara sauce.

PORK STEAKS

The pork steak is an absolute must-have at any St. Louis summertime barbecue – and plenty of local restaurants serve this popular cut, too. The pork steak comes from a pig's shoulder. While it isn't necessarily the best cut of meat, the pork steak is made but its loyal cadre of students seems to have made the transition just fine—thanks in large part to the dart boards and pool tables on the mansion's third floor.

NADOZ $$

3701 Lindell Blvd., 314/446-6800,
www.nadozcafe.com
HOURS: Mon.-Fri. 7 A.M.-8 P.M., Sat. 8 A.M.-8 P.M., Sun. 10 A.M.-2 P.M.
Located in the first floor of the renovated Coronado Building (a former hotel and current apartment complex), Nadoz is a slightly more upscale café with slightly more upscale prices to match. With a display case of chocolates and pastries that are as beautiful to look at as they are delicious to devour, Nadoz sets its sights a bit higher than your average corner bakery. Likewise, its sandwiches, panini, and crepes bring a European flair to the neighborhood, making it the ideal spot for a quick, light lunch. The grilled salmon BLT with pesto mayonnaise will haunt your dreams after one bite, and the café's salad creations take lettuce to delicious new heights. Nadoz also offers a Sunday brunch that ranks as one of the city's finest.

fork-tender by simmering for hours in barbecue sauce.

ST. PAUL SANDWICH
Yes, it's a little strange that something called a "St. Paul sandwich" originated in St. Louis. And, in all honesty, the St. Paul sandwich itself is a little strange: Take an egg foo yong patty, apply a liberal amount of mayonnaise and a handful of dill pickles, and fold the whole shebang between two slices of Wonder bread. The St. Paul sandwich is getting harder and harder to find, but it can still be ordered at most chop suey places in the city.

GOOEY BUTTER CAKE
Don't call it a baked good – call it a baked *great*. So delicious that some sweet-toothed tourists have carried it back on the plane with them, the gooey butter cake is a true St. Louis original. Recipes vary from bakeshop to bakeshop, but all start with a solid foundation of butter and yellow cake, topped with a cream-cheese mixture and sprinkled with confectioner's sugar. Saint Louis Bread Co., a café empire based here in town (it's called Panera elsewhere), serves gooey butter danishes. At Veruca in Benton Park, pastry chef extraordinaire Mathew Rice bakes gooey butter cookies. There's even a shop on the southside devoted solely to the GBC (Gooey Louie, 6483 Chippewa St.).

THE CONCRETE
For more than 75 years, St. Louisans have flocked to Ted Drewes custard shops. The legendary frozen custard, served out of two southside locations (one at 6726 Chippewa St., the other at 4224 Grand Blvd.), is unparalleled. The most popular Ted Drewes treat is The Concrete: thick custard blended with any number of ingredients and served in an iconic yellow cup. Before your server hands you The Concrete, she'll probably turn it upside down. Don't panic – that's just to prove that the custard's so thick that the spoon won't fall out. Try the Fox Treat, a Concrete with hot fudge, raspberries, and macadamia nuts.

RESTAURANTS

CONTEMPORARY AND NEW AMERICAN

CHEZ LEON ❸❸❸

4580 Laclede Ave., 314/361-1589,
www.chezleon.com

HOURS: Tues.-Thurs. 5:30-10 P.M., Fri.-Sat.
5:30-11 P.M., Sun. 5-9 P.M.

Chez Leon, a traditional upscale French bistro, keeps its many fans happy by turning out consistently great food. Service at this white-tablecloth restaurant is always crisp and friendly; in fact, service here is probably the best in the entire Central West End. The Francophile fare at Chez Leon remains respectfully true to its roots. Consider the popular "3 Plats" prix-fixe menu: a special that, for just $40, allows diners the choice of an incredible entrée (such as veal scallops in a white wine-mushroom sauce, or grilled salmon with a tarragon cream sauce) and two accompanying sides. The lovely wine list is primarily French (no big surprise there), but do know that most bottles will quickly boost your dinner tab into the three-digit range. If you're in St. Louis during the warm months, be sure to request a seat on Chez Leon's gorgeous sidewalk patio. Just squint a little, and you might think you're dining in the middle of a Parisian *arrondissement*.

FIVE ❸❸❸

4317 Manchester Ave., 314/535-5553,
www.fiveinthegrove.com

HOURS: Tues.-Thurs. 5:30-9 P.M., Fri.-Sat.
5:30-10 P.M.

Chef Anthony Devoti took a chance when he opened Five in the up-and-coming Grove area of the Forest Park Southeast neighborhood—not exactly anyone's first destination for contemporary bistro fare. But Devoti has the chops in the kitchen to convert skeptics into fans, and Five is an excellent choice for a fine meal. The small menu features local producers, when possible, resulting in terrific beef, lamb, and even rabbit dishes. A four-course tasting menu, with wine pairings, is a steal at $60. The restaurant frequently hosts special wine dinners as well as movie nights.

MOXY CONTEMPORARY BISTRO ❸❸❸

4584 Laclede Ave., 314/361-4848,
www.moxybistro.com

HOURS: Mon.-Fri. 11 A.M.-11 P.M., Sat.-Sun.
5 P.M.-midnight

Moxy is a cozy modern bistro, all dressed up with an urban-lounge feel. It occupies a small storefront (maybe 15 tables) near the corner of Euclid and Laclede, and offers excellent fusion dishes alongside a menu of old-fashioned cocktails and inventive infusions. Though the fare here is constantly evolving (chef Eric Brenner makes it a point to use height-of-the-season, local ingredients), favorite standbys include lobster potstickers, duck breast with a bacon-butternut hash, and a heavenly sticky toffee pudding. Moxy's $35 prix-fixe menu includes an entrée, appetizer, and dessert; this is one of the best values in town, and a great way to get to know this popular place. If you're traveling with several friends, ask to sit at the long table on Moxy's cool mezzanine level. And be sure to set aside time for an aperitif or nightcap at the bistro's wraparound bar, where friendly urbanites flock nightly.

REVIVAL ❸❸

3800 Chouteau Ave., 314/771-3939,
www.revivalstl.com

HOURS: Tues.-Thurs. 11 A.M.-4 P.M. and 5-10 P.M.,
Fri. 11 A.M.-4 P.M. and 5-11 P.M., Sat. 5-11 P.M.

When Revival opened its doors in 2007, it had big shoes to fill. This restaurant, which specializes in what's best described as "gourmet comfort food," occupies the former King Louie's space—and you'd be hard-pressed to find a St. Louis foodie who doesn't wax nostalgic about that dearly departed bistro. Fortunately, Revival more than fills the void left by its predecessor. Chef Cary McDowell puts elegant twists on Southern classics, turning out plates of fried okra and veal sweetbreads with equal facility. Service can be scattered at times, but meals at Revival are leisurely affairs, so you may not even notice a lag. Absolutely save room for pastry chef Carolyn Downs's ingenious desserts, such as the bourbon balls or the warm chocolate bread pudding with Dr Pepper sauce.

☾ TERRENE ⚫⚫⚫

33 N. Sarah St., 314/535-5100, www.terrene-stlouis.com

While red bricks are still the most common color found in post-industrial St. Louis, a handful of the city's chic establishments have gone green. Take Terrene, for example. Located on the outskirts of the Central West End, this spacious restaurant is eco-friendly in every way: The owners stock their pantry with seasonal fare from local farmers, and the vegetable oil from their fryer fuels a neighbor's biodiesel car. Fortunately, the cooking is as strong as the environmentalism. Terrene offers an excellent selection of small plates, such as mussels in basil-pine nut pesto and white-wine broth, as well as entrées like a bouillabaisse with pan-seared tilapia, shrimp, bay scallops, and seasonal vegetable vermicelli. Reserve a table on the lovely outdoor patio for full eco-appreciation.

© AMY FERGUSON

RESTAURANTS

Terrene goes green with locally sourced foods and an eco-chic design.

INDIAN AND NEPALESE
EVEREST CAFÉ AND BAR ⚫⚫

4145 Manchester Ave., 314/531-4800, www.everestcafeandbar.com

HOURS: Mon.-Wed. 11:30 A.M.-2:30 P.M. and 5-9 P.M., Thurs.-Sat. 11:30 A.M.-2:30 P.M. and 5-9 P.M.

It's not every day that you have the opportunity to eat Nepalese food, but after you taste the outstanding cuisine at Everest, chances are you'll want to eat Nepalese food . . . every day. Owner Devi States recently moved his popularrestaurant from a desolate edge of downtown to the groovier environs of the Grove, but the excellent food remains the same. Because of Nepal's geographic location, the nation's cuisine shares some traits with Chinese and Indian cooking. At Everest, the emphasis is on nutrition; all dishes are sourced from local ingredients and prepared without dairy products. The sizzling lamb *tarkari,* with its side of decadent (yet butter-free!) lentil soup, is particularly delicious.

RASOI ●●

25 N. Euclid Ave., 314/962-5757, www.rasoi.com
HOURS: Mon.-Thurs. 11 A.M.-2:30 P.M. and 5-10 P.M., Fri.-Sat. 11 A.M.-2:30 P.M. and 5-10:30 P.M., Sun. 11 A.M.-2:30 P.M. and 5-9 P.M.

Fans of Rasoi's affordable afternoon buffet will remember the restaurant's less auspicious beginnings in an unassuming storefront around the corner. This popular Indian restaurant has been in the Central West End for more than 10 years and opened the doors of its present location in late 2007. The bright, colorful, beautiful space is a more fitting showcase for the bright dishes served here, including lobster *dosa* (a rice crepe stuffed with lumps of tender sweet lobster meat, sweet potato, and South Indian spices) and classic *tikka masala*. The lunch buffet, which is still served daily, offers Rasoi's most popular dishes and comes highly recommended.

PIZZA

VITO'S ●

3515 Lindell Blvd., 314/534-8486, www.vitosstl.com
HOURS: Mon.-Tues. 11 A.M.-10 P.M., Wed.-Thurs. 11 A.M.-midnight, Fri. 11 A.M.-3 A.M., Sat. 5 P.M.-3 A.M.

Vito's has flourished in the Midtown neighborhood by relying on the premise that people like really good pizza. It sounds simple, but in a town where cracker-thin pizza crust is a litmus test for St. Louis pride, Vito's stands by its Sicilian-style crust and above-average toppings (think pine nuts and

portobello mushrooms). A long-time favorite of college kids and downtown businesspeople alike, the weekday lunch buffet (with all-you-can-eat pizza, salad, pasta, and soup) runs 11 A.M.–3 P.M. The dinner menu offers more Italian favorites, and both the comfy dining room and the airy patio make a great pre-show stop before going to the nearby Fox Theatre. Those looking for a late-night drink or snack will appreciate Vito's 3 A.M. closing time on Fridays and Saturdays—because, really, it's *always* time for pizza.

DRESSEL'S PUB ●

419 N. Euclid Ave., 314/361-1060, www.dresselspub.com
HOURS: Mon.-Sat. 11:30 A.M.-1:30 A.M., Sun. 11:30 A.M.-midnight, kitchen hours Mon.-Thurs. 11:30 A.M.-11:15 P.M., Fri.-Sat. 11:30 A.M.-11:45 P.M., Sun. 11:30 A.M.-10:15 P.M.

While Welsh food can be a tricky style to define, we know a thing or two about Welsh beers—clean, crisp, and with the perfect amount of bite. Luckily, Dressel's knows a few things about Welsh beers too, and the cozy bar and grill keeps more than a few on tap, along with more traditional Irish and English varieties of lager and stout. The menu features typical pub grub (burgers, Reubens, and the like) as well as more continental fare (the steamed mussels are a treat), but the real draw is the housemade potato chips. Paired with either malt vinegar or the pub's cheesy, tangy rarebit sauce, the chips alone are worth the trip. Those looking for a place to enjoy a relaxing pint can retire to the Pub Above, where a fireplace, full bar, and pool table provide the ideal oasis away from the world outside.

LLYWELYN'S §

4747 McPherson Ave., 314/361-3003,
www.llywelynspub.com

HOURS: Bar open Mon.-Sat. 11 A.M.-1:30 A.M.;
kitchen open Mon.-Thurs. 11 A.M.-11 P.M., Fri.-Sat.
11 A.M.-midnight, Sun. noon-10:30 P.M.

There are three Llywelyn's outposts in St. Louis now, but the original location of this popular Welsh pub feels the coziest and most authentic. On nice days, patrons pack the patio and enjoy people-watching on the upscale, gallery-lined McPherson Avenue. (The newly expanded beer garden out back is great, too.) Visitors can choose from an impressive selection of beers and brown spirits, as well as a number of traditional Welsh and American pub dishes. The crisp fried pickle spears should not be missed—nor should Llywelyn's signature rarebit, which can be ordered with house-made chips or atop a grilled hamburger.

▮ SCHLAFLY TAP ROOM §§

2100 Locust St., 314/241-2337,
www.schlafly.com

HOURS: Mon.-Tues. 11 A.M.-9 P.M., Wed.-Thurs.
11 A.M.-10 P.M., Fri.-Sat. 11 A.M.-midnight, Sun.
noon-9 P.M.

A genuine brewpub, the Schlafly Tap Room serves rustic English, German, and American fare designed to complement the popular microbrews created on premise. Service can be hit-or-miss, particularly during peak hours, but most servers will be happy to recommend pairings when the menu does not. Of particular note are the house-made soft pretzels and the most excellent fish-and-chips in town. Housed in a beautiful historic building, the Tap Room is an ideal place for casual dining and leisurely drinking. But weekend diners, beware: Conversation becomes difficult when boisterous crowds fill the high-ceilinged dining room and adjacent bar.

SOUL FOOD
▮ SWEETIE PIE'S §

4270 Manchester Ave., 314/371-0304

HOURS: Tues.-Sat. 11 A.M.-8 P.M., Sun.
11:45 A.M.-8 P.M.

Located in the historic Grove neighborhood, Sweetie Pie's may remind visitors of the soul-food cafeterias that are blissfully abundant in the South. This popular spot is owned by Robbie Montgomery, a former backup singer for Ike Turner whose musical talent is matched only by her culinary abilities. Every morning around 11, Montgomery's congenial staff places soul-food standards (okra, mac 'n' cheese, oxtail stew) on the 14-foot line. Items are priced per piece, so just point to what you'd like and have it dished up by the heaping slotted spoonful. Crowd favorites include the bread pudding, fried chicken, and collard greens—but really, everything here is good. Just be sure that your schedule leaves time for an afternoon nap.

RESTAURANTS

Soulard and Lafayette Square   Map 3

AMERICAN
THE SHANGRI-LA DINER $

2201 Cherokee St., 314/772-8308,
www.theshangriladiner.com

The Shangri-La puts on one of the best, busiest Sunday brunches in the city—and offers some vegetarian versions of diner classics, from the classic Reuben to the chocolate shake. Shangri-La's owner, Patrice Mari, got her start by catering an immensely popular brunch at the South City coffee shop MoKaBe's. Hers was one of the very, very few all-vegetarian brunches in town; the tofu scrambles, divine eggless quiches, and stuffed crème-brûlée French toast were in such high demand that Mari eventually decided to open her own place. Today, this bright and whimsical space offers a full lunch and dinner menu—but it's the Sunday brunch that really packs 'em in.

CAJUN AND CREOLE
NORTON'S CAFÉ $

808 Geyer Ave., 314/436-0828,
www.nortonscafe.com

HOURS: Mon.-Thurs. 11 A.M.-11 P.M., Fri.-Sat.
11 A.M.-midnight, Sun. 11 A.M.-10 P.M.

Soulard is a neighborhood in which outdoor drinking and dining is a fine art. Most of the area's best spots offer alfresco seating, which many diners prefer to being cooped up indoors. Norton's spacious, sunken patio is one of the absolute best in Soulard. Billed as a "New Orleans–style courtyard" that can seat up to 200 patrons, Norton's patio provides a shady, secluded spot to dig into the restaurant's Cajun-inspired fare. Entrées include jambalaya and red beans and rice, and sandwiches continue the N'awlins theme with

the excellent Cajun Hot Link (an andouille sausage given a St. Louis twist with the addition of Provel cheese) alongside burgers and other standard bar fare. If you visit during the humid, muggy months of July and August, you could be convinced that you've been transported to the Big Easy.

CONTEMPORARY AND NEW AMERICAN
FRANCO $$$

1535 S. 8th St., 314/436-2500,
www.eatatfranco.com

HOURS: Mon.-Thurs. 11 A.M.-2 P.M. and 5-10 P.M.,
Fri. 11 A.M.-2 P.M. and 5-11 P.M., Sat. 5-11 P.M.

The name refers to owner Tom Schmidt's nephew—look for the photograph of a toddler just inside the entrance—but Franco does in fact offer a contemporary American take on classic French bistro cuisine: escargot, house-made pâté, sweetbreads, and mussels. Don't miss the *pommes frites* (that's, uh, French for French fries), either on their own or with a juicy wood-grilled steak. Seafood dishes are also a good bet. With high ceilings, exposed brick, large windows, and a cool mural above the open kitchen, Franco is one of the most attractive dining spaces in town. The vibe suits both a romantic dinner for two and a night on the town with pals.

(NICHE $$$

1831 Sidney St., 314/773-7755,
www.nichestlouis.com

HOURS: Mon.-Thurs. 5:30-9 P.M., Fri.-Sat.
5:30-10 P.M., Sun. 5-9 P.M.

Niche owner and executive chef Gerard Craft is the brightest star of the current dining scene in St. Louis. In 2008, he was the first St. Louis chef to be named one of *Food & Wine* magazine's "Best New Chefs." Despite all the acclaim, Craft's focus remains the food. His restaurant is lovely but unpretentious, and his dishes aim for purity of flavor. Often a single unexpected ingredient will elevate a dish from excellent to sublime, like a pairing of white-chocolate hummus with lamb or watermelon with blackfin tuna. Pastry chef Mathew Rice's indulgent, whimsical desserts are so fantastic that Craft recently opened a bakeshop, Veruca, next door.

DESSERT
C BAILEYS' CHOCOLATE BAR $

1915 Park Ave., 314/241-8100,
www.baileyschocolatebar.com
HOURS: Mon.-Sat. 4 P.M.-1 A.M., Sun.
4 P.M.-midnight

Just *try* not to feel romantic at Baileys' Chocolate Bar. The restaurant's seductively dim lighting, flickering candle sconces, and surplus of red roses make it impossible not to feel a bit giddy. Dave Bailey (the young restaurant impresario who's also responsible for fabulous downtown creperie Rooster) has crafted a menu of high-quality decadence. Sure, there are cheese plates and pizzettas, but locals flock here for the chocolate. Desserts include Fudgy Truffle Chocolate Cake, Chocolate Sundae Overdrive, and Chocolate Voodoo Bread Pudding. Want to have your chocolate and drink it too? Order from the extensive chocolate martini menu, which boasts varieties from Thin Mint to white chocolate. Since its 2004 opening, Baileys' has been one of the most popular places in town—so be prepared to wait for a table on weekends.

© AMY FERGUSON

RESTAURANTS

Indulge your senses at Baileys' Chocolate Bar, the hottest date spot in Lafayette Square.

MEXICAN
ARCELIA'S MEXICANA RESTAURANT $

2001 Park Ave., 314/231-9200
HOURS: Mon.-Thurs. 11 A.M.-2 P.M. and 5-9 P.M.,
Fri.-Sat. 11 A.M.-10 P.M., Sun. 11 A.M.-9 P.M.

Located right across the street from beautiful Lafayette Park, Arcelia's is one of the city's most beloved Mexican restaurants. The fare served here runs the typical taco-burrito-enchilada gamut, but there are also some delicious family favorites. Try the *enchiladas de crema* (which are baked with mild green chiles and served with a decadent sour cream sauce) and traditional *pozole* (pork-and-hominy soup). The salsa and guacamole are consistently fabulous. And if you skipped breakfast, be sure to atone with the excellent *huevos rancheros*.

LA VALLESANA ⑤

2818 Cherokee St., 314/776-4223

HOURS: Daily 11 A.M.-8 P.M.

La Vallesana, a brightly painted walk-up taco stand at the corner of Cherokee and California, offers one of the tastiest lunch bargains in the city. A generously stuffed burrito (with grilled chicken, steak, or shrimp) is only $6, and it comes with chips and a side of homemade guacamole. The ever-popular *torta* or two *tacos al pastor* can be had for a mere $5. Beloved by neighborhood residents and out-of-town gourmands alike, this *taquería* is an absolute hive of activity during afternoon hours. La Vallesana is located in the Hispanic pocket of Benton Park, just a couple blocks west of Cherokee Street's antique row. Stop here after your antique-shopping adventure, and do stay for dessert. The handmade ice cream bars are divine.

TAQUERÍA EL BRONCO ⑤

2812 Cherokee St., 314/762-0691

HOURS: Tues.-Sun. 10 A.M.-8 P.M.

This small, welcoming storefront *taquería* is just one of a handful like it in this predominantly Hispanic area, but it is among the very best. While many *taquerías* in the neighborhood only offer walk-up service, El Bronco features table service. This is the perfect place for a quick, inexpensive sit-down meal. From the treating-you-like-family service to the outstanding complimentary red and green salsas, El Bronco hits all the right notes. Menu standouts include *tacos al pastor* and chunky, impeccably fresh guacamole. This is also one of the few *taquerías* in town with a liquor license. Visitors can enjoy a great margarita or beer with their delicious from-scratch meal, making El Bronco a perfect first stop for a fun night on the town.

PIZZA

JOANIE'S PIZZERIA ⑤

2101 Menard St., 314/865-1994,
www.joanies.com

HOURS: Sun.-Thurs. 11 A.M.-11 P.M., Fri.-Sat. 11 A.M.-midnight

While it's a fact that Joanie's Pizzeria has an indoor dining room, most long-time patrons have never sat in it. The pizzeria's patio, guarded by wrought-iron fences and tasteful brickwork, is an idyllic setting, perfect for sharing one of Joanie's not-too-thin/not-too-thick pizzas and a bucket of beers. The pizza menu offers the build-it-yourself basics, but take a gamble and try one or two of the house specialties: Franco's Cajun Pride features seasoned ground beef, black olives, and cayenne pepper, while Joanie's Favorite Veggie takes a healthier path with fresh spinach, yellow squash, and garlic. Joanie's also offers a few basic pasta dishes (spaghetti, cannelloni, lasagna) and a handful of hot and cold sandwiches.

South City
Map 4

AMERICAN
CITY DINER $

3139 S. Grand Blvd., 314/772-6100,
www.citydiner.us
HOURS: Mon.-Thurs. 7 A.M.-11 P.M., Fri.-Sat.
24 hours, Sun. closes at 10 P.M.
City Diner is a southside classic. This big,
bright restaurant feeds hungry families out
for Sunday supper, rushed businesspeople
in need of a quick bite, and raucous bar-
hoppershoping to counteract the booze
with a plateful of greasy goodness. The
food is straight-up diner fare (hand-cut
fries, club sandwiches, biscuits and gravy)
with a few unexpected twists (like a delicious veggie burrito). The young, tattooed
waitstaff moves through the room with
efficiency and good cheer, even when the
bar crowds get ornery. Walls are adorned
with vintage movie posters and album covers, and the shady back patio is the perfect
perch for people-watching. If you can get
the green light from your cardiologist, try
the meatloaf omelet.

COURTESY DINER $

3153 S. Kingshighway, 314/776-9059
HOURS: Sun.-Mon. 6 A.M.-10 P.M., Tues.-Thurs.
6 A.M.-4 A.M., Fri.-Sat. 24 hours
Miss the old-fashioned American diner?
The tradition thrives at the Courtesy,
one of St. Louis's most beloved late-night
hangouts. The place may not look like
much, but the "hiya-sweetie" service is
delightful and the food is straight-up
delicious. The Courtesy makes a mean
cheeseburger, which just might drive you
crazy with hungry anticipation as it sizzles
on the flat-top grill. Chili mac, a Midwestern favorite, is served by the heaping
bowlful here. And don't miss the chance to
try a true St. Louis tradition: the slinger.
For the uninitiated, that's a hamburger
patty topped with two eggs, hash browns,
chili, and cheese. St. Louisans have long
counted on late-night Courtesy slingers to
stave off next-morning hangovers. Need
another reason to check this place out? The
Courtesy has one heck of a jukebox.

IRON BARLEY $$

5510 Virginia St., 314/351-4500,
www.ironbarley.com
HOURS: Mon.-Thurs. 11 A.M.-10 P.M., Fri.-Sat.
11 A.M.-11 P.M.
The food at Iron Barley is as delightful as
owner-chef Tom Coghill's ebullient personality. The menu also shares Coghill's
fine sense of adventure and fun. While the
dishes at Iron Barley could be best catego-
rized as "comfort food," Coghill's playful
recipes promise something far more interesting than your typical mac 'n' cheese.
The schnitzel and spaetzle—hammered-
thin pork (not veal) atop ethereally light
noodles, topped with a savory brown
gravy—is excellent, as are the bacon-studded
green beans that often accompany it. Coghill also offers overstuffed "sammiches"
and Southern classics like barbecued
shrimp. Live acoustic music sets the folksy
vibe most weekend nights. Iron Barley recently received star treatment on the Food
Network's *Diners, Drive-Ins, and Dives,* so
curious crowds may cause a spike in the
usual waiting time.

MOM'S DELI $

4412 Jamieson Ave., 314/644-1198

HOURS: Mon.-Sat. 8 A.M.-8 P.M., Sun. 8 A.M.-6 P.M.

In these days of deconstructed dishes and re-imagined entrées, it's refreshing to know that the humble sandwich remains a paragon of simplicity and do-it-yourself ingenu-ity. And in a city peppered with plenty of fine delis, Mom's Deli stands tall in the St. Louis Hills neighborhood thanks to its old-school charm and, of course, the un-beatable sandwiches. The storefront shop houses fridges full of beer and soda and a fine selection of chips and snacks, but you're here for the meat counter. Sidle up

TO MARKET, TO MARKET

Whether you're looking for a quick take-and-heat meal or have the capability to turn out an entire feast in your hotel's kitchenette, you'll find plenty of gro-cery options in St. Louis. Hometown chain **Schnucks** (multiple locations, including 6600 Clayton Rd., Richmond Heights) is a favorite among residents, thanks to low prices, a broad wine and beer selection, and the availability of neighborhood-specific food items (the Schnucks on the Hill has a particularly great assortment of Italian meats and cheeses). **Dierbergs** (multiple locations, including 8450 Eager Rd., Brentwood) is another popular option, although items tend to be a little bit pricier.

Visitors staying in the Central West End should be sure to check out **Straub's** (302 North Kingshighway Blvd., addi-tional locations in Webster Groves and Clayton). This small market boasts one of the best takeout counters in town; the potatoes Dauphine and homemade macaroni and cheese are out of this world. There are also several outposts of affordable-gourmet fave **Trader Joe's** (the most centrally located is at 48 Brent-wood Promenade Ct., Brentwood), along with two **Whole Foods** locations (the clos-est one to the city proper is at 1601 South Brentwood Blvd., Brentwood).

If you're in St. Louis between April and October, check out one of the many farmers markets. The most well-known is **Soulard Farmers Market** (730 Car-roll St.), but in recent years others have popped up all over town. **Tower Grove Farmers Market** (in Tower Grove Park, off Arsenal St.) bustles with life on Sat-urday mornings. You'll find plenty of produce, organic meats, and fresh flow-ers – plus lemonade stands and a fire truck that dishes out ice cream. The **Ma-plewood Farmers Market,** which unfolds Wednesday afternoons in the parking lot of **Schlafly Bottleworks** (7260 South-west Ave., Maplewood), has the added amenities of live music and cold beer.

When you visit the Grand South Grand district, stop in **Jay's International Market** (3172 South Grand Blvd.). This globally minded market carries every-thing from miso to challah and tamarind sodas to Pocky. Plus, Jay's is ultra-affordable (tea lovers will find excellent varieties for less than three bucks a box). There are a number of authentic Mexican markets on Cherokee Street, including **El Torito Supermarket** (2753 Cherokee St.), and University City and Olivette are home to dozens of Asian markets, including **Seafood City** (7733 Olive Blvd. University City).

and order any of the deli's signature sandwiches—Mom's Special is a best-seller, with a thick stack of turkey, ham, and roast beef brought to life by tangy 1,000 Island dressing. Better still is Ron's Special, a spicy mélange of salami, pepper jack cheese, and mustard. Be prepared to wait in line on the weekends, but once you have paid for your feast you can dine on one of the outdoor tables or picnic at one of the nearby neighborhood parks.

SCHLAFLY BOTTLEWORKS ⑤⑤

7260 Southwest Ave., Maplewood,
314/241-2337, www.schlafly.com
HOURS: Sun.-Tues. 11 A.M.-9 P.M., Wed.-Thurs.
11 A.M.-10 P.M., Fri.-Sat. 11 A.M.-11 P.M.

Visitors to the Schlafly Bottleworks in downtown Maplewood can tour the microbrewery's facilities, then enjoy the fruits of the brewers' labor in the clean, casual atmosphere of the adjacent restaurant. The Bottleworks offers a wide selection of locally sourced dishes, including an excellent free-range bison burger, and most items are listed with a recommended beer pairing. Consider taking a refillable jug of fresh-poured beer out with you when you leave—these half-gallon "growlers" make an excellent addition to the hotel minifridge.

ASIAN
FU MANCHU ⑤⑤

7336 Manchester Ave., 314/647-3331
HOURS: Mon.-Fri. 11 A.M.-11 P.M., Sat.-Sun.
5-11 P.M.

Future restaurant entrepreneurs, take note. Mike Johnson, the powerhouse restaurateur behind this playful Asian-fusion restaurant, has built a successful mini-empire in St. Louis. His efforts are sometimes met with mixed reviews (El Scorcho, the quasi-Mexican restaurant right down the block from Fu Manchu, is hopelessly bland), but he often hits the mark. Fu Manchu is a great place for inventive cocktails (many are made with sake) and yummy small plates. Specialties include silver-dollar-sized Kobe burgers, delectable Korean pork ribs, crab Rangoon made with real crab meat (a rarity in the Midwest), and asparagus tempura. The crowd here is young, the light-hearted decor is fun (when it doesn't venture too far into stereotype territory), and the bar is open until 1:30 A.M.

KING & I ⑤

3157 S. Grand Blvd., 314/771-1777,
www.thaispicy.com
HOURS: Tues.-Thurs. 11 A.M.-2:30 P.M. and 5-9:30 P.M., Fri. 11 A.M.-2:30 P.M. and 5-10 P.M., Sat. noon-3 P.M. and 5-10 P.M., Sun. noon-3 P.M. and 5-9 P.M.

There is good Thai food all over the St. Louis region, but city-dwellers have a special affection for King & I. This South Grand stalwart is one of the oldest—and best—Thai restaurants around. The menu sometimes veers into cutesy territory (Thai ravioli, Thai fajitas), but the perfectly prepared curries more than make up for the misguided attempts at Asian fusion. The green-curry dishes are particularly delicious; sweet coconut milk tempers the spicy, addictively good sauce. Soups, including shrimp *tom yum,* are also excellent. Service is brisk but friendly, and the prices are great. Plus, you can soothe your burning tongue with a traditional Thai iced coffee, the Thai beer Singha, or a "Siam Stinker"—that's rum, brandy, sloe gin, and fruit juice.

LEMONGRASS $

3161 S. Grand Blvd., 314/664-6702,
www.lemongrass-rest.com

HOURS: Tues.-Thurs. 10 A.M.-10 P.M., Fri.-Sat.
11 A.M.-11 P.M., Sun. 10 A.M.-10 P.M.

Nestled in a sunny space on South Grand's
ethnic-restaurant row, LemonGrass offers some of the best Vietnamese cuisine in
town. The restaurant underwent a serious
makeover a couple years ago (fortunately,
the owners kept the kitschy-fabulous metal
lobsters that decorate the walls). Lemon-
Grass's menu seems as massive as a Pynchon
novel, but don't worry: The servers are happy
to recommend their favorites—and, be-
sides, everything here is good. Traditional
spring rolls are packed with smoky pork,
cool shrimp, and fresh vegetables. Steaming
bowls of *pho* (Vietnamese noodle soup) are
the ultimate in comfort food. For a real treat,
try *com thit nuong dac biet:* charbroiled pork,
egg cake, and pork skin served over rice and
topped with an over-easy egg.

PHO GRAND $

3195 S. Grand Blvd., 314/664-7435,
www.phogrand.com

HOURS: Mon. 11 A.M.-10 P.M., Wed.-Thurs.
11 A.M.-10 P.M., Fri.-Sat. 11 A.M.-11 P.M., Sun.
11 A.M.-10 P.M.

When it comes to good Vietnamese food,
St. Louis is fortunate to have an embarrass-
ment of riches. Pho Grand is perhaps the
best-known Vietnamese restaurant in town,
thanks to a decade-plus of serving authentic dishes to loyal crowds. The restaurant's
popularity can lead to lengthy waits (particularly on Friday and Saturday nights), but
your patience will be rewarded with great
food and gracious service. Try the *banh xeo:*
ethereally light rice-flour crepes, filled with

pork, shrimp, and crunchy bean sprouts.
Pho Grand is particularly accommodating of
large crowds, which means the decibel level
can get fairly high, but there are also plenty
of nooks fit for quiet conversation.

BOSNIAN

GRBIC $$

4071 Keokuk St., 314/772-3100,
www.grbicrestaurant.com

HOURS: Tues.-Fri. 11 A.M.-9:30 P.M., Sat. 4-10 P.M.,
Sun. 3-8 P.M.

You'll find Grbic in the predominantly Bosnian neighborhood south of Gravois Road,
in a huge old building that was once a busy
neighborhood dairy. The German masonry
of this enormous space complements Grbic's
Eastern European cuisine quite nicely. The
menu features Hungarian goulash and German spaetzle, but branch out and try such
Bosnian favorites as *cevapi* (spicy, finger-length
beef sausages) and *palacinke* (dessert crepes
filled with chocolate sauce, whipped cream,
and walnuts). Members of St. Louis's Bosnian
community frequently gather at Grbic to celebrate important occasions, and that warm,
familial vibe is definitely extended to visitors.

COFFEEHOUSES

MURDOCH PERK $

5400 Murdoch Ave., 314/753-9126,
www.murdochperk.net

HOURS: Tues.-Fri. 7 A.M.-9 P.M., Sat.-Sun.
8 A.M.-9 P.M.

Over the past few years, a sleepy little stretch
of the St. Louis Hills neighborhood has been
invigorated by the flourishing businesses on
Murdoch Avenue. There are delis, specialty
shops, and a few popular watering holes, but
Murdoch Perk serves as the hub for much
of the neighborhood activity. The coffee

house and eatery (housed in a former dry-cleaning shop) offers the standard frou-frou coffee drinks and serves breakfast all day, offering a number of sweet crepes and some fabulous Belgian waffles. Savory crepes are available for lunch and dinner, along with some lighter-fare sandwiches and salads. The main dining room is cozy but can often be crowded, though on pleasant days the patio is quiet and shaded. Murdoch Perk may be tucked away in a little pocket of the city's south side, but the spot is worth finding if only to feel like a native St. Louisan.

CONTEMPORARY AND NEW AMERICAN
THE SHAVED DUCK $$

2900 Virginia Ave., 314/776-1407,
www.theshavedduck.com
HOURS: Tues.-Sat. 5-10 P.M. (bar open until 12:30 A.M.)

The Shaved Duck is a treasure. A cozy European bistro tucked into a lovely residential area, this restaurant, which opened in 2008, is already one of St. Louis's best. Chef Brendan Noonan uses local ingredients whenever possible, and his inventive preparations allow individual elements—like perfectly grilled peaches or meltingly tender duck confit—to shine. The small dining room's dark woods and navy accents suit the simple but elegant pass-around menu items. Standouts include a rabbit cassoulet served over green lentils and skinny *frites* cooked in duck fat. The libation list is full of surprises, like an orange-rosemary mojito. A local brew guru consulted on the beer list, and as a result The Shaved Duck serves hard-to-find beers like Rogue's Morimoto Imperial Pilsner—*on tap!* This little restaurant never, ever fails to impress.

ETHIOPIAN
MESKEREM ETHIOPIAN RESTAURANT $

3210 S. Grand Blvd., 314/772-4442,
www.meskeremstl.com
HOURS: Mon.-Thurs. 11 A.M.-11 P.M., Fri.-Sat. 11 A.M.-midnight, Sun. 11:30 A.M.-10 P.M.

Visitors seeking a unique dining experience have plenty of options on this ethnically diverse South City boulevard—but Meskerem surely offers one of the most distinctive. Locals love this Ethiopian restaurant's congenial staff, strong spiced tea, and authentic *wat* (savory stew). No utensils are on the tables here; just use your right hand and a piece of spongy *injera* bread to scoop up tender cubes of lamb, beef, and roasted bone-in chicken, as well as lentils and vegetables. A blend of traditional Ethiopian spices punctuates every plate, and the familiar staple ingredients make this unfamiliar cuisine thoroughly comforting, especially on a cold day. Vegetarians will adore the smoky, savory greens and refreshing *tinatim* salad.

ITALIAN
MANGIA ITALIANO $$

3145 S. Grand Blvd., 314/664-8585,
www.dineatmangia.com
HOURS: Mon.-Thurs. 11:30 A.M.-10 P.M., Fri.-Sat. 11:30 A.M.-10:30 P.M., Sun. 10 A.M.-4 P.M. (brunch) and 5-10 P.M.

Mangia Italiano (just call it "Mangia" if you want to sound like a local) is a hip hangout that happens to serve absolutely delicious food. The pasta is the biggest draw—in fact, Mangia's handmade noodles are so popular that the restaurant packages them for sale at many local farmers markets and organic grocery stores. Perennial favorites include Vermicelli G.O.C. (garlic, olive oil, and cheese) and mushroom tagliatelle in a sun-dried-tomato cream sauce. Nightly specials always make use of the freshest seasonal ingredients. If you don't want your pasta with a side of cigarette smoke and rock 'n' roll, be sure to arrive before 10 P.M.—at that time, Mangia assumes its identity as one of the south side's most popular bars.

ONESTO ❸❸

5401 Finkman St., 314/802-8883,
www.onestopizza.com

HOURS: Mon.-Thurs. 11 A.M.-10 P.M., Fri.-Sat. 11 A.M.-10:30 P.M., Sun. noon-9 P.M.

Few people in St. Louis know pizza as well as the Racanelli family. Onesto's head pizza-baker and pasta-maker, Vito Racanelli, is a Brooklyn transplant who comes from a long line of spoon-wielding Sicilians. Vito believes that nothing should be more honest than

food, so each of his artisan pizzas, salads, and pasta dishes is made from scratch with the freshest ingredients available. Visitors to this casual bistro should seize the opportunity to try real fettuccine, served in the traditional style (topped with an egg yolk). Delicious brick-oven-baked pizzas include the Queen Margherita (fresh plum tomato sauce, mozzarella, and basil) and the Mad Cajun (shrimp, andouille sausage, fire-roasted peppers, and jalapeños).

STELLINA PASTA CAFÉ ❸

3342 Watson Rd., 314/256-1600,
www.stellinapasta.com

HOURS: Tues.-Thurs. 10 A.M.-9 P.M., Fri.-Sat. 10 A.M.-10 P.M.

Ask a St. Louisan where to find the city's best sandwich, and you'll hear all sorts of different answers. Ignore them. The best sandwich in

Stellina Pasta Café is a gourmet treasure on the south side.

© JAMEY TOCHTROP

St. Louis is Stellina Pasta Café's "South Side Smoke": pulled pork topped with caramelized onion and smoked gouda cheese on ciabatta bread seasoned with sea salt. Is it messy? Well, yes, but so is life. But if you must be fancy, co-owner and chef Jamey Tochtrop serves three pasta dishes each day, all of which feature fresh homemade pasta. Tochtrop's wife, Lisa, creates Stellina's delicious desserts. A small gem worth seeking out.

MEXICAN
EL BURRITO LOCO $
3611 Bates Ave., 314/457-8600
HOURS: Mon.-Thurs. 11 A.M.-8 P.M., Fri.-Sat. 11 A.M.-9 P.M.

Popular with families and penny-pinching students alike, El Burrito Loco serves up huge, meal-and-a-half burritos. Many fast-food Mexican joints claim burrito supremacy, but they don't have a thing on El Burrito Loco. These are the real deal: homemade tortillas (wheat, corn, or flour) filled with everything from chipotle-stewed chicken to chorizo. El Burrito Loco also offers plenty of vegetarian options, including the El Primo, which includes such ingredients as guacamole and spicy fried potatoes. Meals at this family-run restaurant begin with chips and a mildly fiery salsa, and non-burrito choices include excellent tamales, quesadillas, and *tres leches* cake.

PIZZA
BLACKTHORN PIZZA & PUB $
3735 Wyoming St., 314/776-0534,
www.gatewaytothewest.com/blackthorn
HOURS: Daily 5-11:45 P.M.; bar open until 1 A.M. Mon.-Sat., midnight Sun.

Blackthorn Pizza & Pub serves up a slice of southside life—in addition to Chicago-style pies so good that they justify the hour-plus wait. Order a pitcher of beer (Blackthorn keeps a nice rotation of microbrews and imports on tap), slide into a wooden booth, and see why St. Louisans have been coming here for more than 20 years. The laid-back neighborhood vibe and friendly competition (air hockey, anyone?) are appealing, to be sure. But it's the pizza—with its perfectly chewy crust, kicky tomato sauce, and bubbling mozzarella cheese—that makes this place legendary. If the super-dense Chicago-style pizza seems a bit daunting, go for an equally delicious thin-crust pie.

RESTAURANTS

Dogtown and the Hill   Map 5

AMERICAN
FELIX'S ⑤
6335 Clayton Ave., 314/645-6565,
www.felixsrestaurant.com
HOURS: Mon.-Fri. 4 P.M.-1:30 A.M., Sat.
11 A.M.-1:30 A.M., Sun. 11 A.M.-midnight

One of the best things about the Dogtown neighborhood is the gastronomic diversity found in such a small swatch of town. While you can find some of the town's best fried chicken and hamburgers in Dogtown, Felix's offers a slightly lighter menu and a more up-scale (if still casual) vibe. The menu is heavy on appetizers, wraps, and single-serving pizzas, and the corner spot has become a haven for pork lovers thanks to its great barbecue ribs. But Felix's is as much a bar as it is a grill, as the locals who populate the bar-stools will tell you. There is a nice wine and martini list, and the dining room plays host to live local music a few nights a week.

GREEK
OLYMPIA KEBOB HOUSE & TAVERNA ⑤
1543 McCausland Ave., 314/781-1299
HOURS: Mon.-Wed. 11 A.M.-10 P.M., Thurs.-Sat.
11 A.M.-11 P.M., Sun. 11 A.M.-9 P.M.

Olympia's lightning-fast service, friendly atmosphere, and large patio make it the go-to Greek spot for locals. In addition to the basic gyro (served with steak fries), the menu offers such Mediterranean staples as *moussaka, spanokapita,* and the ever-popular flaming *kasseri* cheese. Diners should not overlook the *avgolemono* (creamy lemon-chicken soup with tender grains of orzo) or garlic-heavy hummus. Fans of the Greek aperitif ouzo will be happy to find it here, served in a snifter with a couple of coffee beans.

ITALIAN
AMIGHETTI'S BAKERY AND CAFÉ ⑤
5141 Wilson Ave., 314/776-2855,
www.amighettis.com
HOURS: Mon. 8 A.M.-3 P.M., Tues.-Fri.
9 A.M.-7 P.M., Sat. 9 A.M.-5:30 P.M.

A true family-run business, Amighetti's has been in operation on the Hill since 1921. This quaint bakeshop and deli is best known for the eponymous Amighetti's Special, a loaf of freshly baked bread piled high with ham, roast beef, Genoa salami, brick cheese, and pepperoncinis. Amighetti's also offers a long list of variations on this perennially popular deli sandwich, alongside such pasta dishes as *cavatelli con broccoli* (shells and broccoli in a

© AMY FERGUSON

Olympia's popular patio is the perfect backdrop for enjoying tasty Greek fare.

RESTAURANTS

marinara-spiked cream sauce). The café's casual, counter-service dining attracts families with kids, and those visiting on a weekend afternoon should expect a long (and noisy) wait. Today there are three Amighetti's locations in the St. Louis area, but only the original shop bakes its own bread fresh daily.

GIOIA'S DELI ❸

1934 Macklind Ave., 314/776-9410
HOURS: Mon.-Fri. 9 A.M.-4 P.M., Sat. 9 A.M.-3 P.M.
The Gioia family opened its namesake grocery store in 1918. The store was sold in 1980, but Gioia's Deli remains one of the city's best sandwich shops, its modest location in keeping with the family-friendly Hill neighborhood. Gioia's signature dish features its homemade hot salami (also known as *Salam de Testa*), a delicious blend of beef and that St. Louis specialty, pig snout. Not adventurous enough for pig snout? Don't worry. There are plenty of other terrific Italian lunchmeats, including Genoa salami and mortadella. Save room for the homemade Italian ices.

PIZZA

🄲 PIZZA-A-GO-GO ❸

6703 Scanlan Ave., 314/781-1234,
http://pizzaagogo.blogspot.com
HOURS: Sun.-Tues. and Thurs. 4-9 P.M., Fri.-Sat.
4-10 P.M.
Pizza-a-Go-Go is a no-frills pizza joint. No checks. No credit cards. No beer—but you're welcome to bring your own. You order your pie at the window, then sit down in a vinyl chair to wait. So why make a special trip to Pizza-a-Go-Go? Because there is great happiness in simple pleasures, and this pizza is simply the best. Because this is a true St. Louis institution, open since 1964. Because Paul LaFata (son of Frank,

the original owner) takes great pride in making from-scratch crust. The toppings run the gamut from Canadian bacon to anchovies, although you may want to do like the locals and order "The Special": a classically delicious pie topped with sausage, pepperoni, mushroom, green pepper, and onion.

PUB FOOD

MICHAEL'S BAR & GRILL ❸❸

7101 Manchester Ave., Maplewood,
314/644-2220
HOURS: Mon.-Sat. 11 A.M.-1:30 A.M., Sun.
11 A.M.-midnight
You may have to hoof it across busy Manchester Avenue to get to Michael's, but the food here is worth any Frogger-style peril. This St. Louis institution serves up the platonic ideal of bar fare, in addition to a full complement of excellent Greek cuisine (courtesy of owner Michael Malliotakis). Of particular note are the juicy burgers and the falling-off-the-bone-tender lamb shanks. And if you want a solid introduction to toasted ravioli—a much-beloved part of the St. Louis food pantheon—order up a basket here. Michael's is crowded most of the time, but with seating available on two levels and on the patio, the wait is rarely intolerable. Plus, there's usually a Cardinals, Blues, or Rams game on TV.

PAT'S BAR & GRILL ❸

6400 Oakland Ave., 314/647-6553,
www.patsbarandgrill.com
HOURS: Mon.-Thurs. 6 A.M.-10 P.M., Fri.
6 A.M.-10:30 P.M., Sat. 9 A.M.-10:30 P.M., Sun.
10 A.M.-9 P.M. (brunch 11 A.M.-2 P.M.); bar open
Mon.-Sat. until 1:30 A.M., Sun. until midnight
Hanging out at Pat's is a lot like hanging out in your favorite uncle's rec room—that is, if

your uncle happened to pour perfect pints of Guinness and make the best fried chicken in town. The ideal neighborhood spot, Pat's boasts great live music, nice-as-can-be staff, and fried fare that can stand up to a beer or three. Plus, this is a real Irish bar—no pre-packaged shamrock kitsch here, just genuine good cheer and food that'll put some meat on your bones. Try the hubcap-sized onion rings and the chicken-fried-steak sandwich, or show up in the A.M. for eggs and bacon. On weekday mornings, Pat's offers breakfast for just $2.49.

(SEAMUS MCDANIEL'S ⑤

1208 Tamm Ave., 314/645-6337,
www.seamusmcdaniels.net
HOURS: Mon.-Fri. 11 A.M.-10 P.M., Sat. 11 A.M.-11 P.M.

This family-owned Dogtown pub honors the neighborhood's Irish heritage—both in its name and in its sizable selection of Irish spirits. Visitors will feel at home within about 30 seconds of setting foot in the place; Seamus McDaniel's convivial atmosphere and gracious service always make certain of that. The food here isn't fancy, but it is very, very good. The huge hamburgers are among the best in town, and the rib-eye sandwich with sautéed mushrooms and onions is also a sure bet. Act like a true St. Louisan by ordering a basket of toasted ravioli and a house salad (but no matter how delicious you find the dressing, don't ask for the recipe—it's a well-guarded family secret). Seamus McDaniel's spacious patio is *the* place to be in Dogtown on a warm Friday or Saturday night.

TAPAS

GUIDO'S PIZZERIA AND TAPAS ⑤⑤

5046 Shaw Ave., 314/771-4900,
http://guidosmo.tripod.com
HOURS: Sun.-Thurs. 11 A.M.-11 P.M., Fri.-Sat. 11 A.M.-midnight

A St. Louis original: The Carretero family hails from Spain but opened their restaurant in the heart of the city's Italian neighborhood. What to do? Serve both Spanish tapas as well as pizza and other Italian fare, all of it tasty, all of it an extraordinary value. The authentic tapas dishes include thinly sliced Spanish chorizo and Serrano ham, *albondigas* (delicious meatballs), baked goat cheese, and lots of seafood. Italian fare features crowd-pleasers like spaghetti and meatballs and lasagna. The thin-crust pizza is fantastic, whether you order it with mozzarella or with St. Louis's inexplicably beloved Provel cheese.

MODESTO ⑤⑤

5257 Shaw Ave., 314/772-8272,
www.modestotapas.com
HOURS: Mon.-Thurs. 5-10 P.M., Fri.-Sat. 5-11 P.M.

A fixture on the St. Louis dining scene since 2001, Modesto embodies the convivial spirit of traditional Spanish-style dining. Menu classics include *bisteq a la cabrales* (grilled hanger steak with goat cheese), *gambas al ajillo* (shrimp with garlic and peppers), delicious paellas, and house-made sangria. Frequently topping local polls as the "best place to take a large group," Modesto can get absolutely packed on weekends. Make a reservation, or pass the time with all the pretty people in the bar area. Thanks to its cosmopolitan vibe, quality ingredients, and gracious staff, this Spanish restaurant holds its own in a neighborhood where Italian restaurants typically rule.

Delmar Loop and University City   Map 6

AMERICAN

◖ BLUEBERRY HILL ⑤

6504 Delmar Blvd., University City,
314/727-4444, www.blueberryhill.com

HOURS: Daily 11 A.M.-9 P.M.; nighttime grill menu
offered Mon.-Sat. 9 P.M.-midnight, Sun. 9-11 P.M.

Blueberry Hill is popular with hungry
tourists looking to refuel after a day of
shopping in the Loop. But this legendary
Delmar Boulevard restaurant/bar/night-
club/museum of Americana is a favorite
among locals, too. The menu features one
of the best burgers in town, in addition
to perfectly crisp onion rings, spicy "buf-
falo" fries, hearty daily soups, and much
more. Blueberry Hill is owned by Joe Edwards, the beloved St. Louis visionary
who is largely responsible for the Delmar
Loop's success (and whose impressive
collection of American kitsch is on full
display throughout the venue). Service can
be slow at times, but don't fret: Just drop
a few more coins in the stellar jukebox or
order another pint from Blueberry Hill's
expansive beer list.

THE FATTED CALF ⑤

12 S. Bemiston Ave., Clayton, 314/726-1141,
www.fattedcalfburgers.com

HOURS: Mon.-Sat. 11 A.M.-8 P.M.

Open since 1966, The Fatted Calf is a downtown Clayton institution. But unlike some
institutions, the Fatted Calf doesn't rest
on its laurels. The copper counters gleam
brightly, the service is great time after time,
and the burgers are so good as to be downright addictive. Everything is impeccably
fresh; your burger won't sizzle on that grill

© BRAD HINES

On warm spring days, Blueberry Hill serves up great people-watching opportunities.

RESTAURANTS

top until you place the order. A panoply of toppings and numerous cheeses are available, but it's tradition at the Fatted Calf to order the soft cheddar. This heavenly cheese, served up with the aid of a tiny ice-cream scoop, melts instantaneously on the hot burgers (and doubles as a guilty-pleasure dip for your fries). There's more on the menu than just beef—heck, there's even a good swordfish sandwich—but you'd be remiss not to have a Fatted Calf burger. Check out the website to get a glimpse of the Fatted Calf's history, along with one of the funniest screeds against pampered college students you're likely to see on a restaurant site.

FITZ'S AMERICAN GRILL & BOTTLING WORKS $

6605 Delmar Blvd., University City, 314/726-9555, www.fitzsrootbeer.com
HOURS: Mon.-Thurs. 11 A.M.-11 P.M., Fri.-Sat. 11 A.M.-midnight, Sun. 11 A.M.-10 P.M.

Located in the heart of the bustling Delmar Loop, Fitz's is brimming over with charm and nostalgia. As bottlers of fine, frothy root beer and orange pop (among other flavors), Fitz's hearkens back to the days of soda shops and dime stores, though its modern dining room is remarkably kitsch-free. The menu is fairly typical, offering a mishmash of American favorites and TGI Friday's-inspired concoctions, though its list of gourmet burgers is extensive. You would be remiss if you didn't try a frosty mug of the home-brewed root beer, and on certain days you can even see the bottling process take place in the restaurant's on-site bottling facility. Fitz's prides itself on being kid-friendly, so bring the youngsters.

REARN THAI $$

7910 Bonhomme Ave., Clayton, 314/725-8807
HOURS: Mon.-Thurs. 11 A.M.-8:30 P.M., Fri.-Sat. 11 A.M.-9:30 P.M.

Just a hop-skip-jump from central Clayton's downtown drag sits Rearn Thai, a paragon of Thai cuisine. The dining room isn't anything fancy, but the food is out of this world. Unlike other Thai restaurants in the area, Rearn Thai doesn't change its recipes to placate American palates. The food here is complex, spicy, and sophisticated. Even standards like green curry are elevated by the perfectly calibrated give-and-take of ingredients like lime juice and coconut milk. A cooling papaya salad, or *som tum,* helps counter the rice and noodle dishes' spiciness. And be sure to order a Thai iced coffee.

THAI PIZZA CO. $

608 Eastgate Ave., 314/862-4429
HOURS: Mon.-Thurs. 11:30 A.M.-10 P.M., Fri.-Sat. 11:30 A.M.-midnight, Sun. 11:30 A.M.-10 P.M.

The culinary world has been inundated with misguided attempts at "Asian fusion." Fortunately, pizza and Thai food turn out to be a match in gustatory heaven. The crust here is St. Louis–style, which means it's thin, crisp, and never overwhelms the savory combinations atop it. Thai Pizza Co. is owned by the Prapaisilapa family, whose mini-empire of successful restaurants is responsible for introducing Thai to the Loop. Pizza options include an astoundingly tasty chicken-satay pie, with peanut sauce and a hearty sprinkling of cilantro. More traditional Thai dishes are available—but if you're eating at a place called Thai Pizza Co., you probably want to go with the house specialty.

CONTEMPORARY AND NEW AMERICAN

🄲 ATLAS 🄢🄢🄢

5513 Pershing Ave., 314/367-6800,
www.atlasrestaurantstl.com

HOURS: Tues.-Sat. 5:30-10 P.M. (Fri.-Sat. bar
until 11 P.M.)

After five years, Atlas remains one of the
best-kept secrets in town. The husband-
and-wife team of Michael Roberts and
Jean Donnelly—he is the executive chef;
she does desserts and oversees the front
of the house—turn out classic bistro fare
that is neither fancy nor pretentious. It is
simple, and simply delicious. The menu
changes seasonally, but count on outstanding seafood, pork, and lamb dishes. The
steak frites is always a winner, especially
the absolutely perfect French fries. Choos-
ing just one or two desserts is difficult,
but the *marjolaine,* with both dark chocolate and almond and hazelnut meringue,
is incredible.

RIDDLE'S PENULTIMATE CAFÉ & WINE BAR 🄢🄢

6307 Delmar Blvd., University City,
314/725-6985, www.riddlescafe.com

HOURS: Tues.-Thurs. 5-11 P.M., Fri.-Sat.
5 P.M.-midnight, Sun. 5-10 P.M.

Riddle's Penultimate has been in business
on the Delmar Loop for 23 years, and the
crowd here is as eclectic as the restaurant's
history and menu are long. Chef-owner
Andy Ayres offers something for everyone:
a laid-back bistro atmosphere, a sidewalk
patio, live music, an extensive wine list
(Riddle's was one of the first wine bars in
St. Louis), and a "bill of fare" featuring
a blend of old and new. Rotating specials
showcase the season's regionally sourced

ingredients, although the menu also
offers a few dishes that have remained un-
changed for years—such as the veal Dijon
(slices of veal served sautéed with mushrooms and served with a creamy mustard
sauce) and the fantastic Memphis-style
barbecued pork.

MIDDLE EASTERN

AL-TARBOUSH 🄢

602 Westgate Ave., University City,
314/725-1944

HOURS: Mon.-Sat. 11 A.M.-8 P.M., Sun. noon-6 P.M.

Despite the haphazard assemblage of about
six Formica-topped tables, Al-Tarboush
is not primarily a restaurant. Rather, it's a
Middle Eastern deli that inspires great loyalty among Loop residents. Slide open the
self-serve glass cases, and you'll find the
best hummus, tabbouleh, and baba gha-
noush in the city, as well as small containers
of tangy feta and marinated olives. Hot food
is available, too: Falafel sandwiches and beef
shawarma can be ordered at the counter, as
can an incredibly addictive garlic-chicken
wrap. Slabs of baklava await your impulse
purchase at the register.

GYRO HOUSE 🄢

571 Melville Ave., University City, 314/721-5638

HOURS: Daily 11 A.M.-10 P.M.

This Delmar Loop restaurant is a defi-
nite favorite among local worker bees and
hungry, cash-strapped students. Gyro
plates, gyro sandwiches, and falafel are
served in generous portions and top out at
less than 10 bucks. You won't find much
else here—save for some baklava and an
assortment of bottled and fountain
drinks—but who needs frills when lunch
is this cheap and tasty?

HARVEST $$$

1059 S. Big Bend Blvd., Richmond Heights,
314/645-3522, www.harveststlouis.com
HOURS: Tues.-Thurs. 5:30-9:30 P.M., Fri.-Sat.
5:30-10 P.M., Sun. 5-9 P.M.

Harvest was one of the first restaurants to introduce seasonal, market-driven cuisine to St. Louis. Over a decade later, it remains one of the city's best restaurants, due to owner and executive chef Stephen Gontram's commitment to excellence. Though the menu changes frequently, you'll be sure to find delicious beef, lamb, pork, and seafood dishes. If the gnocchi appetizer is available, you must order it. Harvest is also one of the few high-end restaurants in town to offer a "spa menu" of dishes low in calories but not in flavor. The restaurant's bread pudding has attained legendary status among local foodies.

PIZZA

IL VICINO $

41 N. Central Ave., Clayton, 314/727-1333,
www.ilvicino.com
HOURS: Mon.-Thurs. 11 A.M.-10 P.M., Fri.-Sat.
11 A.M.-11 P.M., Sun. 11 A.M.-10 P.M.

The lunch crowd at Il Vicino ranges from Armani-suited Clayton power brokers to frugal Washington University students. This pizzeria is part of a small national chain, but nothing feels slick or corporate about it. Instead, Il Vicino is a charming place for an affordable meal—and the wood-oven pizzas are outstanding. Gourmet combinations (such as "The Melanzane," with grilled eggplant, artichoke hearts, oven-roasted tomatoes, and fresh oregano) elevate these personal-size pizzas far above ho-hum lunch fare. Salads, panini, and calzones are also available, although it's the pizzas—and the unfailingly cheery service—that keep the crowds coming back.

RACANELLI'S $

6655 Delmar Blvd., University City,
314/727-7227, www.racanellis.com
HOURS: Mon.-Thurs. 11 A.M.-10 P.M., Fri.-Sat.
11 A.M.-11 P.M., Sun. 11 A.M.-9 P.M.

Racanelli's offers New York–style pies at Midwestern prices. The beloved mini-chain has five area locations, each with its own personality and loyal clientele. Dough is made on location daily, spread thick with tomato sauce and whole-milk mozzarella, then baked to crisp and bubbly perfection in brick ovens. Go the traditional pepperoni-and-mushroom route, or choose from a tempting array of specialty toppings that includes sundried tomatoes, grilled chicken, artichoke hearts, feta cheese, and fresh garlic. Single slices are perfect for a cheap lunch on the go. Other locations are in the Central West End, Webster Groves, Kirkwood, and Fenton.

ST. LOUIS PIZZA HAUS $

6602 Delmar Blvd., 314/862-4287, University
City, www.stlouispizzahaus.com
HOURS: Mon.-Thurs. 11 A.M.-10 P.M., Fri.-Sat.
11 A.M.-11 P.M., Sun. noon-11 P.M.

Prior to St. Louis Pizza Haus's opening in 2005, flyers appeared in the Delmar Loop. "The Trick Is in the Bricks!" they proclaimed. And: "The Haus Is Boss." These days, the Haus is still pretty boss, thanks to those aforementioned bricks—and to the high-quality ingredients used throughout the menu. Pizzas here are cut into square slices, and the wonderfully chewy crust provides a solid foundation for piled-high toppings. The traditional pies are best, but pizza lovers with a sense of adventure (and a big appetite) should also try the awesome Leroy's Special (pepperoni, mushrooms, onions, bacon, cheddar, and mozzarella). St. Louis Pizza Haus is run by the Beau-

boeuf family, whose friendly service is absolutely unparalleled.

Greater St. Louis
Map 7

AMERICAN
NATURAL FACT DELI $

20 Allen Ave., Webster Groves, 314/961-2442, www.naturalfact.com

HOURS: Mon.-Sat. 11 A.M.-9 P.M., Sun. 11 A.M.-7 P.M.

The Natural Fact Deli is a wonderful neighborhood spot tucked away in a Webster Groves shopping center. The food here is impeccably fresh, with the emphasis—as the name implies—placed on organic, healthy ingredients. But this is no tofu-and-sprouts-only joint. There *are* plenty of vegetarian options, like awesome hummus and a great meatless burger. But there are also excellent chicken wraps (try the Blanco Burrito, stuffed with baked chicken breast, brown rice, green onions, salsa, and cheese) and a B.L.A.S.T. sandwich (that's bacon, lettuce, avocado, sprouts, and tomatoes). Soups rotate daily and are almost always a winning proposition. Natural Fact carries a nice selection of wines and craft beers, too. Dine-in service can be agonizingly slow, but take-out service is efficient.

CONTEMPORARY AND NEW AMERICAN
BIG SKY $$$

47 S. Old Orchard Ave., Kirkwood, 314/962-5757, www.allgreatrestaurants.com

HOURS: Tues.-Thurs. 5:30-9:30 P.M., Fri. 5:30-10:30 P.M., Sat. 5-10:30 P.M., Sun. 4:30-9 P.M.

Big Sky's updated comfort food and somewhat outdated decor (think "early-'90s

eclectic") cater to the well-to-do crowds from Webster Groves and surrounding suburbs. But anyone who appreciates good food will likely love Big Sky's perfectly portioned, well-executed dishes, and the chefs incorporate local ingredients wherever possible. Big Sky is also one of the few St. Louis–area restaurants to prominently feature a selection of Missouri wines. Service is smooth and professional, and reservations are strongly recommended on weekends. Must-try dishes include the restaurant's signature cheddar-cheese macaroni with fresh sage and smoked bacon, and a four-ounce tenderloin with Maytag blue cheese butter.

NACHOMAMA'S $

9643 Manchester Rd., Rock Hill, 314/961-9110

HOURS: Mon.-Thurs. 11 A.M.-9:30 P.M., Fri.-Sat. 11 A.M.-10 P.M.

From the outside, Nachomama's looks like it was designed by a misguided gringo. There are the bright-red peppers painted on the shingles. The metal cut-out *cabelleros* slouching against the side of the building. And, come on, that name: *Nachomama's?* Step inside, though, and you'll find Mexican fare that's impeccably prepared and incredibly good. This beloved Rock Hill restaurant puts all other fast-casual Mexican food to shame. The house-made guacamole is kissed with lime and served with warm chips. Spinach enchiladas, verdant and delicious, will win over the most stubborn carnivore. Fish tacos are so tasty, you'd swear you were eating them beachside in Baja. Complete the experience with a tamarind soda or a margarita.

PUB FOOD

GROWLER'S PUB $

38 S. Lindbergh Blvd., Sunset Hills, 314/984-9009 and 783 Old Ballas Rd., Creve Coeur, 314/432-3110, www.saucemagazine.com/growlerspub

HOURS: Mon.-Sat. 11 A.M.-1 A.M., Sun. 11 A.M.-midnight

The eponymous "growler" is a 64-ounce mug of beer, and it's certainly popular with the thirsty locals who line up along the restaurant's mahogany bar. This neighborhood pub touts a selection of 133 different beers (33 on draft, 100 by the bottle), and a cold beer is the perfect complement to Growler's book-length, high-sodium menu of pub classics. The Lindbergh location boasts a shady garden that draws crowds throughout the summer months, and both locations offer the warm, casual atmosphere typical of family-owned drinking establishments. Try the hand-cut potato chips served with house-made onion dip, or the BLT made with applewood-smoked bacon and served on buttery Texas toast.

NIGHTLIFE

Don't let the hard-working Midwestern ethos fool you: St. Louis is *not* a city that turns in early. While it's tough to find a meal after midnight here, the drinking-and-dancing scene stays hot till at least 1:30 A.M. (and many places keep their doors open until 3 A.M.). The diversity of St. Louis's neighborhoods is reflected in the city's nightspots. In the trendy Washington Avenue district downtown, dressed-to-impress twentysomethings sample sushi and martinis, or order up premium bottle service at the many VIP booths. On the city's south side, a more relaxed vibe rules, although elegant wine bars are as common as smoky taverns. Bars near the major universities cater to the student demographic by offering cheap beer and well drinks, nightly food specials and popular music.

Live music has always played a major role in St. Louis's cultural identity, from Miles Davis's early gigs to sold-out performances by Nelly and other hip-hop stars. St. Louis fosters a thriving jazz, blues, hip-hop, alt-country *and* indie-rock scene, so there are plenty of options on any given night. National touring bands also make it a point to stop here (although some bypass St. Louis in favor of the college towns of Columbia and Lawrence, Kansas), and with

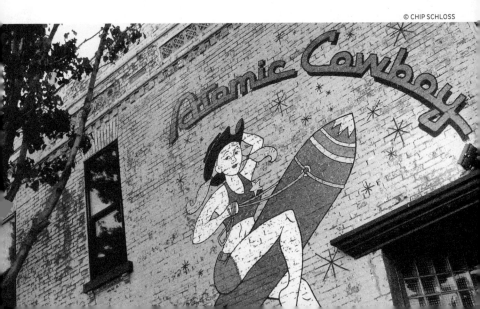

NIGHTLIFE

HIGHLIGHTS

LOOK FOR **(C** TO FIND RECOMMENDED NIGHTLIFE.

(C Best Underground Club: The Billiken Club is literally underground, in the food court of the Saint Louis University student union. But those humble digs don't keep the Billiken from booking top indie acts like Mountain Goats and Do Make Say Think – and the sound is surprisingly excellent. Best of all, there's no charge for any of the shows (page 77).

(C Best Place to See Live Music: Off Broadway is all about the music, and rare is the night when the place isn't packed. Off Broadway devotees truly support live shows, and the turnout is strong for local and national acts alike. Drinks are cheap, the sound is great, and recently the whole place went smoke-free (page 78).

(C Best Place for the Blues: At **B.B.'s Jazz, Blues, & Soups,** passion for the blues is palpable. Late greats Johnnie Johnson and Bennie Smith had regular gigs here, and the place is always packed with casual fans, aficionados, and legends in the making (page 79).

(C Best Pub: Spend an hour or two at the **The Scottish Arms,** and you'll think you've been transported to Edinburgh. The Scotch selection is unparalleled, the kilt-wearing servers are friendly and knowledgeable, and there's always football – the real kind – on the television. Order cock-a-leekie pie or haggis to complete the experience (page 88).

(C Best Subterranean Bar: Sol is one of the most beautiful bars in St. Louis, in terms of both design and clientele. The gorgeous space is located under popular Midtown coffee shop The Grind; just descend the stairs and experience a slice of nightlife unparalleled in the city (page 91).

(C Best Cocktail List: Nhat Nguyen runs one of the friendliest bars in South City – and he also happens to cultivate one fantastic cocktail list. The drink menu at **Urban** incorporates fresh, height-of-the-season fruits and puts inventive twists on classic combinations (page 92).

(C Best Late-Night Bar: At some 3 A.M. bars, the late hours are the only selling point. Not so at **Atomic Cowboy,** where there are selling points by the score – including an expansive patio with an outdoor fireplace, stellar DJ nights, monthly burlesque shows, and perhaps the best margaritas in town (page 93).

(C Best New Old Bar: The **Old Rock House** is a reincarnation of a legendary St. Louis saloon, and it's one of the most interesting places to open in the past few years. Enjoy live music on the main floor and the mezzanine, or head to the basement for scotch, cigars, and conversation. No matter where you are in the Old Rock House, you'll feel like part of St. Louis history (page 94).

(C Best Wine Bar: Spending time at **33 Wine Shop & Tasting Bar** is a lot like hanging out in a really cool friend's amazing wine cellar. In this case, the friend is owner Jake Hafner, and his wine collection is both unparalleled and affordable. Enjoy your vino in the lovely smoke-free bar, or head outside to the lushly landscaped patio (page 97).

the exception of huge arena shows, ticket prices are very affordable. In fact, one of the best venues in town, the Billiken Club, puts on all its shows for the ultra-affordable price of "free." Local publications, such as *St. Louis Magazine* and *Riverfront Times*, do an excellent job of listing almost every upcoming show.

Live Music

ROCK CLUBS

◖ THE BILLIKEN CLUB

21 N. Grand Blvd., 314/977-2020, www.myspace.com/thebillikenclub

HOURS: Call for hours

`Map 2`

Located in a corner of Saint Louis University's Busch Student Center, the Billiken Club plays host to national and local rock 'n' roll bands several times a month during the school year. By day, the space operates as a food court, but the small stage has supported many up-and-coming independent bands. The shows are booked by a group of ears-to-the-ground SLU students, making the Billiken Club a great spot to experience new music and relive your college days (the cheap draft beer should help jog some collegiate memories as well). The best part? Every show is free and open to the public.

CICERO'S

6691 Delmar Blvd., University City, 314/862-0009, www.ciceros-stl.com

HOURS: Mon.-Sat. 11 A.M.-12:30 A.M.; Sun. 11 A.M.-11 P.M.

`Map 6`

Cicero's is a no-frills, three-in-one entertainment destination. This Delmar Loop stalwart offers a restaurant, a bar (with one of the best beer lists in the city), and a music venue. The decor ain't much to look at, but Cicero's charm is in its eclecticism and its come-one-come-all ethos. In the mood for folk music? Jam bands? Straight-out rock? Undoubtedly, there's something on Cicero's packed music schedule to suit your tastes. The venue books some national acts, but you're more likely to stumble across a great local band here. Wednesday nights draw a fun-loving karaoke crowd, and many Sundays are reserved for open-mic performances. The stage at Cicero's has hosted pretty much everything—up to and including a popular local production of *Hairspray*.

CREEPY CRAWL

3524 Washington Blvd., 314/531-3885, www.creepycrawl.com

HOURS: Nightly until 1:30 A.M.

`Map 2`

St. Louis's best-known punk-rock club isn't quite as creepy or claustrophobic as its name implies, but the venue is certainly more austere than many others in town. No matter—music fans flock to the Creepy Crawl to discover new local talent and hear on-the-verge national acts, not to soak up the ambience. Located in the Grand Center arts district, this dark club adds a little spit and gristle to the neighborhood. The Creepy Crawl is one of only a few local venues that welcome an all-ages audience.

NIGHTLIFE

THE DUCK ROOM

6504 Delmar Blvd., University City,
314/727-4444, www.blueberryhill.com
HOURS: Doors open at 8 P.M. nightly
Map 6

Tourists and locals alike regularly flock to
Blueberry Hill, the epicenter of the Delmar Loop, which pairs a fine hamburger
with a museum's worth of pop-culture
knickknacks and rock 'n' roll memorabilia.
Music fans have their own reason for finding
their thrill at Blueberry Hill, as the downstairs Duck Room is one of the city's best
live-music venues. Named in honor of St.
Louis guitar hero Chuck Berry's signature
"duck walk," the Duck Room hosts a good
mix of new talent and music-scene veterans.
The room can only hold a few hundred, so
shows are often intimate affairs, and the
cellar-like atmosphere gives the impression
of a well-heeled basement gig.

LEMMONS

5800 Gravois Ave., 314/481-4812,
www.myspace.com/lemmons
HOURS: Mon. 4 P.M.-1 A.M., Tues.-Sat.
4 P.M.-2 A.M.
Map 4

Lemmons is an out-of-the-way club near
South City's southern fringe, but fun-seekers
have no trouble finding it. The venue's
concert calendar reads like a who's-who in
local music, but Lemmons is far more than
just a rock club. The trivia nights (with
accompanying hot-wing specials) are legendary. An all-you-can-eat pizza buffet and
one-dollar drink specials are available during
Lemmons's frequent movie nights. Worried
that pizza at a rock club might be subpar?
Don't fret. Lemmons serves the Blackthorn
Pub's deservedly famous deep-dish pizza.

Off Broadway plays host to some of the
hottest local and national acts.

◖ OFF BROADWAY

3511 Lemp Ave., 314/773-3363,
www.offbroadwaystl.com
HOURS: Call for hours
Map 3

Tucked away in the shadows of the long-
dormant Lemp brewery (and not far from
the Anheuser-Busch brewery and tour facility), Off Broadway is a little oasis of rock
and folk music. The tall ceiling and wood-
paneled walls are reminiscent of an old-
time saloon, and that vibe only intensifies
when one of many local country-influenced
bands performs in front of the stage's red
velvet curtain. While Off Broadway is a favorite spot for local groups, many touring
artists—including Andrew Bird, Jolie Hol-
land, and the Hold Steady—have made the
club their go-to spot when coming through
town. The club recently went smoke-free

(a welcome but rare thing in St. Louis), which reinforces Off Broadway's status as a listening room.

THE PAGEANT
6161 Delmar Blvd., 314/726-6161, www.thepageant.com
HOURS: Vary by show
Map 6

Built in 2000 on the eastern end of the Delmar Loop, The Pageant remains an anchor in this thriving cultural district. With a seating capacity of more than 2,000, The Pageant is *the* spot for mid- to upper-level touring bands. The balcony provides cushy seats and decent sight lines, although dedicated fans often prefer to nestle up to the stage on the ground floor. Bookings at The Pageant tend toward rock and pop, with the occasional hip-hop or hard-rock act thrown in. Most shows here are all-ages, though over-21 patrons can enjoy or a pre- or post-show drink at the attached Halo Bar, which serves until 3 A.M.

THE WAY OUT CLUB
2523 S. Jefferson Ave., 314/664-7638
HOURS: Mon.-Sat. 9 P.M.-1:30 A.M.
Map 3

Dropping by The Way Out Club is a simultaneous glance into the future and a step into the past: You can get a look at some of St. Louis's newest young bands while hanging out in a much hipper version of your grandparents' basement. The decor is a hodgepodge of beautiful trash—B-movie posters, old televisions, garage-sale junk, and vintage swag lamps mesh to create a one-of-a-kind atmosphere. Most bands that play the club veer towards loud, fast rock 'n' roll, and the slew of regulars will be happy

to give you a thumbnail sketch of St. Louis's underground music history. While the musical performances can be hit or miss, The Way Out is worth stopping by, if only for a drink.

JAZZ AND BLUES CLUBS
◖ B.B.'S JAZZ, BLUES, & SOUPS
700 S. Broadway, 314/436-5222, www.bbsjazzbluessoups.com
HOURS: Daily 6 P.M.-3 A.M.
Map 1

This legendary nightspot's name sums up its offerings quite neatly. B.B.'s Jazz, Blues, & Soups is dedicated to preserving and showcasing great music, and features live jazz and blues acts seven nights a week. Blues legend Oliver Sain made frequent appearances in the club's early days. Today, B.B.'s hosts dozens of legends in the making, from both the local and the national scene. The cover here is usually between $5 and $10—and worth every penny. Drinks are inexpensive, the band plays late (often until 2:30 A.M.), and those staying for the duration can sate their hunger with B.B.'s down-home Southern menu.

BROADWAY OYSTER BAR
736 S. Broadway, 314/621-8811, www.broadwayoysterbar.com
HOURS: Sun.-Thurs. 11 A.M.-1:30 A.M., Fri.-Sat. 11 A.M.-3 A.M.
Map 1

Broadway Oyster Bar has so much confidence in its live shows that it offers them with a return policy. As a prominently placed sign proudly announces: All of the music here is "guaranteed or your money back." Returns, however, are probably few and far between. Broadway Oyster Bar is

NIGHTLIFE

The New Orleans–style food at Broadway Oyster Bar is great, but the live music is even better.

a beloved institution. The kitchen dishes out some of the best Creole and Cajun food in the city—but it's the music that really draws crowds. Lauded as one of the country's top blues joints, the Broadway Oyster Bar frequently hosts national touring acts. On warm nights, the party moves outside to the spacious patio, which doubles as a popular post-game destination for Cardinals fans.

JAZZ AT THE BISTRO

3536 Washington Ave., 314/289-4030, www.jazzstl.org

HOURS: Opens Tues.-Sat. at 5 P.M. for dinner; shows at 8:30 P.M. and 10:15 P.M.

Map 2

Jazz at the Bistro is the official performance venue of Jazz St. Louis, a highly respected nonprofit dedicated to the preservation of jazz in America. St. Louis's jazz history runs deep. Such legends as Miles Davis, Josephine Baker, and Julius Hemphill have called the area home. The bistro pays tribute to these jazz heroes by showcasing the talents they've influenced. The intimate, cabaret-style venue attracts a diverse audience, albeit one with deep pockets—tickets can be fairly expensive. Still, the aural history here is worth experiencing. And don't be surprised if a living legend drops in; after a recent performance at the Sheldon Concert Hall, Wynton Marsalis and his band stopped by for a drink.

SPRUILL'S

2625 Stoddard St., 314/533-8050, www.spruillsinternationalcatering.com

HOURS: Tues.-Sun. 5 P.M.-2 A.M.

Map 2

The foundation for St. Louis's rich jazz and blues tradition was laid in the city's predominantly African American clubs. Spruill's is one of the remnants of that dying legacy. Though an older, mellower crowd tends to frequent the place, it's still the kind of joint with metal detectors at the entrance (and bathrooms that are best avoided). Hip-hop takes over on weeknights, but Saturdays and Sundays are jazz nights and feature two stages, plus a buffet cooked up by the catering company with which the club shares the building.

Dance Clubs

DANTE'S

3221 Olive St., 314/652-2369,
www.dantesstl.com

HOURS: Call for hours

`Map 2`

This spacious Midtown building has played host to a number of restaurants and clubs; as soon as one hot spot loses its luster, another moves in. Dante's has been going strong for several years now—and shows no signs of slowing down. The place gets wall-to-wall packed on weekend nights. Dante's is a European-style dance club with a large college-student following, and such top DJs as Tiesto, John Digweed, and Dave Aude spin here with surprising frequency. There are plenty of "theme" parties, too, so check the website to find a night devoted to your favorite kind of music (hip-hop, house, Latin, rock, and goth sets occur weekly). Despite its collegiate patrons and its proximity to Saint Louis University, Dante's isn't a place for cheap drinks. You won't find any dollar pitchers here; instead, the club stocks its back bar with premium liquors and offers a VIP bottle service. A lot of pretty people show up here, but Dante's is no glorified meat market—this is a place where music lovers come to dance for hours on end.

LA ONDA

4920 Northrup Ave., 314/772-0877,
www.myspace.com/clublaonda

HOURS: Thurs.-Sat. 9 P.M.-3 A.M.

`Map 5`

La Onda just might be the most authentic Latino bar in the city, and it's certainly one of the most popular. Vast and warehouse-like, La Onda draws a mainly Hispanic crowd and features live bands throughout the week. The party vibe is strong, and the crowds are here to dance. Your high-school Spanish might draw good-natured jibes, but after a few rounds, you'll be able to take it all in stride. As is true in the best Mexican bars, tequila can be ordered by the shot or the bottle; the latter option is iced tableside. La Onda is in a transitioning neighborhood, and all revelers must pass through metal detectors. Once inside, though, the atmosphere is pure fun. On many weekend nights, real-deal Mexican-food vendors park their carts right outside the club—after a night of dancing and drinking, few things taste better than an authentic taco.

NIGHTLIFE

MANDARIN LOUNGE

44 Maryland Plaza, 314/367-4447,
www.mandarinlounge.net

HOURS: Wed. 9 P.M.-1:30 A.M., Thurs.-Sat.
8 P.M.-1:30 A.M.

Map 2

The Central West End's only rooftop club can, at first glance, seem like a secret club or a well-appointed tree house: Mandarin is accessible via a pedestrian walkway near the recently revamped Maryland Plaza Fountain. Soon after the doormen let you into the elevator, you'll enter the low-lit, red-walled lounge. The bar space is open and fluid, with a few snug booths available, but the real draw is the open-air rooftop bar, which offers a lovely view of the always-bustling West End nightlife. Like the bar's decor, the drink menu takes a few cues from the Far East, with cocktails like the Geisha Blossom (vodka, green tea, and peach nectar) and the Shanghai Cosmo (raspberry vodka, Cointreau, and white cranberry juice). You may not find yourself transported to an exotic locale in Asia when you party at Mandarin, but you will be able to dance and drink on one of the city's finest perches.

THE PEPPER LOUNGE

2005 Locust St., 314/241-2005,
www.thepepperlounge.com

HOURS: Wed.-Sun. 9 P.M.-3 A.M.

Map 2

Although it's at a bit of a remove from Wash. Ave.—the city's main dancing-and-drinking drag—The Pepper Lounge is worth seeking out on it own merits. This club, built inside an old Eastman Kodak warehouse, is a favorite of many St. Louis trend-setters. Some clubs care more about raking in the cover charges than creating ambiance, but not The Pepper: It's as beautiful as it is popular. Some revelers may be bummed by the (tiny) size of the dance floor, but those looking to chill with friends will be delighted by the expansive bar and ample, plush seating. (VIP booths are available for a steep premium.) The Pepper regularly hosts some of the best DJs in town, including a few who spin excellent old-school hip-hop.

RUE 13

1311 Washington Ave., 314/588-7070,
www.rue13stl.com

HOURS: Mon.-Fri. 5 P.M.-3 A.M., Sat. 7 P.M.-3 A.M.

Map 1

As the well-worn adage goes, looks can be deceiving. The fresh flowers, leather couches, and late-night sushi bar position Rue 13 as an upscale lounge. And, indeed, the place was originally intended as a hip nightclub for moneyed young urbanites. Today, it serves a fun-loving college crowd. The university set arrives in droves to take advantage of Rue 13's daily $1 drink specials. The club reaches fever pitch at around 10 P.M. on Saturday nights, when all eyes turn to the scantily clad burlesque dancers of the Alley Cat Revue.

VIVA

408 N. Euclid Ave., 314/361-0322,
www.clubvivastl.com

HOURS: Tues.-Sat. 8 P.M.-1:30 A.M.

Map 2

This hip Central West End nightspot is one of the few salsa clubs in town. Don't know how to salsa? Not to worry—just stop in a bit early, and take a free salsa class before the dance floor heats up. The classes attract droves of people, all ready to let their hair down and learn one of the world's most sensual dances. The vibe at Viva is warm and welcoming, and despite being open since 1997, the club hasn't lost any of its panache. If you need a little liquid courage before you hit the dance floor, try the pisco sour.

YEMANJA BRASIL

2700 Missouri Ave., 314/771-7457,
www.brazildining.com

HOURS: Call for hours

`Map 3`

Yemanja Brasil is an unremarkable restaurant, but the weekends-only Latin dance club above it is a gem. Yemanja draws a young crowd (composed primarily of international students from Washington University and Saint Louis University), and the snug club is always filled to capacity. The venue's appeal is in its intimacy and otherworldliness—in other words, a late night in a strange place can be a whole lot of fun. At around 11 P.M., the bartenders start pouring strong mojitos. Then, someone turns up the salsa music. Combine the good Puerto Rican rum, the swirling lights, and the sultry tunes, and you have an evening that's intoxicating in every sense of the word.

NIGHTLIFE

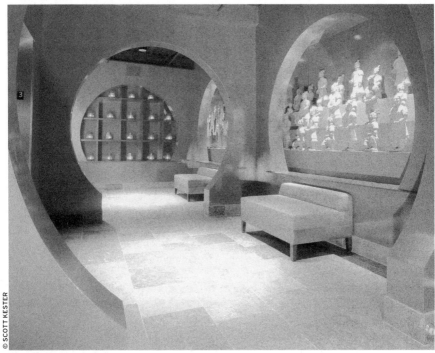

© SCOTT KESTER

West End's Mandarin Lounge

Bars

TAVERNS AND SPORTS BARS

THE ARENA BAR AND GRILL
5760 West Park St., 314/646-7171
HOURS: Mon.-Sat. 11 A.M.-1 A.M.
Map 5

The regulars at this quirky little Dogtown dive are fiercely loyal. Many have been coming here since the days of the old St. Louis Arena. That sports venue fell victim to controlled demolition in 1999, the Blues moved to Scottrade Center downtown, and this friendly bar is all that remains. If you're looking to drink on the cheap, the Arena is there for you. Drink specials often include $1 beer bottles and $2 shots. True Arena devotees head here for a two-martini lunch; the tiny corner kitchen serves up surprisingly great sandwiches and appetizers. You may not be a regular, but chances are you'll feel like one by the time last call rolls around.

THE CHURCH KEY
4127 Manchester Ave., 314/601-3828,
www.thechurchkeystl.com
HOURS: Thurs.-Fri. 4 P.M.-1:30 A.M., Sat. 6 P.M.-1:30 A.M.
Map 2

The Church Key is a drop-dead-gorgeous bar built on the solid foundation of two strong St. Louis traditions: Catholicism and beer. Behind The Church Key is the Bellon family, owners of a local salvaging company. The Bellons rescued the remains of St. Aloysius Gonzaga, a demolished church in the Hill neighborhood, and transported them to the up-and-coming Grove. Behold: The Church Key, a stunning space full of original stained glass and burnished-wood pews for seating. (The bar is made from the choir loft.) The beer list is 40 brews deep, and every night brings a different—and super-cheap—happy-hour special. Service is unfailingly cheerful. And you don't even have to go home smelling like an ashtray, because The Church Key is smoke-free.

THE FAMOUS BAR
5213 Chippewa St., 314/832-2211,
www.thefamousbar.com
HOURS: Mon.-Fri. 3 P.M.-1:30 A.M., Sat. 5 P.M.-1:30 A.M.; happy hour Mon.-Fri. 3-7 P.M.
Map 4

Named in honor of the old Famous-Barr department store that used to anchor the nearby corner of Chippewa and Kingshighway, the Famous Bar has gained a bit of local fame in its own right for its speakeasy-esque atmosphere. It's hard to miss the throwback vibe upon entering the Famous Bar—the staff sport ties and blue jeans from behind the massive mirrored bar, and the cocktail and martini menu hearkens back to days of long-stemmed glasses and stiff libations. If you are a lighter drinker, don't fret: The bar has a nice selection of draft and bottled beers available, and the Bloody Mary menu is unrivaled (approach the Cajun Mary with caution—it kicks). The club books live blues, jazz, and rock on the weekends, and a cover charge applies on those nights.

THE HIDE AWAY
5900 Arsenal St., 314/645-8822
HOURS: Mon.-Sat. 11 A.M.-1:30 A.M., Sun. noon-midnight
Map 5

Beloved by local hipsters and septuagenarians alike, this dimly lit lounge offers a fun departure from the typical St. Louis bar scene. You won't find thumping bass or pink mixed drinks here. Instead, regulars order rail drinks or sip Budweiser from the bottle. Mark Dew, The Hide Away's blind pianist, takes requests from the crowd, and it's a rare night when *someone* doesn't get up to slow dance. Libations are cheap, the mood is relaxed, and the age range is fascinating— there aren't many other places that draw college kids *and* retirees.

ICE AND FUEL

215 N. Kirkwood Rd., 314/822-0494, www.stl-eat.com/Ice.html

HOURS: Mon.-Sat. 11 A.M.-1:30 A.M., Sun. noon-midnight

Map 7

A straightforward, just-good-folks bar in the heart of Kirkwood, Ice and Fuel pours some of the coldest drafts in the neighborhood. You shouldn't go out of your way to visit Ice and Fuel, but if you're already in

---

BAR-HOP LIKE A ST. LOUISAN

Sure, you can check out the bars that all the tourists know about – in fact, you *should*, because many of these nightspots are rich with St. Louis history. But if you really want to feel like a local, spend an evening visiting the city's more under-the-radar watering holes. Here, you're likely to meet interesting people and hear some great stories.

Start off at **The Royale** (3132 South Kingshighway). Local impresario Steven Fitzpatrick Smith has quickly turned this shotgun space into a favorite local hang, thanks to excellent DJ nights, way-above-average food, and tasty drinks. The libation menu itself is a crash-course in St. Louis neighborhoods and landmarks; try the River Des Peres, a martini turned deliciously dirty by kalamata olives.

If you can't find a seat at the super-popular Royale, check out the equally beloved but far less crowded **CBGB** (3163 South Grand Blvd.), a true dive bar (so dive-y, in fact, that it does not have a phone). The drinks are cheap and the folks are friendly – just be aware that the place gets seriously smoky as the night goes on.

Soulard is the Holy Grail for many a bar-hopping St. Louisan. Cheap drinks and an impressive bars-to-block ratio make it easy and fun to check out plenty of spots. Don't-miss destinations include **The Great Grizzly Bear** (1027 Geyer Ave.), which has an excellent patio; **Nadine's Gin Joint and Café** (1931 South 12th St.), which almost always feels like a rockin' neighborhood block party (thanks to inexpensive booze, shuffleboard, and darts); and **Hammerstone's** (2028 South Ninth St.), which frequently hosts great jazz and R&B acts.

Looking to catch a game? Blues, Cards, and Rams fans eschew the corporate-feeling sports bars and head instead to **Tom's Bar & Grill** (20 South Euclid Ave.). This Central West End institution has lots of screens, lots of beer, and lots of deep-fried bar fare. If you're feeling a bit fancier, head for the **M Lounge** (4584 Laclede Ave.), a chic-but-cozy nightspot with a speakeasy vibe. This bar is above Moxy Bistro, and many St. Louisans have yet to find out about it. Shh!

NIGHTLIFE

the Kirkwood area, it's worth a stop. The bar keeps 15 beers on tap, and the kitchen turns out satisfying bar fare, including hot wings and sandwiches. The multiple TVs at this sports-themed bar make it a great place to catch a game. Just be sure that the words "Go Cubs!" don't escape your lips.

IRON HORSE SALOON
7928 S. Broadway, 314/631-3141
HOURS: Mon.-Sat. 11 A.M.-1:30 A.M., Sun. 5-9 P.M.
Map 7

Ranked among the oodles of bars in St. Louis, Iron Horse Saloon is rather unremarkable. This is a genuinely middle-of-the-road sort of place, although there is absolutely nothing wrong with that. The smoky shotgun bar is as good a place as any to start your night, and it's close to several other worthwhile restaurants and clubs. Iron Barley, Off Broadway, and the Broadway Athletic Club share this scruffy saloon's blue-collar neighborhood and charm. Best to stop here for a little pre-drinking before you head to your big destination.

JOHN D. MCGURK'S
1200 Russell Blvd., 314/776-8309,
www.mcgurks.com
HOURS: Mon.-Fri. 11 A.M.-1:30 A.M., Sat. 11:30 A.M.-1:30 A.M., Sun. 3 P.M.-midnight
Map 3

St. Louisans love Irish pubs, and St. Louisans love patios. Enter John D. McGurk's: a classic Irish pub with one of the biggest, prettiest patios in town. The staff here is delightful, and the menu features well-prepared pub food with the occasional upscale twist. Those looking for a snuggly tête-à-tête will love McGurk's cozy hand-carved booths, which weave through the bar's three main rooms. If barroom conviviality is more your style, join

in the raucous fun on the covered patio. The weekend crowd is young and collegiate—feel free to wear your university sweatshirt—and the party grows louder as the night goes on.

THE MACK
4615 Macklind Ave., 314/832-8199
HOURS: Daily 11 A.M.-1 A.M.
Map 4

Sometimes, upon stepping into a neighborhood bar, an out-of-town visitor feels ill at ease. That's never the case at The Mack (named for its location on Macklind Avenue), where the staff and the regulars are wonderfully welcoming. The vibe here reflects the hospitable, laid-back nature of the surrounding Southampton neighborhood—and the bartenders are happy to catch you up on all the local gossip. Buckets of beer are cheap, darts and air hockey are available in the back room, and if you're smart you'll come hungry. In-the-know locals swear by The Mack's food, which includes an awesome Mexican pizza and, on Sundays, stellar fried chicken. The hot wings are always a great accompaniment to the bar's $2 drafts.

MORGAN STREET BREWERY
721 N. 2nd St., 314/231-9970,
www.morganstreetbrewery.com
HOURS: Tues.-Sun. 11 A.M.-2:30 A.M.
Map 1

Much of the once-thriving Laclede's Landing district has gone to seed in recent years. The district's anchor—the legendary rock club Mississippi Nights, which hosted everyone from Uncle Tupelo to Nirvana—was shuttered in 2007, and much of the Landing's "cool" factor seemed to go with it. Still, must-visit stalwarts remain, and one of those is Morgan Street Brewery. This spacious microbrewery blends in perfectly with the brick and cobblestone surrounding it, and the handcrafted beers are divine. Award-winning brewmaster Marc Gottfried creates his beers on-site. Particularly good (when they're in season; Gottfried won't pour beers that are not seasonally appropriate) are the rich Doppelbock (available in winter) and the sweet-and-spicy Cobblestone Steam Lager (on tap year-round, thanks to its ability to pair well with absolutely everything). A nice menu, with dishes that are way beyond basic bar food, complements the beer selection.

MR. B'S
5800 Southwest Ave., 314/645-5912
HOURS: Mon.-Fri. 11 A.M.-1:30 A.M., Sat.
4 P.M.-1:30 A.M., Sun. 2 P.M.-midnight
Map 5

This wood-paneled neighborhood bar has the feel of hunter's lodge and is a great place for a drink and a bite on a cold winter evening. Mr. B's cozy atmosphere, stiff drinks, and simple Italian dishes are guaranteed to send you back into the chilly night air with a warm and satisfied glow. The service here is arguably the friendliest in the neighborhood, and the patrons are mostly older Italian-Americans from the surrounding Hill—meaning you're likely to catch some lively conversations. This is a bar full of regulars, and they love to debate everything from politics to bocce ball.

PEPPER'S BAR AND GRILL
5452 Gravois Ave., 314/352-9909
HOURS: Mon.-Sat. 11 A.M.-1:30 A.M., Sun.
11 A.M.-midnight
Map 4

Pepper's, a friendly pub in the Southampton neighborhood, boasts some great vintage

details and fully stocked shelves. Something of a bartenders' bar, Pepper's attracts a crowd that's middle-aged and a little sedate, but the atmosphere provides a nice reprieve from the hubbub of the city's trendier nightspots. The quiet space, warm colors, and upholstered booths make this a great place to catch up with friends, and the food isn't bad either. Favorites include an outstanding Pepper's burger with fries and an absolutely crave-worthy breaded pork tenderloin.

RILEY'S PUB
3458 Arsenal St., 314/664-7474
HOURS: Call for hours
Map 4

Riley's Pub is only a couple of blocks east of South Grand Boulevard's bustling commercial strip, but this corner tavern still manages to feel like a neighborhood spot, a place where everyone might not know your name but sure are glad you came. Bottle and draft beer is reasonably priced, and in spite of the Budweiser memorabilia on the walls, a decent selection of brews is available. The kitchen turns out thin-crust pizzas to sate your munchies. The only potential drawback is the copious cigarette smoke.

ROSIE'S PLACE
4573 Laclede Ave., 314/361-6423
HOURS: Mon.-Sat. 10 A.M.-1:20 A.M.
Map 2

Hidden among the expensive French restaurants and upscale nightclubs of the Central West End is Rosie's, a window into St. Louis's blue-collar, Budweiser-swilling soul. An eclectic mix of grizzled old barflies and slumming Washington University grad students belly up to the bar of this tiny, narrow dive. It's cash-only and there's no beer

NIGHTLIFE

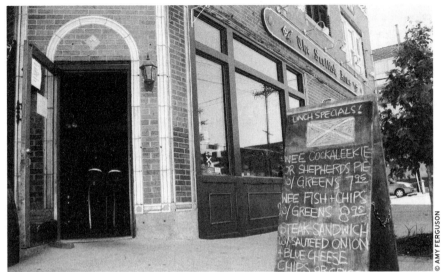
Looking for a wee taste of the highlands? You'll find it – and a world-class whiskey selection – at The Scottish Arms.

on tap, just dirt-cheap bottles of Bud and some of the stiffest cocktails in town. The sole diversion is a jukebox heavy on Motown and Bon Jovi, which provides the soundtrack as the friendly bartenders, a muscle-bound ex-Mixed Martial Arts fighter and Rosie herself, do their best to keep the thirsty patrons from staggering home before last call.

THE SCOTTISH ARMS

8 S. Sarah St., 314/535-0551,
www.thescottisharms.com
HOURS: Mon. 5-9 P.M., Tues.-Sat. 11 A.M.-2 P.M.
and 5-10 P.M., Sun. 10 A.M.-2 P.M. and 5-9 P.M.; bar
open until 1:30 A.M. Tues.-Sat. and until midnight
Sun.-Mon.
`Map 2`

St. Louis has a glut of Irish bars, and even a few decent Welsh ones, but the Scottish Arms does more than its share to represent the British Isles. Owner Alistair Nesbit brings the spirit of his native Aberdeen to the heart of the

Midwest. As befits a bar that hearkens back to the highlands, the whiskey selection is among the best in town, and the beer list is heavy on dark, crisp U.K. brews. The dark wooden bar and low-glowing lights make for a suitably snug atmosphere, and the menu sails high above normal pub-grub fare. Delicacies like Scotch eggs (hard-boiled eggs cooked in sausage batter) and bangers-and-mash are must-haves, and the gastronomically adventurous will want to save room for haggis, the (in)famous Scottish dish of stuffed sheep's intestines.

SKYBOX SPORTS BAR AND GRILL

800 N. 3rd St., 314/241-5100,
www.skyboxstl.com
HOURS: Mon.-Fri. 11 A.M.-1:30 A.M., Sat.
4 P.M.-1:30 A.M., Sun. 4 P.M.-midnight
`Map 1`

Skybox brings light and life back to the on-the-brink Laclede's Landing area, and although this upscale sports bar is quite new, the buzz is already strong. A likely reason for the positive vibes is Skybox's ownership: It's a joint venture between rap star (and native St. Louisan) Nelly and athletes Marshall Faulk, Darius Miles, and Larry Hughes. Those heavyweights stop in when they can, but this bar is cool even without celebrity spottings. Eighty-plus gigantic TVs make it an ideal place to catch practically any game, and the space itself is bright and beautiful. Gamers will love the fact that they can play Guitar Hero (along with a number of sports titles) right at their booths. The extensive food menu features fun takes on bar classics, along with less-traditional items like shrimp tacos and freshly baked cornbread with honey-butter. Worried you'll miss a key play? Don't fret: There are TVs in the bathrooms, too.

34 CLUB

34 N. Euclid Ave., 314/367-6674
HOURS: Mon.-Sat. 3 P.M.-1:30 A.M.
Map 2

Those who describe their favorite drinks with adjectives like "stiff" and "potent" will want to belly up to the 34 Club's bar. This shotgun space has little in common with high-rent neighbors like Sub Zero Vodka Bar and Brennan's Wine Bar, but it has a charm all its own. If your evening calls for something a little more down-and-dirty, make a beeline for the 34 Club. The clientele here is economically and culturally diverse, and while there are plenty of regulars, they won't make out-of-towners feel out of place. Just look for the vintage neon window sign at the corner of Laclede and Euclid. That means you've arrived at the 34 Club, the neighborhood tavern that's been holding down this block for 60 years.

TIN CAN TAVERN & GRILL

3157 Morganford Rd., 314/865-3003,
www.tincantavern.com
HOURS: Mon.-Sat. 11 A.M.-1 A.M., Sun.
11 A.M.-midnight
Map 4

Many St. Louisans go to Tin Can for the food—and rightfully so. This South Tower Grove spot puts cool twists on down-home favorites (where else in town can you order a basket of mini-corn dogs?). But as delicious as the food is, it's the beer selection that has elevated Tin Can to local-legend status. There are roughly a gazillion beers available, from lowbrow brews like Hamm's and Schlitz to fancier beers like Young's Chocolate Stout and Boddington. Do know that Tin Can takes the "Can" part of its name seriously. With the exception of three or four rotating seasonal beers, all suds come ensconced in aluminum. But that's part of the charm here—that, along with the raucous local music and the anything-goes decor.

THE VENICE CAFÉ

1903 Pestalozzi St., 314/772-5994,
www.thevenicecafe.com
HOURS: Bar open Mon.-Sat. 4 P.M.-1 A.M., kitchen open Mon.-Thurs. 4-10 P.M., Fri.-Sat. 4-11 P.M.
Map 3

The Venice Café might be a bit of a misnomer, as this popular joint serves food only during the summer months. But the Caribbean-influenced fare isn't what draws crowds to the Venice. Instead, people flock to Pestalozzi Street for the Venice's super-cool—and downright surreal—vibe. The patio could be described as "postmodern," or even "apocalyptic," with its combination of colorful mosaics, headless Barbie dolls, quirky fountains, and mannequin parts. The building's

NIGHTLIFE

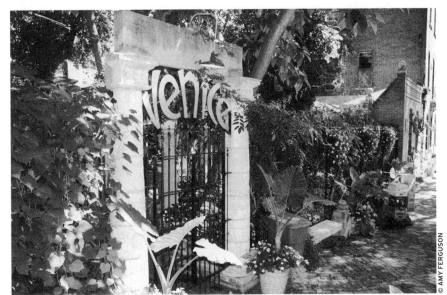

© AMY FERGUSON

Act like a local and head for The Venice Café – beloved by St. Louisans for more than 20 years.

interior features more of the same, as well as a private second-floor bar that feels like the best treehouse ever. The Venice Café's wild whimsy attracts patrons of all ages, as it has for the past 20 years. A small stage often hosts musicians and poets.

MARTINI BARS
ABSOLUTLI GOOSED

3196 S. Grand Blvd., 314/772-0400, www.absolutligoosed.com

HOURS: Wed.-Thurs. 4 P.M.-midnight, Fri. 4 P.M.-1:30 A.M., Sat. 5 P.M.-1:30 A.M., Sun. 4 P.M.-midnight

Map 4

The classic martini had its resurgence a few years ago, along with zoot suits and swing music, but the modern drinker wants a little sweetness mixed in with the potent stuff. Drinkers know Absolutli Goosed as a haven of flavored cocktails: Many of the

concoctions take inspiration from the candy aisle (like the Three Musketeers Martini), while others offer updates on classic drinks like margaritas and cosmopolitans. The bar is successful at attracting a mixed crowd from the diverse South Grand neighborhood, and it's a common sight to see gay, lesbian, and straight clientele rubbing elbows and tippling tall-stemmed drinks in the bar's tight quarters.

CAFÉ EAU

212 Kingshighway Blvd., 314/454-9000, www.chaseparkplaza.com

HOURS: Sun.-Thurs. 6 A.M.-10 P.M., Fri.-Sat. 6 A.M.-11 P.M.

Map 2

The Chase Park Plaza is legendary, and Café Eau is at its heart. Hotel guests begin trickling in around 10 P.M.—and, given the Chase's status as *the* hotel for visiting luminaries and well-heeled locals, the people-watching opportunities are ample. Café Eau has a decent wine list, but the expertly made cocktails are the real draw. It's hard not to feel elegant when sipping a martini in one of the city's most historic hotels. Patrons can also take their drinks to the poolside deck, where an outdoor fireplace keeps things toasty year-round.

THE RITZ-CARLTON LOBBY LOUNGE
100 Carondelet Plaza, Clayton, 314/863-6300
HOURS: Mon.-Sun. 11 A.M.-11 P.M., tea service Thurs.-Sun. 1:30-3:30 P.M., sushi bar Tues.-Thurs. 5-8 P.M. and Fri.-Sat. 5-10 P.M.
Map 6

Don't feel like shelling out big bucks for a night's rest at the Ritz-Carlton? You can still experience the hotel's legendary opulence and topnotch service by grabbing a drink in the Lobby Lounge. The room is absolutely beautiful, with dark woods and luxurious couches that practically demand intense, hours-long conversation. Drink specials change with the season, and by-the-glass wine selections are solid if not wildly interesting (the bottle list, on the other hand, is stellar). You'll pay a premium for drinking at the Ritz; glasses of wine are between $12 and $18, and cocktails are usually around $10. But the experience is worth it, and if you dress to impress, no one will know that you're just passing through for a drink.

◖ SOL
4241 Lindell Blvd., 314/534-1300
HOURS: Tues.-Sat. 7 P.M.-1:30 A.M.
Map 2

There is a bit of a Clark Kent-Superman situation going on with Sol. The bar is located in the back of The Grind, a collegiate coffeehouse on the eastern edge of the Central West End. But walk through the muted white hallways, take a trip down a stairwell, and all of a sudden you enter a modern update of the Prohibition-era speakeasy. Sol exudes a relaxed, lounge-y vibe with a tall ceiling, private booths—and enough wine, beer, and spirits to flood a small village. The ambience is upscale without being snooty, and the cool stone walls provide a little oasis from the nearby pubs and nightclubs.

SUB ZERO VODKA BAR
308 N. Euclid Ave., 314/367-1200,
www.subzerovodkabar.com
HOURS: Mon.-Sat. 4 P.M.-1:30 A.M.
Map 2

As one might expect, given the name, Sub Zero offers an enormous selection of imported vodka and every mixer imaginable. But there's much more to the place than

Sub Zero serves martinis, with zero attitude.

NIGHTLIFE

© AMY FERGUSON

that, and a daytime visit is much different from a nighttime one. If you're interested in sipping a good martini in a lounge atmosphere, stop by during the late afternoon, when the place is almost sanctuary-like in its cool stillness. At night, Sub Zero caters primarily to the well-shod baby-boomers who shuffle in from the city's suburban enclaves. Sushi and gourmet burgers are both available until 1 A.M.

THE U LOUNGE
609 Eastgate Ave., 314/721-9168
HOURS: Daily until 1:30 A.M.
Map 6

The U Lounge shares a space (and an owner) with the Asian fusion restaurant 609. That restaurant has seen better days (plus, Asian fusion just feels kind of 2003), but the U Lounge still packs 'em in. The Modernist furniture, trance-y dance music and high-end cocktails set the U apart from its more casual Loop neighbors. There's a nice selection of sake here, as well as martinis that incorporate the popular Japanese spirit (the 609 Signature, with unfiltered sake and charbay green tea, is particularly good). Hookahs are also available, along with a list of tobacco flavors that reads like a Baskin Robbins menu. Take your hookah to the semiprivate rooms toward the back, and you'll feel like you're in Marrakesh. (That is, until someone wanders by with a Bud Light and a plate of toasted ravioli.)

◖ URBAN
3216 S. Grand Blvd., 314/772-3308
HOURS: Mon.-Sat. 5 P.M.-1:30 A.M.
Map 4

Though its name might suggest sleek sophistication, laid-back Urban feels more like an underground bar than a trendy lounge. Owner

Nhat Nguyen has designed a drink menu that will appeal both to the *Sex and the City* culties—the pomegranate cosmopolitan is labeled as Oprah's favorite drink, after all—and the cocktail connoisseurs. Drinks that have jumped the shark elsewhere are given smart, tasty twists here, like the lemongrass mojito. And the "Gin Garden"—a refreshing blend of gin, muddled cucumbers, and apple juice—just might be the perfect summer drink. Most nights, DJs spin in the sedate lounge area.

VAN GOGHZ
3200 Shenandoah Ave., 314/865-3345,
www.vangoghz.com
HOURS: Tues.-Thurs. 4-11 P.M., Fri.-Sat. 4 P.M.-1:30 A.M., Sun. 10 A.M.-5 P.M.
Map 4

Coffee shop by day and elegant cocktail lounge by night, Van Goghz shines

Stop in the versatile Van Goghz: Chill coffee spot by day, happening martini lounge by night.

in its two distinct roles. Free WiFi and a full-service brunch menu bolster this southside spot's daytime charms, while a seemingly endless list of wines, beers, and inventive martinis keeps the evening crowd coming back. This is a busy place, but the vibe is low-key, and there's never any pressure to vacate your seat. Quite the opposite; bartenders encourage leisurely conversation over drinks and small plates. The happy-hour specials (on both cocktails and food) make Van Goghz a popular stop with the after-work set. On nice nights, Van Goghz offers sidewalk seating.

3 A.M. BARS
☾ ATOMIC COWBOY

4140 Manchester Ave., 314/775-0775, www.atomiccowboystl.com
HOURS: Wed.-Sat. 5 P.M.-3 A.M.

`Map 2`

Atomic Cowboy is a natural extension of owner Chip Schloss's magnetism and energy. Schloss is playing an instrumental role in the redevelopment of the entire Grove area, but Atomic Cowboy is at the epicenter of his efforts. The term "bar" does the venue an injustice, as it's also a lounge, dance club, art gallery, and late-night restaurant. On one side of the Cowboy, there are booths and high tables; on the other, there are living room–style arrangements of vintage Atomic Age furniture. The incredibly popular patio is shaded by a 1940s-style Quonset hut, and a roaring outdoor fireplace makes it possible to drink alfresco even on chilly nights. The crowd and the music are always eclectic, the Baja-Mexican food is tasty, and the atmosphere is 100 percent fun.

DELMAR RESTAURANT & LOUNGE

6235 Delmar Blvd., 314/725-6565
HOURS: Daily 5 P.M.-3 A.M.

`Map 6`

With cushy red booths, potent cocktails, low lighting, and live music, the Delmar truly delivers that classic lounge vibe. A longtime anchor for the funky Delmar Loop district, this hot spot is a favorite for jazz heads and DJ-loving college kids alike. The food is reliably tasty, the straightforward wine list doesn't disappoint, and the service is friendly, not stuffy. Plus, the bar remains open until 3 A.M., making it a preferred destination for a diverse late-night crowd.

MANGIA ITALIANO

3145 S. Grand Blvd., 314/664-8585, www.dineatmangia.com
HOURS: Mon.-Sat. 11:30 A.M.-3 A.M.

`Map 4`

Mangia Italiano may be beloved for its homemade pastas and cheap-and-tasty lunch buffet, but South Grand night owls know it as *the* place to be after midnight. Mangia is one of the very few 3 A.M. bars in the district, so it's not uncommon to see hordes of revelers heading here after the other bars call it an "early" night at 1:30 A.M. The huge, inviting space features two bars, a subterranean space for special events, a small elevated stage, an expansive wall mural by legendary southside artist Wayne St. Wayne, and a charmingly mismatched assemblage of 1950s Formica tables and vinyl chairs. The seating is plentiful, making Mangia the perfect place for large groups who come here for the bar's weekly jazz gigs, rock shows, DJ sessions, and karaoke contests. Those sensitive to smoke should be aware that the bar gets a bit hazy as the night progresses.

NIGHTLIFE

NICK'S PUB

6001 Manchester Ave., 314/781-7806

HOURS: Mon.-Fri. 11 A.M.-3 A.M., Sat. 5 P.M.-3 A.M., Sun. 5 P.M.-3 A.M.

Map 5

Even if it is your first time coming through the doors, Nick's Pub will likely seem familiar: The green-and-white color scheme, the tall pints of beer, and the live folk music may make you think you've stumbled into an actual pub in Ireland. Every city needs a good Irish bar, and this is one of St. Louis's most comfortable. The menu offers good, greasy bar food, but the real draw is the pub's many facets: The beer garden is lovely in warm weather, and the upstairs area attracts all sorts of gamers. Dartboards, pool tables, and a slew of vintage arcade games await those with a competitive streak, and the shuffleboard table is perpetually packed. Nick's has a 3 A.M. license, making this a popular last stop for the under-30 crowd.

◖ OLD ROCK HOUSE

1200 S. 7th St., 314/588-0505, www.oldrockhousestl.com

HOURS: Mon.-Thurs. 11 A.M.-1:30 A.M., Fri. 11 A.M.-3 A.M., Sat. 5 P.M.-3 A.M.

Map 3

The Old Rock House represents one of the more exciting developments near St. Louis's riverfront. Built as a reincarnation of the *original* Old Rock House—a rowdy riverside saloon rumored to draw everyone from shipping tycoons to Mark Twain himself—this new music venue is as gorgeous as it is ambitious. Thanks to an excellent renovation job, the Old Rock House seems like a historic landmark in the making. The original Old Rock House was demolished to make way for the Gateway Arch, but this new iteration takes

the mantle quite effectively, with its intricate brickwork and gleaming wood floors. Within the venue's 6,000 square feet are three levels of seating; local and national bands rock out on the main floor and the mezzanine. The Old Rock House serves up great burgers and barbecue, and drink specials are abundant. Those looking for quiet conversation can repair to the cigar-and-scotch lounge in the basement.

SANDRINA'S

5098 Arsenal St., 314/601-3456, www.sandrinasstl.com

HOURS: Daily 4 P.M.-3 A.M.

Map 4

The old Sandrina's was a classic St. Louis Italian restaurant, serving the neighborhood with tasty if predictable red-sauce pasta and the like. The new Sandrina's features a revamped menu and a 3 A.M. liquor license. The food veers more towards bistro fare (pork chops, pizza, a few pasta dishes), but the nightlife provides a little snapshot of the surrounding Hill neighborhood. Once the area restaurants have shut down for the night, it seems that most of the waiters, bartenders, and kitchen staff make a beeline for Sandrina's to share war stories, a few laughs, and (of course) a couple more drinks. If the main floor gets too crowded, try the upstairs pool room, where an ancient 45-RPM jukebox spins out forgotten classics.

THE UPSTAIRS LOUNGE

3131 S. Grand Ave., 314/773-3388, www.upstairslounge.com

HOURS: Mon.-Sat. 6 P.M.-1 A.M., Sun. 6 P.M.-midnight

Map 4

This pocket-sized bar is located directly above Mekong, a Vietnamese restaurant at the corner of Grand Boulevard and Hartford Street. Mekong backs up to yet another smoky nightspot, the Jade Room, but the Upstairs Lounge is where the action is. The entrance is easy to miss—look for the lozenge-shaped Lounge sign above the door. A narrow set of stairs takes you past dingy, graffitied walls, but then the door opens on a scene of thumping music, friendly scenesters, and potent drinks. Do expect to pay a cover, and possibly a steep one. The Upstairs regularly hosts prominent out-of-town DJs, and you will be asked to pay a premium for it.

Wine Bars

BRENNAN'S WINE BAR AND CIGAR SHOP

4659 Maryland Ave., 314/361-9444

HOURS: Mon.-Thurs. 2:30 P.M.-1:30 A.M., Sat. noon-1:30 A.M.

Map 2

Though located at a busy intersection frequented by people who want to see and be seen, Brennan's remains one of the best-kept secrets in St. Louis—many of the locals don't even know about this outstanding wine and cigar bar. Perhaps that's because this single address is home to four locales in one. You've got your main-floor wine and cigar storefront, which provides cash-and-carry wines by the bottle. During warm-weather evenings, the outdoor patio serves as an excellent post for people-watching, and on chilly winter nights, the basement speakeasy scotch bar provides a welcome coziness. Finally, the second-floor Maryland House is popular with both the primped and the laid-back, offering wines by the glass, cheese plates, and a casually cool vibe.

ERATO

3117 S. Grand Blvd., 314/664-6400, www.eratowines.com

HOURS: Mon.-Sat. 2 P.M.-1:30 A.M., Sun. 2 P.M.-midnight

Map 4

Erato is sleek enough to attract the trendy and spacious enough to accommodate those who want a more sedate evening. The wine list is broad (though not deep), and the by-the-glass selection rotates with some regularity. The beer list balances

© AMY FERGUSON

At Brennan's, you can sip wine on the patio or descend to the speakeasy-style cigar bar.

NIGHTLIFE

Sasha's Wine Bar & Market, in the chic DeMun neighborhood of Clayton

both the popular brews and a few unusual selections. The bar's specialty cocktails include a tasty (and strong) mojito and that old-school classic, the Pimm's cup. There is live music almost every night and free tango lessons weekly. Of special note: Erato is entirely smoke-free.

REMY'S KITCHEN & WINE BAR

222 S. Bemiston Ave., Clayton, 314/726-5757, www.allgreatrestaurants.com

HOURS: Lunch Mon.-Fri. 11:30 A.M.-2 P.M.; dinner Mon.-Wed. 5:30-10 P.M., Thurs. 5:30-11 P.M., Fri.-Sat. 5:30-11:30 P.M.

Map 6

A *Wine Spectator* Award of Excellence winner eight times over, Remy's is a place that's serious about good wine. The good thing is, no one here takes *themselves* too seriously; the decor is at once classy and whimsical, the servers have great senses of humor, and the wine list is well-cultivated and creative. It's not uncommon to see a businessperson or professor tucked into a corner table, reading a book and working his or her way through a wine flight. The flights change monthly and offer sippers the opportunity to try some truly amazing vino. Summertime flights often include gorgeous Alsatian varietals, while winter flights showcase hearty Cab blends. The food at Remy's is hit-or-miss, but you can't go wrong with the cheese plate and the stuffed grapevine leaves.

SASHA'S WINE BAR & MARKET
706-C De Mun Ave., Clayton, 314/863-7274
HOURS: Mon.-Sat. 11 A.M.-1 A.M., Sun.
11 A.M.-midnight
Map 6

Sasha's Wine Bar & Market is exactly the kind of hidden-away, low-key spot people seek out to unwind over a glass of wine (or three). Situated in a quiet, residential neighborhood you'll wish you could call your own, Sasha's faces a tranquil park, making its outdoor seating a perfect refuge from the city's hustle-bustle. And when those patio tables are full, indoor patrons still can enjoy the benefit of a breezy summer night: The French doors are frequently flung wide, bringing the outdoors in. The lengthy wine list ensures there's something for every palate, and the crepes, pizzas, and other small plates guarantee you won't be drinking on an empty stomach.

33 WINE SHOP & TASTING BAR
1913 Park Ave., 314/231-9463, www.33wine.com
HOURS: Tues.-Thurs. 3:30 P.M.-midnight,
Fri.-Sat. 3:30 P.M.-1 A.M.
Map 3

33 Wine Shop & Tasting Bar—33 to its regulars—is one of the city's hidden gems, a beautiful (and smoke-free) bar with a tremendous wine list, friendly and exceptionally knowledgeable staff, and one of the funniest menus that you'll ever read. In fact, owner Jake Hafner's tasting notes and random musings are so hilarious that the front cover of the menu begs you not to steal it. That menu provides great choices at every price point, with only a modest markup if you enjoy a bottle (or two) at the bar. The beer selection is excellent, too. In nice weather, 33's backyard patio is a lovely place to while away an evening.

Gay and Lesbian

ATTITUDES
4100 Manchester Ave., 314/534-0044,
www.attitudesnightclub.com
HOURS: Wed. 9 P.M.-3 A.M., Fri. 9 P.M.-3 A.M., Sat.
6 P.M.-3 A.M.
Map 2

Today, the disco-style dance floor at this popular lesbian bar looks a little dated. Attitudes opened its doors more than 20 years ago, and it bears the hallmarks of LGBT clubs from the mid-1980s: nondescript building, tinted windows, tiny foyer. These secretive measures were put in place to protect patrons; while the Grove is now a flourishing gay-friendly neighborhood, that wasn't

always the case. Still, even though Attitudes could use some sprucing up, it's a great place to drink and dance. And don't be scared off by the name—the attitudes on display here are friendly, outgoing, and laid-back.

CLEMENTINE'S
2001 Menard St., 314/664-7869,
www.clementinesbar.com
HOURS: Mon.-Sat. 10 A.M.-1:30 A.M., Sun.
11 A.M.-midnight
Map 3

The city's oldest gay bar, Clementine's occupies a pretty brick building in the historic Soulard neighborhood. The bar primarily serves a

NIGHTLIFE

leather crowd: Men come here to meet up, to hang out, and to have a bite at the adjoining Oh My Darlin' Café. Clementine's proximity to the annual Mardi Gras celebration makes it a particularly popular destination for the LGBT community each February.

THE COMPLEX

3515 Chouteau Ave., 314/772-2645,
www.complexnightclub.com
HOURS: Tues.-Sun. 9 P.M.-3 A.M.

Map 2

Like a deep-rooted weed growing from a sidewalk crack, The Complex rises up from one corner of an industrial park in Midtown, beneath the Kingshighway Bridge. But the barracks-like jumble of chain link and sheet metal outside have nothing on the dark, sweaty labyrinth inside. People don't come to The Complex for the atmosphere. They probably don't come here for the thrumming techno and gay house, or for the bad bar food and disco-lit dance floor. But partiers continue to arrive in droves each weekend—to meet, to dance, and, if all goes well, to hook up. The bartenders are amicable and the drinks are powerful. The Complex is a fun place for anyone on the prowl.

JJ'S CLUBHOUSE

3858 Market St., 314/535-4100,
www.jjsclubhouse.com
HOURS: Daily 3 P.M.-3 A.M.

Map 2

This exclusively male gay bar on Market Street is the largest bear and leather scene in the city. Those looking for outgoing leather daddies will certainly find an active little enclave here, as well as pool tables (free Sundays and Mondays), dartboards, and a busy calendar of events. Every year, JJ's hosts the Mr. Midwest and Missouri Leather contests, the Mr. Heartland Bear contest, and a popular regional bear event called Hibearnation. This 3 A.M. spot welcomes people of other orientations, but female bar-hoppers should know that J.J.'s is not particularly touted for its friendliness to women.

NOVAK'S

4121 Manchester Ave., 314/531-3699,
www.novaksbar.com
HOURS: Daily 4 P.M.-1:30 A.M.

Map 2

Many people know Novak's as the biggest lesbian bar in St. Louis, but the crowd at this busy social hub is welcoming to all. Lesbians, gay men, and straight folks mingle nightly here. Owner Nancy Novak describes her role as "throwing a party for a living," and that's quite accurate. The monthly events calendar is packed with trivia contests, singles nights, washers tournaments, and drag shows. Anyone who feels bored with the St. Louis scene needs only to head down to Novak's, where there's something happening every night. The game room offers pool tables and dartboards, and the patio is one of the best in the city. Heck, Novak's even makes a great burger.

ARTS AND LEISURE

St. Louis boasts a thriving fine-arts scene, both in rarefied museum exhibits and in funky galleries. Entrepreneurial artists have turned much of the city's raw warehouse space into showrooms and studios for up-and-coming talent. St. Louis also reveals its wonderfully quirky side with museums that have nothing to do with portraits or Picassos—American Kennel Club Museum of the Dog, anyone?

Theater is also an important part of St. Louis's cultural identity, and the city hosts numerous theatrical companies. While the theater community sometimes argues over whether a midsize city can support so many different groups, most plays and musicals here are high-caliber. Particularly noteworthy is the St. Louis Black Rep, the nation's largest African American theater company.

Of course, entertainment in St. Louis isn't always about gallery openings and theatrical shows. This is a great city in which to let loose and have a great time; the sheer number of fairs and festivals practically mandates it. Visitors will find abundant options in any season, from the raucous Mardi Gras celebration (second only in size to New Orleans's annual party) in spring to the St. Louis Jazz & Heritage Festival in the summer to winter's Robert Burns Night.

HIGHLIGHTS

LOOK FOR ◖◗ TO FIND
RECOMMENDED ARTS AND ACTIVITIES.

◖◗ **Best Art Museum:** A work of art in itself, the **Contemporary Art Museum St. Louis** brings the world's most talented artists to the heart of St. Louis. But the museum also gives local talents plenty of credit – and it's that sense of community that makes the Contemporary so appealing, so respected, and so successful (page 101).

◖◗ **Best Acoustics:** Known as the "Carnegie Hall of St. Louis," the **Sheldon Concert Hall** does justice to many visiting luminaries with its near-perfect acoustics. The Sheldon also houses a small but beautiful art gallery (page 107).

◖◗ **Best Seat in the House:** With more than 4,000 seats, a gorgeous Baroque interior, and the renown of the largest Broadway houses in the nation, the **Fox Theatre** is the perfect place to see a musical, enjoy a concert – or just take a tour (page 108).

◖◗ **Best Theater Company: St. Louis Black Rep** is the largest African American theater company in the United States, and its shows are consistently stellar. Performances take place in the gorgeously renovated Grandel Theater in Grand Center (page 109).

◖◗ **Best Place for Movies and Martinis:** The **Moolah Theatre & Lounge,** a former Shriners Temple, boasts a full evening's entertainment under one roof. Grab a pre-show martini, watch a first-run movie (while sitting on a plush leather couch), and then repair to the basement for a few frames of bowling (page 111).

◖◗ **Best Summer Festivals:** The **Festival of Nations** in Tower Grove Park is hosted by the International Institute and celebrates the food, dance, and art of St. Louis's many cultures. **PrideFest** brings the city's LGBT community together for three days of parades, performances, and camaraderie (pages 113 and 114).

◖◗ **Best Art Festival:** While some art fairs seem stuffy and staid, **ArtOutside** brings a sense of pure fun (plus beer!) to the proceedings. Peruse awesome, affordable work by some of St. Louis's best artists; you're sure to find something you'll love (page 115).

◖◗ **Best Park for Joggers: Forest Park** is the perfect place for casual joggers and marathoners-in-training alike. The park's jogging path is 7.5 miles long and wraps around the circumference of St. Louis's urban oasis (page 118).

◖◗ **Best Urban Bike Route:** The **Bike St. Louis** route originally extended 20 miles from Forest Park Parkway to the Gateway Arch, and now it's been expanded by 50 miles. Along the way, colorful Bike St. Louis signposts direct cyclists to city neighborhoods, attractions, and other points of interest (page 120).

◖◗ **Best Way to Feel Like a True St. Louisan:** No matter how the team is doing – whether the season culminates in a World Series win or a pre-playoffs elimination – St. Louisans stay true to the **St. Louis Cardinals.** Take in a game at the new Busch Stadium, and be sure to wear red (page 123).

Sports also are a key element of the city's cultural fabric. There are very few casual sports fans in St. Louis. Instead, there are sports lovers—and sports fanatics. The city is home to three major professional teams: the Cardinals (baseball), the Rams (football), and the Blues (ice hockey). Even when these teams are less than stellar (we're looking at you, 2008–2009 Rams), many St. Louisans stay loyal, and you'll find neighborhood sports bars packed on game nights.

While St. Louis isn't known for its die-hard citizen-athletes (no one will mistake St. Louis for, say, Denver or Austin in that regard), many St. Louisans lead very active lifestyles. The city's parks provide perfect terrain for joggers, runners, and roller-bladers. In recent years, a dedicated group of cyclists has worked to make the city streets safer for those who commute on two wheels rather than four. Today, the bike trails and lanes are clearly marked, and the city's biking routes can provide visitors with a lovely tour de St. Louis. If you travel with your golf clubs, be sure to reserve a tee time at Forest Park; this beautiful course is open to the public.

The Arts

MUSEUMS
AMERICAN KENNEL CLUB MUSEUM OF THE DOG
1721 S. Mason Rd., 314/821-3647,
www.akc.org/affiliates/museum
HOURS: Tues.-Sat. 10 A.M.-4 P.M., Sun. 1-5 P.M.
COST: $3 adult, $1 child
Map 7

If your idea of fine canine art involves dogs playing poker, you may want to expand your view at the American Kennel Club Museum of the Dog. This exhibition space, located in the gorgeous Queeny Park, is home to the nation's largest collection of dog paintings. That may sound quirky, but the museum's aims are straightforward and sincere: They honor the elegance and faithfulness of the American dog. The paintings are touching homages to some of the world's most elegant breeds. Set aside an hour or two to see the 700 works on display here—and to admire the Jarville House, the lovely 18th-century home in which this collection is kept.

CONTEMPORARY ART MUSEUM ST. LOUIS
3750 Washington Blvd., 314/535-4660,
www.contemporarystl.org
HOURS: Tues.-Sat. 10 A.M.-5 P.M., Thurs. 10 A.M.-8 P.M., Sun. 11 A.M.-4 P.M.
COST: $5 adult, $3 senior, free for students and children
Map 2

The Contemporary Art Museum St. Louis is the crown jewel of Grand Center, an area that is fast becoming the city's preeminent arts district. The Contemporary, St. Louis's premier institution for contemporary art and outreach, opened its doors in 2002 and hosts six to eight world-class exhibitions each year. The Contemporary's featured artists range from internationally acclaimed veterans to local rising stars. Past exhibitors include Yoshimoto Nara, Cindy Sherman, Jim Hodges, and Maya Lin. Don't miss the opportunity to peruse the Contemporary's Flat Files; you can open the files and peruse the works of artists of the Midwestern heartland.

ARTS AND LEISURE

THE ART OF THE FAMILY VACATION

Families who visit St. Louis are in luck. Rather than being forced to seek out the local Chuck E. Cheese outpost, parents can introduce their kids to wonderful cultural activities. St. Louis's thriving art scene is kid-inclusive, thanks to places like the **Craft Alliance** (6640 Delmar Blvd.). Just down the street from the Craft Alliance, the **Center of Creative Arts** (524 Trinity Ave., University City) offers dance and theater workshops and a student acting company for the younger set. COCA's many performances are open to the public; affordable tickets make a COCA show the perfect choice for a family outing.

In Maplewood, **Piwacket Theatre** (2810 Sutton Blvd.) produces amazing shows. This performance company puts unexpected twists on classic tales (consider the upcoming **Alice@wonder .com**), often with the help of gorgeously made puppets. If the kids dig the fanciful shows at Piwacket, they're sure to

also love **Bob Kramer's Marionettes** (4143 Laclede Ave.). Kramer's beautiful marionettes – each of which takes nearly 1,500 labor hours to create – come to splendid life in offbeat shows like *The Enchanted Toyshop.*

If your kids aren't yet keen on "traditional" museums, take them to an out-of-the-ordinary place like **City Museum** (701 N. 15th St.) or the **American Kennel Club Museum of the Dog** (1721 S. Mason Rd.). Kids who grew up with Thomas the Train will definitely want to check out the **Museum of Transportation** (3015 Barrett Station Rd., Kirkwood), which is chock-full of model trains, automobiles, trolley cars, and full-size locomotives (there's even a mini-train on which kids can ride). At the **Saint Louis Artists' Guild** (2 Oak Knoll Park, Clayton), the Monsanto Children's Gallery always displays artwork by local students. Kids are sure to be inspired when they see their peers' work in such a beautiful setting.

© ALISE O'BRIEN

Center of Creative Arts

© RAY MARKLIN/LAUMEIER SCULPTURE PARK

Laumeier Sculpture Park boasts an internationally recognized collection of contemporary sculpture, including Mark di Suvero's *Bornibus*, 1985-1987 (left) and *Destino*, 2003 (right).

They are available to the public and provide a glimpse into the area's regional art communities. A free, docent-led tour is offered every Saturday at noon.

LAUMEIER SCULPTURE PARK

12580 Rott Rd., Sunset Hills, 314/821-1209, www.laumeier.com

HOURS: Daily 8 A.M.-sunset; gallery and museum shop open Tues.-Sun. until 5 P.M.

COST: Free

Map 7

Laumeier Sculpture Park collects, commissions, and exhibits monumental contemporary sculptures. Laumeier's 100-plus acres of forest paths and broad lawns provide a backdrop for its internationally acclaimed permanent collection, as well as several touring exhibitions. Artists in the permanent collection include Donald Judd, Sol LeWitt, and Mark di Suvero. The park's small indoor museum displays additional works, including excellent photographs and drawings. Admission to both the sculpture park and the museum is free (except for special events). This is the perfect place for a picnic and afternoon stroll, and visitors should be sure to visit Laumeier's website for a calendar of fun outdoor events. During warm-weather months, the park plays host to live music, festivals, and outdoor movies.

THE MOTO MUSEUM

3441 Olive St., 314/533-3091, www.themotomuseum.com

HOURS: By appointment only

COST: $8 adult

Map 2

Moto Museum founder Steve Smith maintains his rare and vintage motorcycles with

ARTS AND LEISURE

COURTESY OF THE SAINT LOUIS ART MUSEUM

The Saint Louis Art Museum's collection is both broad and deep.

the care and precision of a fine-art curator. Those interested in visiting certainly should, but do know that it's necessary to call in advance. Moto does not keep regular hours. The museum is, first and foremost, a workshop where Smith restores bikes that he has collected from all around the world. Moto also doubles as a super-cool event space.

MUSEUM OF CONTEMPORARY RELIGIOUS ART

3700 W. Pine Blvd., 314/977-7170, www.mocra.slu.edu
HOURS: Tues.-Sun. 11 A.M.-4 P.M.
COST: $5 adult, $1 students and children
Map 2

Saint Louis University is well-respected for its strong Jesuit mission, an approach that places scholarly pursuit far above dogma. The Museum of Contemporary Religious Art exemplifies this mission. The contemplative, sanctuary-like space is filled with pieces that have dialogue with, explore, and even critique matters of faith. The museum has an ecumenical approach, and the artwork here reflects themes of many world religions. Meditation and personal spirituality also inform MOCRA's collection, and the museum hosted the largest-ever U.S. installation of Andy Warhol's *Silver Clouds*.

PULITZER CENTER FOR THE ARTS

3716 Washington Blvd., 314/754-1850, www.pulitzerarts.org
HOURS: Wed. noon-5 P.M., Sat. 10 A.M.-5 P.M.
COST: Free
Map 2

The Pulitzer Center's awe-inspiring galleries and elegant outdoor spaces sprang from the imagination of Pritzker Prize–winning architect Tadao Ando. The Pulitzer, a Modernist work of art in its own right, sits next to the equally stunning Contemporary Art Museum St. Louis (an impressive, much-beloved Richard

Serra sculpture is on permanent display in the two museums' shared courtyard). The Pulitzer's artist roster changes somewhat frequently, and has in recent years included Dan Flavin, Hiroshi Sugimoto, Max Beckmann, and Cy Twombly. The Pulitzer also contributes to literary and performing-arts programs. Visitors are advised to check out the museum's website in advance, as hours are limited.

SAINT LOUIS ART MUSEUM

1 Fine Arts Dr., 314/721-0072, www.slam.org
HOURS: Tues.-Sun. 10 A.M.-5 P.M., Fri. 10 A.M.-9 P.M.
COST: Free (additional charge for select exhibitions)
Map 6

The Saint Louis Art Museum occupies a significant space in the St. Louis landscape, both figuratively and literally. The Beaux Arts–style building, designed in the late 19th century by famed architect Cass Gilbert, sits atop the aptly named Art Hill like a great white palace. Step inside, and you'll find an interior that's just as stunning—and a permanent collection that is both broad and well-culled. Of particular note is the modern-art wing upstairs, which includes one of the best German Expressionist collections in the nation.

ART GALLERIES

BRUNO DAVID GALLERY

3721 Washington Blvd., 314/531-3030, www.brunodavidgallery.com
HOURS: Wed. and Sat. 10 A.M.-5 P.M. or by appointment
COST: Free
Map 2

The Bruno David Gallery is a great side stop for Pulitzer Center visitors attracted by its bright red door. This gallery aims to represent

the bright young talents that museums like the Pulitzer and Contemporary typically miss, and those who follow their curiosity into the heart of this small space will appreciate the innovative and spirited work on display here. Bruno David exhibitions feature the creative projects of local and international talents side-by-side, and represent a variety of media, from sculpture and installation to video and illustration.

PHILIP SLEIN GALLERY

1319 Washington Ave., 314/621-4634, www.philipsleingallery.com
HOURS: Tues.-Sat. 11 A.M.-4 P.M. or by appointment
COST: Free
Map 1

When St. Louis art collectors want the very best in cutting-edge art, they call up Philip Slein—or, better yet, they head to his gallery on Washington Avenue. Thanks to his keen aesthetic sense and dynamic personality, Slein continually brings in artists who are at the top of their game. Frequent exhibitions make the work accessible to those who might not have deep enough pockets to make a purchase. Philip Slein helped bring renowned printmaker Tom Huck to national attention; today, Huck's gigantic and wonderfully grotesque works hang in some of the country's premier museums.

SHELDON ART GALLERIES

3648 Washington Blvd., 314/533-9900, www.sheldonconcerthall.org
HOURS: Tues. and Thurs. noon-8 P.M., Wed. and Fri. noon-5 P.M., Sat. 10 A.M.-2 P.M.
COST: Donation requested
Map 2

The Sheldon Art Galleries are on the basement level of the world-class Sheldon Concert

Hall. Frequently missed by concert attendees (and even by astute gallery-goers), this collection represents one of the St. Louis art community's best-kept secrets. The Sheldon hosts a diverse array of artists and media; one recent exhibit featured photographs accompanied by carefully arranged found objects. The gallery also offers a full schedule of art talks, lunchtime lectures, and master-class workshops, in addition to a wonderful annual children's art show.

WHITE FLAG PROJECTS
4568 Manchester Rd., 314/531-3442,
www.whiteflagprojects.org
HOURS: Wed. noon-7 P.M., Sat. noon-5 P.M.,
or by appointment
COST: Free
Map 2

White Flag Projects offers art lovers an alternative to the often-stuffy exclusivity of the contemporary art world. The artists exhibited here run the gamut from progressive newcomers to internationally acclaimed veterans. The gallery's curators are not partial to any particular medium, but White Flag's focus is on fringe artists. Located in the burgeoning Grove neighborhood, this renovated industrial building provides the perfect backdrop for challenging art. Gallery hours are limited, but visitors are invited to call ahead and schedule a tour.

CONCERTS
FOCAL POINT
2720 Sutton Blvd., Maplewood, 314/781-4200,
www.thefocalpoint.org
Map 4

As the town of Maplewood continues to flourish with new restaurants and attractions, it's comforting to know that the area retains its small-town feel. Across the street from the one-of-a-kind bowlers' haven Saratoga Lanes stands the Focal Point, a listening room that plays host to all sorts of folk art from at home and abroad. Depending on the evening, you may come across a world-class Irish fiddler, a Cajun zydeco dancing exposition, or an expert banjo picker. The room is arranged with a small stage and a few rows of wooden seats, so every performance is intimate and memorable. Most events take place on the weekend, and it's best to check the venue's website for upcoming events.

OPERA THEATER ST. LOUIS
210 Hazel Ave., Webster Groves, 314/961-0171,
www.opera-stl.org
Map 7

Opera Theater St. Louis's intimate home is located on the manicured grounds of Webster University. The company stages a nicely blended repertoire of classic and contemporary productions, from *Madame Butterfly* to *Una Cosa Rara*. Opera Theater St. Louis also hosts an outdoor cocktail hour and picnic prior to several of its spring concerts—the perfect milieu for a date. Visitors are invited to bring their own wine and picnic food, and a local restaurant provides affordably priced boxed dinners for those who come without.

POWELL SYMPHONY HALL
718 N. Grand Blvd., 314/533-2500, www.slso.org
Map 2

This 2,700-seat theater began its life as a vaudeville hall and movie palace. Today it is an acoustic marvel, thanks to a graceful midcentury renovation, and is home to the world-renowned Saint Louis Symphony Orchestra. The Grammy-winning SLSO was founded in 1880 and took up residence at

ARTS AND LEISURE

© KEN HOWARD

Opera Theater St. Louis is a cultural treasure – and a surprisingly great date spot.

the Powell in 1966, thanks to a generous private donation. In addition to its beautiful Versailles-inspired decor, Powell Hall also boasts a permanent acoustic shell. There is simply not one bad seat in the house—the sound at the Powell carries perfectly.

ROBERTS ORPHEUM

416 N. 9th St., 314/588-0388,
www.robertsorpheum.com
Map 1

This beautiful, Parisian-style venue began its life as the American Theatre. The American was built in 1917 by Louis A. Cella, a self-made millionaire with a taste for vaudeville. When vaudeville acts waned in popularity, Warner Brothers purchased the theater and converted it to a movie house. The American was reborn as a performance theater in the 1960s and has hosted hundreds of concerts, musicals, and other

special events. Cary Grant, Mae West, Eartha Kitt, and Henry Fonda all performed here; contemporary acts such as Pearl Jam, Tori Amos, and the Red Hot Chili Peppers have also made appearances. The theater is now named for the Roberts brothers, the dynamic St. Louis duo who purchased it in 2003. Aided by their deep pockets and equally deep respect for local history, the brothers have restored the theater to its original, dazzling elegance.

◖ SHELDON CONCERT HALL

3648 Washington Blvd., 314/533-9900,
www.sheldonconcerthall.org
Map 2

The perfect acoustics of the intimate, early-20th-century Sheldon Concert Hall make it an ideal venue for the wide variety of engagements that take place within. Several chamber and solo concerts are scheduled at the

ARTS AND LEISURE

Catch a Broadway musical or a legendary rock performance at the beautiful Fox Theatre.

Sheldon throughout the year, as are speaking engagements, jazz sessions, and blues concerts. Tickets are typically inexpensive (anywhere from $10 to $50) and can be purchased online at Metrotix.com. The Sheldon is located in St. Louis's Midtown arts district, behind the Fox Theatre, and enjoys the distinction of being one of the area's oldest concert halls.

THEATERS AND THEATER COMPANIES
BLACK CAT REPERTORY THEATRE COMPANY
2810 Sutton Blvd., 314/963-8800, www.blackcattheatre.org

`Map 4`

There are nearly 70 small, independent theater companies in St. Louis—but only a handful of venues in which to enjoy their productions. Black Cat Repertory Theatre is one of the nicest performance spaces in town. This small venue offers cabaret-style seating and a laid-back lounge vibe. Evening playbills showcase contemporary playwrights and edgy scripts, but Black Cat is best known for its daytime performances, when the mood of the place changes entirely. Black Cat is home to Piwacket, a popular children's theater company. For nearly two decades, families have enjoyed Piwacket's whimsical take on classic stories. The puppet shows are particularly delightful.

◖ FOX THEATRE
527 N. Grand Blvd., 314/534-1678, www.fabulousfox.com

HOURS: Tues., Thurs. and Sat. 10 A.M. (tours)
COST: Tues. $5 adult, $3 child; Thurs. and Sat. $8 adult, $3 child

`Map 2`

The Fox Theatre is one of the largest Broadway houses in the country.

Considering its Baroque grandeur (and its 4,192 seats), it's hard to believe this ornate palace began its life as a movie theater—but indeed it did. Opened by cinema mogul William Fox in 1929, this theater was one of the first to show films with audio tracks. The Fox welcomed moviegoers until the 1970s, when the theater briefly served as a live-music venue. In the '80s, a group of private investors purchased the Fox from the city of St. Louis and restored the theater to its original condition. Today the "Fabulous Fox" hosts touring Broadway shows and big-name performers. It is also the headquarters of Fox Theatricals, a Tony Award–winning Broadway production company.

HOTCITY

501 N. Grand Blvd., 314/289-4063,
www.hotcitytheatre.org

Map 2

In 2004, two of the city's most respected fringe theater companies, City Theatre and Hot House Theatre, combined forces to create HotCity. Today the company produces contemporary, issue-oriented theatrical works appreciated by both local and national audiences. HotCity's main-stage productions take place in Midtown's brand-new Kranzberg Arts Center, where the organization will move its offices in 2009. The company's annual Greenhouse New Plays Festival showcases theatrical debuts hand-selected by a jury. The festival has garnered international recognition and takes place during the months of June and July.

NEW LINE THEATRE

www.geocities.com/newlinetheatre

One of the tragedies of local St. Louis theater is the rapid rate at which little companies are losing their venues. Despite not having a permanent theater home, New Line puts on some of the very best stage productions in the city. The company's challenging, buoyant productions have garnered praise from the nation's top theater critics, and the local following is strong. New Line's shows are first-rate—yet, refreshingly, tickets are never more than $20. The company often stages the U.S. premieres of shows by up-and-coming playwrights, and the directors and actors have a particular yen for wickedly entertaining musicals. Visit the company's website for show schedules and locations.

⟨ ST. LOUIS BLACK REP

1717 Olive St., 314/534-3807,
www.theblackrep.org

Map 1

The St. Louis Black Rep is one of the nation's leading African American theater companies. Founded in 1976 by producing director Ron Himes (who is nothing less than a hero in local theater circles), the Black Rep stages plays that are at once challenging and entertaining. Himes has overseen the production of more than 100 shows at the company's home theater, the historic Grandel. The Black Rep is dedicated to the preservation and exultation of black culture through its plays and playwrights. The company produces plays and musicals, and favors inventive interpretations of modern classics by such scribes as August Wilson and Eubie Banks.

ST. LOUIS REPERTORY THEATER

130 Edgar Rd., Webster Groves, 314/968-4925,
www.repstl.org

Map 7

The St. Louis Repertory Theater is a regional, professional playhouse at the top of its game. For more than 40 years, the Rep has staged high-caliber productions in the cushy Loretto-Hilton Center in Webster Groves. The mainstage selections can lean toward the predictable, but the theater's Off-Ramp Series more than makes up for that with its inclusion of excellent, daring selections like *The Lieutenant of Inishmore*. The season typically begins in early September, and the theater goes dark in mid-April. The excellent website includes a listing of all shows, along with online ticket-purchasing capabilities.

STAGES ST. LOUIS

111 S. Geyer Rd., Kirkwood, 314/821-2407,
www.stagesstlouis.org
COST: $46 adult, $43 senior, $24 child

Map 7

Stages St. Louis is one of the city's largest musical-theater production companies. Founders Jack Lane and Michael Hamilton established this professional, nonprofit company in 1987, after meeting on the New York theater scene. In addition to producing around five shows per year, Stages also teaches a host of popular theater workshops. The school, known as the Stages Performing Arts Academy, offers a year-round, comprehensive musical-theater curriculum in dance, voice, drama, and theory. The company and the school are housed in the 380-seat Robert G. Reim Theatre at the Kirkwood Civic Center.

MOVIE HOUSES

CHASE PARK PLAZA THEATER

212 N. Kingshighway Blvd., 314/367-2385,
http://chase.stlouiscinemas.com
COST: $8 adult, $6 student/senior, $5 child, $6 matinee

Map 2

Anytime you see a movie at the Chase Park Plaza, it feels like an event. To reach the box office and theater, you must stroll through the lobby of one of the ritziest hotels in St. Louis, passing limousines in the parking lot, tuxedos in the lobby, and an elegant bar where jazz drifts from the shiny baby grand. The theaters themselves are standard multiplex fare, with all the new releases and an occasional indie hit. But your departure from the theater is far classier than at other movie houses. As soon as the credits roll, ushers stand by the exit doors and offer mints and candy off a silver platter.

HI-POINTE THEATER

1005 McCausland Ave., 314/781-4716,
www.landmarktheatres.com
COST: $8 adult, $6 student/senior, $6 matinee

Map 6

This old-fashioned, single-screen cinema is named for its unique vantage point: The theater sits at the corner of Clayton Road and McCausland Avenue, the highest point in the city. The film du jour at the Hi-Pointe is almost always an acclaimed first-run indie flick, and there are no matinees here, only late-afternoon and evening showings. Some locals fear for the fate of their beloved little theater; the bar next door (also called the Hi-Pointe) drew good crowds but was nevertheless shuttered in 2007. Still, if you're in the mood for a good movie with a side of

St. Louis–style nostalgia, you can't do much better than this.

◖ MOOLAH THEATRE & LOUNGE

3821 Lindell Blvd., 314/446-6868, www.stlouiscinemas.com/moolah/

COST: $8.50 adult, $6.50 student/senior, $5.50 child, $6.50 matinee

`Map 2`

If you set out to create the best movie theater ever, you would end up with the Moolah. For starters, there's a giant 45-foot screen and an ear-splitting sound system. There are plush leather couches, stadium seating with ample legroom, and a balcony that affords a bird's-eye view. Extras include a bar that serves theme drinks for each film (e.g., a "Lord Voldemort Mojito" for *Harry Potter and the Order of the Phoenix*), a bowling alley in the basement, and a beautiful old building with a Masonic history. As for films, the Moolah picks the best new release every few weeks and hosts "Midnight Brew and View" parties on Fridays and Saturdays, which feature all-you-can-drink cocktails and old movies that range from *A Clockwork Orange* to *Top Gun*. The Moolah proves they don't build 'em like they used to—they build 'em better.

TIVOLI THEATER

6350 Delmar Blvd., 314/995-6270, www.landmarktheatres.com

COST: $8 adult, $6 student/senior, $6 matinee

`Map 6`

The Tivoli is one of the very few St. Louis theaters that screen foreign and independent

© AMY FERGUSON

At the Moolah, you can have a top-shelf martini with your first-run movie.

films. The theater has been open since 1924 and has the ambiance to accompany the history, including burgundy curtains in front of the screens, an orchestra pit in one auditorium, and a host of movie memorabilia that runs the gamut from a replica of the statue from *The Maltese Falcon* to a poster for hometown favorite *Meet Me in St. Louis*. Though the Tivoli was renovated in 1995, paring the original massive movie palace expanse into three smaller screening rooms, its iconic marquee remains.

ARTS AND LEISURE

Festivals and Events

WINTER

FIRST NIGHT

Grand Center, 314/289-8121,
www.grandcenter.org/firstnight/
HOURS: 5:30 P.M.-midnight
COST: Free
`Map 2`

This free, family-friendly New Year's Eve event takes place every year in the Midtown arts district. It was created in response to a public need for a fun, safe, and affordable event inclusive of families with children. Activities kick off at 5:30, with a quirky, spirited musical procession (often involving kazoos), and continues until midnight with a full schedule of unique music and comedy performances. The celebration's most popular yearly event, "Field of Chimes," asks attendees to write down their regrets for the past year and then burn them in a symbolic bonfire.

MARDI GRAS FESTIVAL

314/771-5110, www.mardigrasinc.com
COST: Free

This boisterous celebration is one of the city's most well-attended events—and it's also one of the largest Mardi Gras festivals in the entire nation. Usually celebrated during the third weekend in February, the eclectic schedule of events includes a pet parade, a Cajun cook-off, the Taste of Soulard restaurant showcase, and a Weiner Dog Derby. The architecture of Soulard, St. Louis's original French settlement, lends an air of authenticity to the proceedings. Attendees should strongly consider taking public transportation to the event, as parking is quite limited. And while the parades are fine for small children, the street party is not.

SPRING

CINCO DE MAYO FESTIVAL

www.cincodemayostl.com
COST: Free

The Cinco de Mayo festivities in early May are the largest of St. Louis's three annual Hispanic festivals and a testament to the city's booming Latino population. Things took off for the festival after planners partnered with the same folks who coordinate St. Louis's raucous Mardi Gras celebration. Three blocks' worth of Cherokee Street, the city's Hispanic hub, are blocked off to traffic. Vendors temporarily move their shops onto the street and peddle everything from tacos and empanadas to soccer jerseys and custom airbrushed Nikes. There are two stages for live music, with an array of acts from homegrown St. Louis rock to an 18-piece mariachi band. Drinko de Mayo, as the holiday that commemorates the Battle of Puebla is often called, is also the only time that sipping a *cerveza* is permitted on Cherokee, a part of town where liquor laws are unusually strict.

ST. LOUIS JAZZ & HERITAGE FESTIVAL

Shaw Park Clayton, 314/863-0278,
www.saintlouisjazzfest.com
COST: $25 lawn, $75 VIP
`Map 6`

The St. Louis Jazz & Heritage Festival takes place in Clayton every spring, usually during the last Saturday in May, and showcases the finest local and national talents the genres have to offer. A diverse lineup features acts from all across the country and is widely appreciated for the tribute it pays to the genre's Midwestern roots. Gate price pays for first-come-first-serve lawn seats at every show, and the $75 VIP admission gains access to special reserved seating and a free-refreshments tent. This is a one-day event and tickets sell out fast, so admission should be purchased online in advance.

ST. PATRICK'S DAY FESTIVAL

18th St. and Market St., 314/231-2598, www.irishparade.org

COST: Free

Map 1

Every year, more than 250,000 St. Louisanscelebrate their city's proud Irish heritage by attending a St. Patrick's Day Parade in mid-March. There are officially two, one downtown and the other in the formerly working-class, Irish neighborhood of Dogtown. The festival downtown has been taking place for more than three decades and downtown is the "official" location of the event. City officials paint a path of green leprechaun footprints along Market Street each year in honor of the occasion, and a quirky afternoon festival features live Irish music and fare. Yet despite the popularity of this event, the Dogtown iteration is considered the more authentic of the two. Organized by members of the Ancient Order of Hibernians, the Dogtown party features far more local flair. The festival's eccentric little parade chugs down Tamm Avenue, and residents say—only half-jokingly—that the party starts at 6 A.M.

SUMMER

❰ FESTIVAL OF NATIONS

314/773-9090, www.iistl.org/festival.php

COST: Free

Map 4

Sponsored by the International Institute—itself a civic treasure—the Festival of Nations brings the world to Tower Grove

ARTS AND LEISURE

© WAYNE CROSSLIN/INTERNATIONAL INSTITUTE

International dance performances are a big part of the Festival of Nations.

Park each August. Given the sheer number of food stands, artisan booths, and cultural performances, visitors are wise to plan an entire afternoon around this festival. Entrance to the fest is free, as are primo lawn seats for the many stage shows, but food and drinks (and crafts, of course) cost extra. Adventurous gourmands will want to pass up the could-eat-it-anywhere booths selling fried rice and tacos, and head instead to the Bosnian, Peruvian, and Eritrean booths. The gorgeous artisanal items stretch for yards and include delicate silver jewelry, handmade instruments, and chic, vibrant dresses. Performances—many of them traditional dances, such as the Highland fling—are not to be missed. This is the perfect place to introduce children to the big, big world around them—and to remind yourself that we truly are a nation of immigrants.

JAPANESE FESTIVAL

4344 Shaw Blvd., 314/577-9400,
www.mobot.org
HOURS: Sat. and Sun. 10 A.M.–8 P.M., Mon.
10 A.M.–5 P.M.
COST: $10 adult, $7 senior, $3 child
Map 4

The Missouri Botanical Garden's annual Japanese festival is a Labor Day weekend tradition that draws visitors from all over the region. This is the garden's most popular yearly event, and pays tribute to the culture behind one of its finest features, the world-renowned Japanese Garden. Events during this jam-packed three-day weekend include sumo wrestling, *rakugo* Japanese comedy, and *taiko* drumming. Japanese food is also available for purchase. The nightly candlelight walks along the Japanese

Garden's serene and meditative paths are worth the price of admission alone, but be sure not to miss the great bonsai exhibit in the main building.

PAGAN PICNIC

Tower Grove Park, (Grand Blvd. and Arsenal St.)
www.paganpicnic.yarrowcoven.org
COST: Free
Map 4

Regardless of one's spiritual inclinations, this yearly event in Tower Grove Park is a worthwhile experience. More a festival then a picnic, the Pagan Picnic is one-stop shopping for everything one needs to live the modern pagan lifestyle. Visitors will find a bevy of unique vendors, plus workshops on everything from building a coven and casting spells to tapping into the universal energy to gain spiritual enlightenment. The popular 15-year-old gathering usually takes place during the first weekend in June and is a labor of love for its supporters. The love is certainly evident in this all-are-welcome event.

☾ PRIDEFEST

Tower Grove Park (Grand Blvd. and Arsenal St.),
314/772-8888, www.pridestl.org
Map 4

St. Louis's annual PrideFest, like most other LGBT pride fests around the nation, takes place in late June to commemorate the 1969 Stonewall Riots in New York City. The concerts, barbecues, contests, dances, and parade at this three-day event attract 100,000 people each year. The majority of PrideFest activities take place in South City's beautiful Tower Grove Park. The dense residential area surrounding the park is known for its gay-friendliness and support of gay-rights issues. After sunset each day, the PrideFest fun continues in the Grand South Grand and Grove neighborhoods. Many bar owners block off streets and sidewalks to accommodate the enormous crowds. In 2009, St. Louis Pride-Fest celebrates its 30th year.

ST. LOUIS SHAKESPEARE FESTIVAL
Forest Park, 314/531-9800, www.sfstl.org
COST: free
`Map 2`

Each year, the St. Louis Shakespeare Festival draws the city residents en masse to Forest Park. And with good reason: There are few better ways to spend a nice evening than with a picnic dinner and free theater. The festival sponsors a different Shakespearean work each season, and shows typically have a creative contemporary spin. Although the festival's mission is charitable in nature, this is professional theater. Productions employ nationally renowned directors, designers, and actors, and shows attract 50,000 people during their month-long run. Performances begin on Memorial Day weekend and run for four weeks; catch the show at 6:30 P.M. every day but Tuesday.

TWANGFEST
314/535-4660, www.twangfest.com
COST: $20

Every year in June, St. Louis's community radio station, KDHX (88.1 FM), hosts an eclectic music festival. Named for its down-home rock and country roots, Twang Fest takes place over the course of a weekend and is one of the largest festivals of its kind in the nation. For three days and nights, local and national acts perform in venues all over the city, from the Duck Room in the Delmar Loop to the Schlafly Tap Room in Midtown. Past acts have included the Old 97's, Centro-Matic, and the Waco Brothers. Proceeds from this perennially popular event support KDHX's excellent public programming.

FALL
ART IN THE PARK
Francis Park (bounded by Nottingham Ave., Tamm Ave., Eichelberger St., and Donovan Ave.), http://stlouis.missouri.org/stlouishills
COST: Free
`Map 4`

The Southampton neighborhood's Art in the Park festival is a relative newcomer on what's quickly becoming the "St. Louis art fair circuit." The charm of this one-day fall gathering is its local focus. Much like Schlafly's annual ArtOutside festival, Art in the Park exhibits the crafts of local artists exclusively. Art in the Park also boasts a classic car show, along with a food court where local restaurant owners share *their* best work. Admission is free, and festivities take place in the neighborhood's beautiful Francis Park on the last Sunday in September.

◖ ARTOUTSIDE
7260 Southwest Ave., Maplewood, 314/241-2337, www.schlafly.com/artoutside.shtml
COST: Free
`Map 4`

Taking place (not-so-coincidentally) the same weekend as the St. Louis Art Fair (usually the first Friday, Saturday, and Sunday in September), ArtOutside offers an alternative to the traditional, pricy art sale. This

ARTS AND LEISURE

yearly festival takes place in the enormous parking lot of the Schlafly Bottleworks and feels like a really great street party—that just so happens to feature really great art. Practically every medium is represented here, from photography to painting to sculpture to printmaking. One of the best things about ArtOutside is that it makes art accessible; festival-goers can spend less than $50 and go home with an original work. Live music provides the soundtrack to your art perusal, and Schlafly keeps the suds flowing.

FALL HARVEST FESTIVAL

Hwy. 100 and I-44, Gray Summit, 636/451-3512, www.mobot.org

Map 7

The St. Louis Fall Harvest Festival is held annually, usually during the second or third week of October. Local restaurants set up tents here, along one of Shaw Nature Reserve's main thoroughfares, and compete with their best fall dishes. An outdoor stage features local musicians, and there are plenty of arts and crafts available for purchase. Gray Summit is a 40-mile drive west of the city, but festival-goers seem to relish the opportunity to spend an afternoon away. This relatively new festival has gained popularity with each passing year. While the Fall Harvest Festival started out small, it now attracts thousands.

GROVE FEST

Manchester Ave. between Sarah and Boyle, www.grovefest.org

HOURS: Sat. 3-11 P.M., Sun. noon-6 P.M.

COST: Free

Map 2

This offbeat weekend festival, which usually takes place in September, celebrates the continued revitalization of the Forest Park Southeast neighborhood. A live-music stage hosts local bands, independent restaurants sell tantalizing food, street performers entertain the crowds, and visitors can browse a block's worth of arts-and-crafts booths. Throughout the weekend, Grove residents work on a colorful new building mural, which is dedicated at the close of the festival. Thanks to this new tradition, there is plenty of public art to complement the Grove's rapidly gentrifying streetscape.

SCI FEST, THE INTERNATIONAL SCIENCE FESTIVAL

5050 Oakland Ave., 314/286-4607, www.scifeststl.org

COST: $6-10

Map 5

The International Science Festival just had its St. Louis debut in 2008, but the future of this weeklong program of workshops, speakers, and films is very promising. Biotechnology is becoming one of the city's most critical and driving industries. The science "magic" performed by such local companies as Monsanto, Pfizer, and Chlorogen is uncoded for the general public here, and the focus of organizers is on St. Louis's youngest residents. Sci Fest aims to inspire future generations of scientists, and although the event has something to interest virtually anyone, it features a full schedule of hands-on children's activities. Festivities take place at the Science Center and James S. McDonnell Planetarium, and admission to each of the various workshops and lectures is around $10.

SHAW ART FAIR

www.shawartfair.com

COST: $5

This proud little weekend-long arts festival has been taking place in October for nearly 20 years but has gained popularity and recognition in only the past few. Today it is one of the city's top art fairs, and it features the work of as many as 135 artists from around the country (including much of the city's nationally recognized local talent), in addition to a live music stage and food from area restaurants. One of the best things about Shaw Art Fair is its location: Stalls are set up along the elegant tree-lined boulevard of Flora Place, in South City's historic Shaw neighborhood. Southsiders love a good brunch, so consider attending the fair's opening-day breakfast feast. Partaking of this particularly well-attended neighborhood meal will net you free, early admission to the event.

ST. LOUIS ART FAIR

314/863-0278, www.saintlouisartfair.com

HOURS: Fri. 5-10 P.M., Sat. 10 A.M.-10 P.M., Sun. 11 A.M.-4 P.M.

COST: Free

The St. Louis Art Fair blossoms to life each year around the first weekend in September on the streets of downtown Clayton. While some art fairs are more kitsch than craftsmanship, the St. Louis Art Fair is the real deal. Price tags can be high, but the work is usually worth it. Spend a nice fall afternoon browsing original pieces by some of the nation's top artists, listening to live local music and enjoying food from more than 20 area restaurants. The artists and craftspeople featured here are hand-selected by a jury, and the St. Louis Art Fair deserves its great national reputation. Be prepared to walk quite a bit—this festival is attended by thousands of St. Louisans every year, so parking spots are at a premium.

Sports and Recreation

PARKS

CARONDELET PARK
S. Grand Blvd. and Loughborough Ave.,
314/289-5330
HOURS: Daily 24 hours
Map 4

Many neighborhoods in south St. Louis are blessed with wonderful public parks. Carondelet, which is nestled in the charming Holly Hills area, is a reminder of the city park's historical role as the epicenter and main meeting place of a neighborhood. The park boasts a bevy of features in a relatively small space. A 1.5-mile walking/biking path surrounds a couple of baseball fields, tennis courts, a few playgrounds, and the best horseshoe pits around. The music stand hosts free concerts during the warm months, and a five-acre, fish-stocked lake attracts plenty of amateur anglers.

FAUST PARK
15185 Olive Blvd., 636/532-7298,
www.co.st-louis.mo.us/parks/Faust_home.html
HOURS: Daily dawn-dusk
COST: Free
Map 7

Faust Park offers far more than the typical playground-and-picnic-shelter routine. In addition to miles of paved walking trails, super-clean picnic and restroom facilities, and a busy events calendar, several popular historic and tourist sites are here; admission costs are nominal. The Sophia M. Sachs Butterfly House is a can't-miss attraction here, as is the beautiful, fully restored 1920s carousel. A bit farther into the park, you'll find a restored 19th-century farm and historic village. This area is open for self-guided tours during the week and docent-led tours on weekends.

(FOREST PARK
Hwy. 40 between Skinker Blvd. and Kingshighway Blvd.
HOURS: Daily 24 hours
COST: Free
Map 2

Forest Park has captured St. Louis's civic imagination for well over 100 years. The huge, verdant park hosted the 1904 World's Fair, and native St. Louisans rightfully associate Forest Park with culture and history. But it's the perfect place for recreation, too. Biking enthusiasts will definitely want to take a bicycle tour, which covers 18 Forest Park attractions in 10 easy miles. Visitors up for an adventure should not miss the Segway tour; tours depart from the Saint Louis Science Center and (after a training session) send riders zinging through Forest Park. If a traditional jog is more your speed, take advantage of the wide, well-paved, seven-and-a-half-mile jogging trail. Paddleboats (which seat up to four adults) are available for rental at $15 per hour, and the views from Forest Park's Grand Basin are magnificent.

HEMAN PARK
7200 Olive Blvd., University City, 314/721-8172,
www.ucitymo.org
HOURS: Daily dawn-dusk
COST: Free
Map 6

This wedge-shaped 85-acre park is a hive of activity during the warm-weather months. The Heman Park swimming pool is an important focal point for the community, as are the large playground and sports fields. Heman offers all of the amenities of a great city park—football and soccer fields, baseball diamonds, and lighted tennis courts can all be found here. Picnic areas are abundant, and restroom facilities are convenient (if not always spotless).

LAFAYETTE PARK

Park Ave. and Mississippi Ave., 314/289-5300
HOURS: Daily 24 hours
Map 3

This 29-acre, Victorian-era park was one of the first public parks to be established in St. Louis. It was dedicated in 1838 and is faced on all sides by some of the city's preeminent historic homes, including several meticulously restored Second Empire–style mansions. Behind the park's massive stone gates, visitors will find a one-acre lake, a playground, a park house, sports fields, and paved trails. Features include beautifully landscaped grounds, an 1870s police station and a pair of Revolutionary War-era cannons that once stood on the deck of a British war ship.

LONE ELK PARK AND
WORLD BIRD SANCTUARY

1 Lone Elk Park Rd., Valley Park, 636/861-3225,
www.co.st-louis.mo.us,
www.worldbirdsanctuary.org
HOURS: Daily 8 A.M.-5 P.M.
COST: Free (donations encouraged)
Map 7

Many native St. Louisans have fond childhood memories of Lone Elk Park, of Sunday-afternoon drives along the road that snakes up and down its tumbling terrain. From the comfort of their vehicle, visitors can observe one of the nation's last remaining bison herds, as well as the wild turkeys, waterfowl, elk, and deer that graze on the park's wild grasses. If you feel inspired to do some grazing of your own, pack a picnic and enjoy it in one of the park's several shelters. The World Bird Sanctuary at Lone Elk's entrance is open to visitors as well and keeps the same hours as the park.

POWDER VALLEY CONSERVATION
NATURE CENTER

11715 Cragwold Rd., Kirkwood, 314/301-1500,
http://mdc.mo.gov
HOURS: Daily sunrise-sunset
COST: Free
Map 7

Those seeking a quick and convenient break from the urban landscape will find it here, in a wild oasis set within the boundaries of the St. Louis suburb Kirkwood. Residents working in this area can enjoy its 112 acres of oak hickory forest and trails (some paved, some unpaved) during their lunch breaks. Travelers are urged to find respite as well. Just one word of warning: The cathedral lofts of Powder Valley's oaks frame views of the Highway 44/270 interchange, so one never quite escapes the sound of the highway here. But that matters little once you've seen the park's breathtaking vistas; from them, you just might acquire an appreciation for the convoluted beauty of nature interrupted by suburban sprawl.

SHAW NATURE RESERVE

Hwy. 100 and I-44, Gray Summit, 636/451-3512,
www.shawnature.org
HOURS: Daily 7 A.M.-sunset
COST: $3 adult, $2 senior, free for children
Map 7

The Ozark landscape of rural Missouri gives travelers a good idea of what this part of the country looked like to its earliest residents. This extension of the Missouri Botanical Garden, established in 1879, seeks to

ARTS AND LEISURE

© MISSOURI BOTANICAL GARDEN

Shaw Nature Reserve, part of the Missouri Botanical Garden system, preserves the flora and fauna of the Ozarks.

preserve a corner of this native environment for decades to come. Less than an hour's drive from the city, Shaw Nature Reserve's 2,500 acres boast a visitor center, a museum, and scenic hiking trails through marshlands, forests, glades, and prairies. The scientific data collected here in wildlife surveys is utilized by ecologists all over the world. The wildflower garden and views of the Meramec River are spectacular.

BICYCLING
BIG SHARK
6681 Delmar Blvd., 314/862-1188,
www.bigshark.com
HOURS: Mon.-Fri. 10 A.M.-8 P.M., Sat.
10 A.M.-6 P.M., Sun. noon-5 P.M.
`Map 6`

Avid cyclists and weekend cruisers alike will find the answer to all their bicycling needs at Big Shark, a friendly, one-stop retail and repair shop on the Loop. The staff at this stylish bike boutique is always courteous and knowledgeable. Whether in the market for a gear ratio built for speed and distance, a bicycle basket, or a powder-blue beach cruiser built for two, the shopper will find answers here. Visit the shop's great website for special weekly discounts and the 411 on local cycling events.

◖ BIKE ST. LOUIS
1000 St. Louis Union Station, Ste. 102,
314/436-7009, www.bikestlouis.org
`Map 1`

For too many years, St. Louis had a reputation of being inhospitable to cyclists. The Midwestern love affair with the automobile and the interstate system made it difficult for bikes to travel safely. Fortunately, Bike St. Louis is changing all of that. Congressman Russ Carnahan and Board of Aldermen president Lewis Reed spearheaded the project, which connects the city's parks to one another via bike-friendly commuter lanes. The original Bike St. Louis route was 20 miles, but a 2008 expansion added 50 more miles—and now cyclists can take the route as far as the River Des Peres Greenway in South St. Louis County and the Mississippi riverfront in North St. Louis. Colorful signs, designed by Kiku Obata, guide riders as they take in St. Louis on two wheels.

GOLF

TRIPLE A GOLF AND TENNIS CLUB IN FOREST PARK
5163 Clayton Ave., 314/652-2433, www.tripleaclub.org
HOURS: Daily 7 A.M.–8 P.M.
COST: $14 weekdays, $16 weekends, $11 after 5 P.M.
Map 5

The Bermuda-grass fairways and bent grass greens of this historic nine-hole course are an urban oasis for St. Louisans. The tight fairways here are woven into the scenic landscape of beautiful Forest Park. The club's recently renovated facilities include meticulously manicured grounds, an updated clubhouse, and a three-hole mini-course for pre-game practice. The course was established in 1897 to provide the public with low-cost athletic facilities, and it continues to fulfill this mission. A round here costs just $14 on weekdays, and cart rental is available for a mere $15 more.

NORMANDIE GOLF CLUB
7605 Saint Charles Rock Rd., 314/862-4884, www.normandiegolf.com
HOURS: Daily 7 A.M.–8 P.M.
COST: $28.50 weekdays, $35 weekends
Map 7

Normandie Golf Club was established in 1901 and claims to be the oldest 18-hole course west of the Mississippi. It's inarguably one of the longer courses in St. Louis, and is prized by locals for its unique routing and tight fairways. Normandie was designed by a disciple of the Scottish legend Old Tom Morris and most recently purchased by locally renowned Walter Thomas Management. Walter Thomas operates many of the area's best courses, and golfers here look forward to a host of promised improvements. Amenities include a full-service pro shop and restaurant.

QUAIL CREEK GOLF CLUB
6022 Wells Rd., 314/487-1988, www.quailcreekgolfclub.com
HOURS: Daily 6 A.M.–8 P.M.
COST: $15–59 (see website for details)
Map 7

The natural streams and narrow rolling fairways of this par-72 course have been the majestic backdrop of two USGA tournaments and a US Open qualifier. Quail Creek is one of the area's most challenging public courses from its back tees and boasts a slope rating of 141, though it does a great job of hosting all play levels. The atmosphere here is casual, and the front tees are playable by all. Quail Creek is only a 25-minute drive southwest of downtown. Its amenities include a full-service pro shop and casual restaurant.

ARTS AND LEISURE

TAPAWINGO NATIONAL GOLF COURSE

13001 Gary Player Dr., 636/349-3100,
www.tapawingogolf.com
HOURS: Daily 7 A.M.-8 P.M.
COST: $25-70 (see website for details)
Map 7

Tapawingo is a Native American word for "place of joy," a fitting summary of the hardwood forests, rolling prairies, and 27 championship holes at this lovely course. Tapawingo is a 20-minute drive from downtown and offers play for golfers of all levels. An undulating front nine and links-style back nine bookend a total of three 18-hole combinations. This par-36 course was designed by golf legend Gary Player, and rates are reasonable considering the amenities, which include majestic 3,520-yard fairways and practice greens regularly visited by wild turkeys, geese, and deer.

BOWLING

EPIPHANY LANES

3164 Ivanhoe Ave., 314/781-8684
HOURS: Call for hours
Map 4

Epiphany Lanes has all the ambiance of a church basement, but really, that's part of its charm. That, and the rock-bottom prices, which will leave you wondering if it's 1972 again. At only $2.25 per game ($1.25 before 6 P.M.), bowling at Epiphany is one of the cheapest dates in town. This church-owned eight-lane bowling alley is near the corner of Jamieson and Arsenal, adjacent to its sister parish, and is one of the last of its kind in the country. Though amenities here are basic, visitors will find everything they need, from shoe rental to a well-stocked bar and basic grill.

PIN-UP BOWL

6191 Delmar Blvd., 314/727-5555,
www.pinupbowl.com
HOURS: Mon.-Thurs. 3 P.M.-3 A.M., Fri.-Sun.
noon-3 A.M.
Map 6

Bowling alley and restaurant by day, see-and-be-seen hot spot by night, this nightclub hybrid is *the* place to go after a concert at The Pageant or dinner on the Loop. Pin-Up Bowl's location is great. It's located in one of the city's prime nightlife districts, and just a couple doors down from one of the city's most popular concert venues. The fun here revolves around classic cocktails, late-night snacks, and midnight bowling. Under the watchful gaze of a museum's worth of Vargas prints, Pin-Up's humming bar serves cocktails until 3 A.M. The kitchen is open nearly as late as the bar (and turns out fun, nostalgic items like grilled-cheese sandwiches and Campbell's tomato soup), and bowling on the 12 full-length lanes is available all night for just $5 a game.

SARATOGA LANES

2725 Sutton Blvd. #A, Maplewood,
314/645-5308, www.saratogalanes.com
HOURS: Mon.-Fri. 2 P.M.-1:30 A.M., Sat.-Sun.
5 P.M.-midnight
Map 4

Saratoga Lanes in Maplewood is one of the last second-floor bowling alleys in the country, and despite the humble appearance of its modest brick facade, it is the pulse of quite a scene. This is a favorite haunt of more than a few St. Louis country-rock legends (and plenty of aspiring ones). There are only eight lanes at Saratoga, and scoring is figured the old-fashioned way. Checkerboard floors and a wall of rec-center lockers make for a retro, kitschy utopia, or at least a worthy tribute

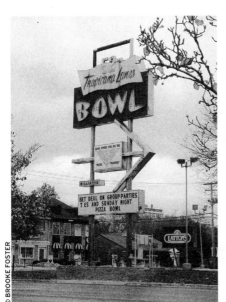

© BROOKE FOSTER

Go bowling at Tropicana Lanes.

to your Uncle Buck's basement bar. No less fabulous for it, the ambiance evolving here seems to be purely accidental.

TROPICANA LANES

7960 Clayton Rd., Richmond Heights, 314/781-0282, www.tropicanalanes.com
WINTER HOURS: Sun.-Tues. noon-midnight, Wed.-Thurs. 10 A.M.-midnight, Fri. 10 A.M.-1 A.M., Sat. noon-1 A.M.
SUMMER HOURS: Tues.-Thurs. and Sun. noon-midnight, Fri.-Sat. noon-1 A.M.
Map 6

This way-popular bowling behemoth is within throwing distance of downtown Clayton and is certainly deserving of its "bowling center" appellation. A good deal broader than any other local alley, Tropicana boasts an impressive 52 lanes, a banquet facility, a lounge, a game room—you name it—and is roughly the size of two *Air Force One* airplane

hangars. This is the perfect place to join a league, host a child's birthday party, or get in a couple of last-minute sets. The sheer size of this place means that there's almost always an open lane waiting, and electronic scoring makes single play a breeze.

SPECTATOR SPORTS
ST. LOUIS BLUES

Scottrade Center at 1401 Clark Ave., 314/421-4400, www.blues.nhl.com
COST: $18-235
Map 1

Located right off Interstate 64 near Union Station and City Hall, Scottrade Center plays host to rock concerts and the occasional basketball tournament, but the tall glass structure is best known as the home of the St. Louis Blues. The hockey squad remains the only St. Louis sports franchise that lacks a championship, but even without Lord Stanley's Cup, the Blues have turned out consistent teams in the past few seasons. The oval seating plan makes for ideal viewing from nearly any angle in the arena, and the cushy blue-and-purple seats make for the most comfortable viewing short of your at-home easy chair. Tickets are fairly easy to come by and can often be purchased on the cheap.

ST. LOUIS CARDINALS

Busch Stadium at 700 Clark St., 314/345-9000, http://stlouis.cardinals.mlb.com
COST: $16-140
Map 1

Fans of the St. Louis Cardinals fancy themselves the best fans in baseball, and their loyalty was rewarded in 2006 with a brand-new stadium. The grand structure stands adjacent to the site of the old Busch Stadium. During their first year in their new digs, the Cards

COURTESY OF THE ST. LOUIS RAMS

aerial view of the Edward Jones Dome, home of the St. Louis Rams

won the World Series, so you would be forgiven for thinking there's a little bit of magic in these red bricks. The sight lines are better at the new Busch (check out the center-field view of the Old Courthouse), and the kid-friendly concessions and accoutrements—including an on-site Build-A-Bear Workshop—make a Cards game an ideal family outing. Single tickets can be purchased in advance or at the box office on the day of the game.

ST. LOUIS RAMS
Edward Jones Dome at 701 Convention Plaza, 314/342-5201, www.stlouisrams.com
COST: $40-125
Map 1

The Rams came to St. Louis from Los Angeles in 1995, and the Edward Jones Dome has been the football team's home turf since then. Attached to the America's Center convention complex, the dome can hold almost 67,000 football fans, and all those seats were filled during the Rams' 2000 run to the Super Bowl.

As is the case with many indoor stadiums, the experience of watching a Rams game can be a little like watching a TV show taping—the bright lights and white roof give the impression of a soundstage, although the action on the gridiron is (ideally) much more engrossing.

GUIDED AND WALKING TOURS
ST. LOUIS WALKING TOURS
701 N. 15th St., 314/368-8818, www.triunecommunications.com/walk
HOURS: Walking tours available Mar.-Nov. Mon.-Sat. 9 A.M.-5 P.M., Sun. noon-5 P.M.
COST: $25 per couple, $60 up to 4 adults, $15 for each additional guest, $10 senior
Map 1

The narrated art and architecture tours of downtown St. Louis introduce travelers to the city's rich and dramatic history through its most important landmarks. Stops include the Wainwright Building (the oldest steel skyscraper on earth) and the world-famous th-

Gateway Arch, the tallest manmade monument in the United States. Every guide is well-versed and as much a storyteller as a docent. The history covered here begins with the territory's early days as the burial grounds of the country's largest tribal culture and then covers the first years as a cultured French Creole village. Bring a pair of comfortable shoes. Tours are 3–5 hours long, and travelers have their choice of three: one that leads sightseers through the western central corridor of the city (Union Station to the Wainwright Building via Market Street and Washington Avenue), one that winds its way along the eastern central corridor (Kiener Plaza to the Mississippi via Washington Avenue and Walnut Street), and a tour that combines both.

MERAMEC STATE PARK CAVE TOUR

115 Meramec Park Dr., 573/468-6072,
www.mostateparks.com/meramec.htm
HOURS: Apr.-May and Sept.-Oct. Thurs.-Mon. 1 and 3 P.M.; June-Aug. daily 9:30 and 11:30 A.M., 1 and 3 P.M.
COST: $6 adult, $5 teen, $4 child
Map 7

This 6,896-acre park offers year-round camping, picnicking, and hiking. Great amenities include inexpensive rental cabins, raft and canoe rentals, and a visitors center, but a trip here isn't complete without a tour of Fisher Cave. Lantern-lit paths lead visitors along an underground stream, past caverns horned with thousands of calcite columns (some of them more than 30 feet tall). This is just one of the park's 40-plus caverns, and it offers some of the most beautiful cave scenes in the country. Naturalist-led tours are available seasonally, between April and October, and travelers should check out the visitors center's cool aquarium display afterward.

OTHER RECREATION
HIDDEN VALLEY

17409 Hidden Valley Dr., 314/938-5373,
www.hiddenvalleyski.com
HOURS: Mon.-Thurs. 1-9:30 P.M., Fri. 1-10 P.M., Sat. 9 A.M.-10 P.M., Sun. 9 A.M.-8 P.M.
COST: $29-70. Price includes ski rental.
Map 7

The Midwest is hardly known for its alpine wonders, but those who hit Missouri with a strange desire to ski *do* have a few options. One of these is Hidden Valley, a pocket-sized ski spot with one lift and 12 runs of varying difficulty. Slopes open in mid-December and close in early March, weather depending, and snow here is predominantly artificial. A popular feature at Hidden Valley is its "Moonlight Marathons." Beginning on December 23, on Fridays and Saturdays, skiers can hit the slopes until 3 A.M.

STEINBERG SKATING RINK

400 Jefferson Dr. (in Forest Park), 314/361-0613,
www.steinbergskatingrink.com
HOURS: Sun.-Thurs. 10 A.M.-9 P.M., Fri.-Sat. 10 A.M.-midnight
COST: Adults $6.50, kids 12 and under $5.50, skate rental $2.50
Map 2

Anyone seeking a wintertime idyll should make skating at Steinberg a priority. For more than 50 years, St. Louis families have flocked to this outdoor rink, which is nestled into Forest Park and provides a picture-perfect winter tableau. On Friday and Saturday nights, the rink stays open till midnight, making it a favorite date destination. The nearby Steinberg Café offers sandwiches and pizzas, plus beer and wine. During the warmer months (March 1 through mid-November), Steinberg hosts sand-volleyball

ARTS AND LEISURE

leagues—but it's the ice-skating that brings people back again and again.

UPPER LIMITS ROCK CLIMBING GYM

326 S. 21st St., 314/241-7625,
www.upperlimits.com

HOURS: Mon.-Fri. noon-10 P.M., Sat. 10 A.M.-8 P.M., Sun. 10 A.M.-6 P.M.

COST: $15 adult day pass, $12 child day pass, $45 family day pass (equipment rental not included)

Map 1

Urbanites interested in honing their mountain-climbing skills—and novices looking for a way to try out the thrilling experience—don't have to travel far. Upper Limits' indoor climbing facilities offer artificial rock faces, equipment, and advice for climbers of all experience levels. The training gym boasts 1,000 square feet of climbing area, experienced instructors, and plenty of classes. Upper Limits is also a great resource for meeting other climbers and planning that next big out-of-state excursion. The gym is only five minutes from downtown, behind Union Station. Yearly memberships are available for repeat visitors.

SHOPS

No one is going to mistake the shopping promenades of St. Louis for those of New York or Los Angeles. That's perfectly fine, because what St. Louis lacks in breadth, it makes up for in quality, ingenuity, and affordability. The relatively low cost of living here makes nearly all price points lower, from the tab at the bar to the receipt from the mall. And the affordable rents allow young entrepreneurs to make a go of it, which is why you'll find many chic stores in up-and-coming districts (such as Maplewood and The Grove). Many St. Louisans are devoted to patronizing independent businesses, and this devotion has kept money in

the local economy and brought new life to many sleepy neighborhoods. The consortium Build St. Louis (www.buildstlouis.org) provides support for local merchants and posts great information about St. Louis businesses on its frequently updated website.

No matter what you're looking for, you're likely to find it in St. Louis. If it's boutique shopping you seek, head downtown to Washington Avenue for high-end pieces by still-under-the-radar designers (labels like Prada and Michael Kors can be found in the shops of Ladue and Clayton). Each neighborhood offers its own unique shopping opportunity. Browse for vintage clothing,

© BROOKE FOSTER

HIGHLIGHTS

LOOK FOR **[** TO FIND RECOMMENDED SHOPS.

[Best Gift Store: There are dozens of wonderful gift shops in St. Louis, with items ranging from the elegant to the quirky. But it's **Plowsharing Crafts'** mission that makes it doubly wonderful; the money spent here goes directly back to artisans in developing nations (page 129).

[Best Independent Bookstore: Left Bank Books is a St. Louis landmark, and with good reason. Not only does this lovely shop carry the best in literary fiction and creative nonfiction, it also has an excellent used-book selection, hard-to-find periodicals, and a schedule of author readings that rivals those in far bigger cities. Say hello to the resident cat, who likes to nap in front of Social Sciences (page 131).

[Best Music Store: Vintage Vinyl is staffed by music lovers; these guys and gals know music up and down, and they can make some great recommendations. Be diligent when searching the CD racks, as local music journalists and DJs frequently offload parts of their collections here (page 132).

[Best Women's Boutique: Ziezo is paradise for the woman with great fashion sense and a little cash to burn. This Loop boutique keeps pace with the latest fashions without ever drifting into trendy impracticality (page 135).

[Best Furniture and Home Decor: Good Works is in the Delmar Loop, on the very same street where Charles Eames has a star on the St. Louis Walk of Fame. That's some nice synergy, as Good Works sells modern, often minimalist furniture undoubtedly inspired by Eames (but at a fraction of the price) (page 137).

[Best Shop for the Home Chef: Kitchen Conservatory provides everything a great home chef could ever desire, from All-Clad pots to Emile Henry ceramic Dutch ovens (page 141).

[Best Kids' Store: If you're tired of Barney, Elmo, and all of their singsongy comrades, head to **City Sprouts.** This adorable Loop shop sells beautiful wooden toys, classic illustrated books, and too-cute-for-words baby duds (page 142).

[Best Place to Pamper Your Pet: Want a tiny plush Porsche for your kitten to nap in? Need a wee Cardinals jersey for your bichon frise? Head to **Lola and Penelope's.** If your pet is traveling with you, make sure to treat her to a pawdicure (page 143).

[Best Aromatherapy: Cassie Buell's Central West End shop, the eponymous **Cassie's Fragrance Boutique and Scent Bar,** is an olfactory treat. Customize your own perfume or body wash with the dozens of scents available at Cassie's, or treat yourself to an Earthly Body's Suntouched soy candle – it burns down into warm massage oil (page 147).

rare recordings, and striking home accents in the Delmar Loop. Find antique radios, Chippendale desks, and 1920s jewelry on Cherokee Street. Discover shelves of used books and fabulous 1950s toasters on Grand South Grand. Wherever your St. Louis travels take you, fun shopping is bound to be right in the neighborhood.

Arts and Crafts

CRAFT ALLIANCE
6640 Delmar Blvd., University City, 314/725-1177, www.craftalliance.org
HOURS: Tues.-Thurs. 10 A.M.-5 P.M., Fri.-Sat. 10 A.M.-6 P.M., Sun. 11 A.M.-5 P.M.
`Map 6`

Visit Craft Alliance one day, and you'll see a beautiful display of handmade clothing. Stop in the next day, and one-of-a-kind home accessories will sparkle in the window. The inventory may change regularly, but one thing is certain: Craft Alliance is no mere gift shop. It is also a thriving community art center where people of all ages learn glass-blowing, ceramics, textile-making, and more. On the second floor of this well-established Loop space, working artists bustle about in their studios. Craft Alliance now operates a huge second store in Grand Center, Midtown's rapidly emerging arts district. No matter which location you choose, your purchase will benefit Craft Alliance's superlative outreach programs.

◖ PLOWSHARING CRAFTS
6271 Delmar Blvd., University City, 314/863-3723, www.plowsharing.org
HOURS: Mon.-Fri. 10 A.M.-6 P.M., Sat. 10 A.M.-5:30 P.M.
`Map 6`

This volunteer-staffed shop has little in common with the big-box decor stores. Plowsharing doesn't rock the world-music XM station or have storewide sales on throw pillows. Instead, this Loop gem offers unique gifts that enrich lives. Plowsharing partners with Ten Thousand Villages, the largest fair-trade organization in the U.S., and money spent here goes right back to artisans in developing nations. In other words, if you spend $30 on a gorgeous hand-carved bracelet from Uganda, your money supports the Ugandan artist who created it. In addition to jewelry, Plowsharing sells home decor, musical instruments, artisanal coffees, and more.

Books and Music

BIG SLEEP BOOKS

239 N. Euclid Ave., 314/361-6100,
www.bigsleepbooks.com
HOURS: Mon.-Sat. 11 A.M.-6 P.M., Sun.
11 A.M.-5 P.M.

Map 2

Mystery readers are a dedicated and dis-criminating bunch—and they'll be thrilled by what they find at Big Sleep Books. This cozy Central West End shop specializes in new and used mystery, detective, and espio-nage tomes (and bibliophiles will love the inventory of rare first editions). Staff mem-bers might seem aloof at first, but they're truly happy to direct aimless shelf-wanderers toward personal favorites. Big Sleep also hosts regular book signings with the genre's up-and-comers.

THE BOOK HOUSE

9719 Manchester Rd., Rock Hill, 314/968-4491,
www.bookhousestl.com
HOURS: Tues.-Sat. 10:30 A.M.-7 P.M.

Map 7

Within the walls of a quaint, two-story Victorian home built in 1865, this indepen-dent shop offers new and used inventory and even rare books. Maybe you'll come across a hard-to-find cookbook in one of the Book House's nine rooms, or perhaps you'll rediscover an old favorite in the bargain basement. Rumor has it that in addition to the two cats that make their home in the Book House, a ghost watches over the tomes by night—and possibly during the day as well! The spooky specter must not scare away too many customers, though, because the shop has been in business for more than 20 years.

DUNAWAY BOOKS

3111 S. Grand Blvd., 314/771-7150,
www.dunawaybooks.com
HOURS: Mon.-Fri. noon-8 P.M., Sat.-Sun.
10 A.M.-8 P.M.

Map 4

Founded by a professional stamp-and-coin auctioneer who always dreamed of owning a bookstore, Dunaway Books is a true treasure. Walt Dunaway used his keen collector's eye to fill the cavernous space with books both beloved and unusual, popular and obscure. Browsers will find books from every genre, although the great-est finds are usually in the literary-criticism and nonfiction sections. Be sure to descend to the store's basement level, which boasts hundreds of nifty old textbooks. Dunaway is always looking to buy, so terrific new books show up daily.

EUCLID RECORDS

601 E. Lockwood Ave., Webster Groves,
314/961-8978, www.euclidrecords.com
HOURS: Mon.-Thurs. 10 A.M.-8 P.M., Fri.-Sat.
10 A.M.-9 P.M., Sun. 10 A.M.-5 P.M.

Map 7

Revered by audiophiles all over the nation, Eu-clid Records offers a trip through the annals of recorded music. The spacious shop's respect-able selection of new and used CDs is eclipsed by its enormous collection of records (there are more than 40,000 titles here). Visitors can also browse shelves of vintage magazines, posters, and other interesting bits of musical ephem-era. Jazz is owner Joe Schwab's greatest area of expertise, but shoppers will find a healthy portion of just about everything. Serious col-lectors may wish to inquire in advance about the un-priced basement stash, which can be browsed by appointment only.

◖ LEFT BANK BOOKS

399 N. Euclid Ave., 314/367-6731,
www.left-bank.com
HOURS: Mon.-Sat. 10 A.M.-10 P.M., Sun.
11 A.M.-6 P.M.
Map 2

Left Bank Books, the city's oldest independent bookstore, sits at the bustling corner of McPherson and Euclid Avenues. The shop was established in 1969, when its progressive social politics and inventory of gay literature were considered risky business. Today, Left Bank serves St. Louis's literati with a thoughtful selection of...pretty much everything. The store carries an estimated 16,000 volumes. New books are upstairs, used books (and a friendly cat) are downstairs, and spirited conversation thrives throughout. Left Bank is a community focal point, thanks to the small but dedicated staff that manages the store's busy calendar of book signings and

© AMY FERGUSON

Well-known authors often visit Left Bank Books — you should, too.

readings. When well-respected authors come through St. Louis, Left Bank treats them like honored guests and long-lost friends.

RECORD EXCHANGE

5320 Hampton Ave., 314/832-2249,
www.recordexchangestl.com
HOURS: Mon.-Thurs. 10 A.M.-8 P.M., Fri.-Sat.
10 A.M.-9 P.M., Sun. 10 A.M.-5 P.M.
Map 4

Devoted, diligent St. Louis music collectors know this shop's cluttered aisles well. On the right day, Record Exchange can be an absolute gold mine, and while the inventory may be less organized and selective than that of local competitor Euclid Records, the great prices reward shoppers who are willing to search. Exploring Record Exchange's room of 45s is a daylong project in itself. Expect to get dusty—but also expect to feel right at home amid the towering stacks of what was once the South Hampton branch of the public library.

SUBTERRANEAN BOOKS

6275 Delmar Blvd., University City,
314/862-2362, www.subbooks.com
HOURS: Mon.-Thurs. 11 A.M.-8 P.M., Fri.-Sat.
11 A.M.-10 P.M., Sun. noon-6 P.M.
Map 6

Many factors go into making a great bookstore: It has to be inviting without seeming too overbearing, be stimulating enough to rouse both your curiosity and your sense of treasure-hunting, and (most important) be exciting enough to inspire you to want to devour every book in sight. With these criteria in mind, the Delmar Loop's Subterranean Books is a great bookstore. What's more, the staff is knowledgeable, helpful, and happy to let you simply browse the stacks. While the store may not bowl you over with its size, Subterranean takes care to stock both popular favorites and obscure gems. The store's loft space often hosts artwork by local artists, ensuring that both the visual arts and the written word continue to earn their proper respect.

⟨ VINTAGE VINYL

6610 Delmar Blvd., University City,
314/721-4096, www.vintagevinyl.com
HOURS: Sun.-Thurs. 10 A.M.-10 P.M., Fri.-Sat.
10 A.M.-midnight
Map 6

Whether you're seeking a just-released album or something more classic, this Delmar landmark is likely to have it. Want an obscure spoken-word album? A compilation of Swedish pop songs? The newest single from an up-and-coming St. Louis rapper? You're in luck at Vintage Vinyl, where it's easy to spend at least an hour wandering through the meticulously organized inventory. Many of Vintage Vinyl's employees have worked in the shop for years and are tireless boosters of the St. Louis music scene. Don't be afraid to ask questions; the clerks here are incredibly well-informed. Just don't be surprised if they grimace when ringing up your Sting album.

Clothing and Accessories

© SARAH KING

At Blush, you'll find chic women's fashions in a delightfully low-key environment.

BLUSH BOUTIQUE

151 W. Jefferson Ave., Kirkwood, 314/965-4411,
www.shopblushboutique.com
HOURS: Mon.-Fri. 10 A.M.-6 P.M., Sat.
10 A.M.-5 P.M., Sun. noon-5 P.M.
Map 7

Sarah King, owner of this inviting Kirkwood boutique, considers herself a disciple of fashion. At Blush, she spreads the good word about affordable, high-quality, leading-edge women's couture. King's preference for up-and-coming designers means you won't be stuck browsing through same-ol'-same-ol' labels, and her collection of accessories (Virgins Saints and Angels jewelry, Melie Bianco handbags, even Voluspa candles) is one of the best in town. Perhaps best of all, you'll never feel rushed or pressured at Blush. King offers outstanding personalized service in addition to other perks like free gift wrap and after-hours appointments.

FIFI'S

6172 Delmar Blvd., 314/773-2234, www.fifs.biz
HOURS: Mon. noon-6 P.M., Tues.-Sat.
11 A.M.-7 P.M.
`Map 6`

FiFi's is directly across from The Pageant, St. Louis's 2,000-seat rock venue. The placement is appropriate, if not intentional. Proprietor Kelly was personally invited to the neighborhood by well-known Delmar Loop developer Joe Edwards, and FiFi's rockabilly-punk apparel and accessoriesare popular with many of the neighborhood's concertgoers. Displays change often and frequently feature local designers. Kelly buys in small quantities to keep her inventory as fresh and hip as the street scene in front of her shop.

MARTE SHOES

1326 Washington Ave., 314/231-2432
HOURS: Mon.-Fri. 9:30 A.M.-5 P.M., Sat.
9 A.M.-2:30 P.M., Sun. 11 A.M.-3 P.M.
`Map 1`

The Alper family knows a thing or two about shoes, as they've helped St. Louisans strut in style since the 1930s. At Marte Shoes, their downtown depot, the knowledgeable staff will personally fit your shoes and special order them if you can't find what you want (though, with 30,000 name-brand shoes in the place, not finding something is a challenge). From a vast array of athletic footwear to downtown-appropriate dress shoes—carried in sizes far beyond the usual range—Marte even puts online shoe shops to shame. One thing is for certain: When you walk out the door, you're walking in shoes that fit.

MEZZANINE

389 N. Euclid Ave., 314/361-3777,
www.shopmezzanine.com
HOURS: Tues.-Sat. 11 A.M.-7 P.M., Sun.
11 A.M.-4 P.M.
`Map 2`

St. Louis ladies are lucky to be able to regularly experience retail therapy at a shop like Mezzanine—if only everyone could! This Central West End mainstay helps anchor a particularly shopper-friendly intersection of the neighborhood, and its airy interior serves up a breath of fresh air and sets the scene for a relaxing shopping experience. With gorgeous clothes from designers such as Rachel Pally and Nanette Lepore—and jewelry selections that are just as stunning—Mezzanine will have you playing dress-up and loving every minute. While the prices at this upscale boutique might be a little on the splurge side from time to time, the sales are amazing and always worth the trip.

MISTER GUY CLOTHIERS

9831 Clayton Rd., Ladue, 314/991-5262
HOURS: Mon., Tues., Wed., and Fri. 10 A.M.-6 P.M.,
Thurs. 10 A.M.-7 P.M., Sat. 10 A.M.-5:30 P.M.
`Map 7`

Mister Guy Clothiers is just the sort of place you can imagine James Bond shopping—the new Daniel Craig–style Bond, that is. Of course, having been in business for more than 30 years, Mister Guy might have clothed Roger Moore, too. Like 007, this Ladue men's shop is not afraid to be both ruggedly manly and perfectly turned out. Case in point: They have cold beer and ESPN in the back, but Vineyard Vines and Robert Talbott in the front (Mister Guy is the exclusive local carrier of the Robert Talbott Estate collection). This high-end shop carries everything from designer jeans to bespoke suits. A full-service boutique, Mister Guy provides free alterations—so while you may not exactly be Bond, you can look like you shop on Bond Street.

MORIS FASHIONS

34 Maryland Plaza, 314/361-6800,
www.morisfashions.com
HOURS: Mon.-Sat. 11 A.M.-7 P.M., Sun. noon-6 P.M.
Map 2

St. Louis isn't home to many dedicated men's shops, but what the city lacks in quantity, it makes up for in quality. And Moris Fashions definitely delivers quality goods. The shirts and jackets are fresh takes on the classics, the jeans and hoodies are cool and stylish, and the accessories, including watches and wallets, are perfect for today's modern man. Located in one of the most upscale St. Louis neighborhoods, Moris Fashions can hook you up with something to wear for nearly every occasion. Expect to find items from Modern Amusement, Ted Baker, and more, and note that the owners are the kinds of nice guys who often write thank-you notes to their customers.

PAPER DOLLS

1021 Washington Ave., 314/621-9696,
www.paperdolls-stl.com
HOURS: Mon. 11 A.M.-5 P.M., Tues.-Thurs. 11 A.M.-7 P.M., Fri.-Sat. 11 A.M.-9 P.M., Sun. noon-5 P.M.
Map 1

This midpriced boutique in the fashionable Washington Loft district carries creative, stylish apparel and great designer jeans. Featured items include the handmade garments of artist Macu and the jeans "Eva Longoria swears by." Sales associates are great at finding your correct inseam amid the heaps of denim, and they are also happy to share stories about Paper Dolls' latest featured designers. The philosophy here is that good fashion should be treated as art, and that fashionistas should stay well-informed.

PITAYA

6632 Delmar Blvd., University City,
314/725-2233, www.pitayaonline.com
HOURS: Mon.-Thurs. 11 A.M.-9 P.M., Fri.-Sat. 11 A.M.-10 P.M., Sun. noon-9 P.M.
Map 6

The cool window displays all along the Delmar Loop make this neighborhood prime territory for impulse purchases. You may not *think* you need new clothes, but you're likely to walk away with a bagful. Pitaya is a place full of fun, flirty clothes that look great on many different figures. It's also a place where, when you do find that cute wrap-dress you didn't know you needed, you can afford to buy it anyway. (Dresses and trousers rarely go above $50, and blouses are even cheaper.) And if you happen to be shopping for, say, a purple top to go with the bracelet you just bought, Pitaya has a clever system made for you: The racks are organized by color. Pitaya makes shopping easy—almost *too* easy.

R·SOLE

6662 Delmar Blvd., University City,
314/721-7653
Map 6

R·Sole has soles—plenty of them: Nike, Vans, Adidas, Artful Dodger, and more. But for a shoe store, the place also has soul. When this retail space debuted in 2006, Delmar Loop shoppers could be forgiven for thinking it was another nightclub, rather than a shoe store. Designed by architects Tobin+Parnes, R·Sole seems to be half-dance club and half-art gallery, displaying high-end, hip-hop–inspired footwear in cut-in niches and on glass ledges lit by color-changing LED. The checkout counter even doubles as a DJ booth, and sometimes music is heard pulsing into the night. These may be sports-styled shoes, but R·Sole's artfully displayed kicks are more for the nightclub than the athletic club.

TANTRUM
6635 Delmar Blvd., University City, 314/783-0527, www.tantrumstl.com
HOURS: Mon.-Thurs. 11:30 A.M.-7 P.M., Fri.-Sat. 11:30 A.M.-8 P.M., Sun. 1-6 P.M.
Map 6

Tantrum holds its own among several great boutiques located on the bustling Delmar Boulevard. One of the best things about this trendy women's store is its versatility. If you're looking for a cute dress to wear on a date, you can find it here. If you'd like a chic top for work, Tantrum's your spot. And even if you're not quite sure what you're looking for, but you know you just want something new, you'll be able to pick out an item or three at Tantrum. What's even better is that you'll be able to afford your selections, too!

TESTIMO BOUTIQUE
9216 Clayton Rd., Ladue, 314/432-5775
Map 7

Ladue's Testimo Boutique has a certain bohemian flair, although not quite in the stereotypical New York boho sense. Rather, at Testimo, the bohemian vibe is reflected in great fashion eclecticism. Buyers here collect a little bit of everything and concentrate more on personal style than on particular brands. Shoppers looking for unique pieces will appreciate the wide variety, from a nice selection of Bulga handbags to Ratna's Western-style shirts and an in-house jewelry brand called Bohemian Rhapsody. In addition to its excellent selection, Testimo offers personal style-consultation services and employs a cadre of friendly shopping assistants.

THE TIME
922 Washington Ave., 314/241-7171, www.thetimeboutique.net
HOURS: Mon.-Wed. 11 A.M.-7 P.M., Thurs.-Fri. 11 A.M.-8 P.M., Sun. 11 A.M.-4 P.M.
Map 1

A great boutique is a reflection of its proprietor. Jennifer Gray, owner of The Time, is a fashionable, risk-taking sort of gal—and she's also refreshingly practical. Gray carries exclusive lines from emerging designers and has a knack for finding clothes that flatter a variety of non-model physiques. Her sales staff is arguably the friendliest in town, and The Time recently relocated to the best storefront on the block. In addition to the racks of chic pieces, this Washington Avenue boutique also houses a full-service salon.

☾ ZIEZO
6394 Delmar Blvd., University City, 314/752-9602
HOURS: Mon.-Thurs. 11 A.M.-8 P.M., Sat. 11 A.M.-9 P.M., Sun. noon-6 P.M.
Map 6

On-the-spot decision-making can be difficult when shopping for clothing, particularly when said clothing is of the high-ticket variety (e.g., "Should I buy the $80 T-shirt to complement the $200 jeans?"). But Ziezo demands and rewards quick thinking.

The shop's owner, Carol Crudden, buys just four to six pieces of each item on her rack, and the inventory moves quickly. For the fashionista who dreads showing up at a party wearing the same dress as someone else, this definitely has its advantages. This Loop boutique carries such popular lines as Miss Sixty and Squasht by Les, and Ziezo offers more Betsey Johnson designs than any other shop in St. Louis.

Gift and Home

BOTANICALS DESIGN STUDIO
3014 S. Grand Blvd., 314/772-7674,
www.botp.com
HOURS: Mon.-Fri. 9:30 A.M.-5:30 P.M., Sat.
10 A.M.-4 P.M.
Map 4

This great South City flower and gift shop is a fun place to browse. Visitors can wander amid two floors of beautiful floral and gift displays. Botanical Design Studio's merchandise is as inventive and sophisticated as its plant arrangements, and the staff here is über-friendly. Those looking for the perfect gift will likely find something here, and the awesome gift-wrapping service is always free. In addition, Botanicals' sought-after tropical plant arrangements can be sent anywhere in the country, and their access to a wide variety of suppliers allows them to meet almost any request.

CATHOLIC SUPPLY
6759 Chippewa St., 314/644-0643,
www.catholicsupply.com
HOURS: Mon.-Fri. 9 A.M.-5:30 P.M., Sat.
9 A.M.-5 P.M.
Map 4

You don't have to be Catholic to appreciate the vast inventory of Catholic Supply. Even more important, the employees here make all shoppers feel welcome, and the store's fascinating stash of theology books is downright ecumenical.

In St. Louis, Catholic Supply is *the* go-to place for school uniforms, christening gowns, and First Communion gifts. There are also a lot of unexpected delights here, like gorgeous prayer candles, Modernist nativity scenes, and kitschy figurines that put Jesus at the center of basketball games, ski outings, and football matches. A mural on the side of the building commemorates John Paul II's 1999 visit to St. Louis. The city's Catholic heritage is strong, and this southside emporium is a must-see for anyone interested in Catholicism.

CENTRO MODERN FURNISHINGS
4727 McPherson Ave., 314/454-0111,
www.centro-inc.com
HOURS: Mon.-Wed. 10 A.M.-6 P.M., Thurs.
10 A.M.-8 P.M., Fri.-Sat. 10 A.M.-6 P.M.
Map 2

Unless you have incredibly deep pockets, you may find yourself doing more browsing than buying at this exclusive modern-furniture gallery. The iconic furnishings on display in Centro's bright, 7,500-square-foot gallery space usually don't sport price tags—so bear in mind the old aphorism: If you have to ask, you probably can't afford it. Still, a visit to Centro is wonderfully worthwhile. Weekly additions to the museum-quality showroom keep visitors abreast of the latest news in the international design and architecture community.

And, despite the super-pricy wares, you won't encounter snobbery here; the very knowledgeable staff is more than happy to answer questions, and the shop's great newsletter is a design resource in itself.

CHEAP TRX

3211 S. Grand Blvd., 314/664-4011, www.cheaptrx.com
HOURS: Mon.-Sat. 10 A.M.-8 P.M., Sun. 11 A.M.-6 P.M.

Map 4

Those interested in a tattoo or piercing to commemorate their St. Louis trip need go no further than Cheap TRX. This friendly Grand South Grand boutique has dedicated its three stories to all those important lifestyle accessories one won't find at Target. In addition to operating the city's oldest and most trusted piercing studio, Cheap TRX now runs a clean and professional tattoo shop. The main floor is dedicated to jewelry, alternative clothing, and unique home accessories, while the 18-and-older basement level is a good deal naughtier. Shoppers are invited to use their imaginations, and the store's friendly, openminded staff is happy to answer any questions about the products on the shelves.

GOOD WORKS

6323 Delmar Blvd., University City, 314/726-2233, www.goodworksfurniture4u.com
HOURS: Mon.-Thurs. 11 A.M.-8 P.M., Fri. 11 A.M.-6 P.M., Sat. 10 A.M.-6 P.M., Sun. 1-5 P.M.

Map 6

Good Works' selection of nicely made, reasonably priced furnishings makes it a popular place for hobbyists and professional designers alike. Every piece—from playfully mod bookshelves to solid-wood coffee tables—reflects topnotch craftsmanship.

The majority of pieces on the showroom floor can be custom-ordered in a variety of fabrics and finishes (although visitors should know that delivery is mostly local and can take up to eight weeks). Good Works also sells great gift items, including elegant vases and trendy barware. The staff is exceptionally helpful.

GRINGO JONES IMPORTS

4470 Shaw Blvd., 314/664-1666
HOURS: Daily 10 A.M.-6 P.M.

Map 4

Mention Gringo Jones to longtime St. Louisans, and they're likely to break into the store's delightfully cheesy jingle ("Gringo Jooooones and me," sung to the tune of Counting Crows' "Mr. Jones"). They're also likely to recommend that you head to Gringo Jones ASAP, because just browsing here is highly entertaining. The inventory reflects a guiding aesthetic principal that can best be described as "whatever-chic," as this import store stocks everything from gorgeous teak benches to surreal lawn ornaments. Gringo Jones's proximity to the Missouri Botanical Garden creates some cool synergy—including a variety of Mexican glass bowls inspired by the work of garden mainstay Dale Chihuly.

GROVE HOME FURNISHINGS

3169 Morganford Rd., 314/776-7898, www.grovefurnishings.com
HOURS: Wed.-Fri. 11 A.M.-7 P.M., Sat.-Sun. 10 A.M.-5 P.M.

Map 4

Much of the Grove Home Furnishings' well-priced collection has been crafted locally, and buyers here have a fondness for the warm, eclectic blend of old and new. Pieces made from salvaged materials are

Many of the pieces at Grove Home Furnishings are made by local artisans.

here are customizable—there's a wide range of fabrics and finishes—making the design possibilities seemingly endless. The shop's roving consultants are happy to give personalized, expert design advice, and a more thorough design consultation is offered for a minimal fee. Considering the quality and creativity found at Intaglia, prices are surprisingly affordable. This locally owned store (which has blossomed into a small national chain) offers financing options for purchases both large and small.

THE LOUISIANA PURCHASE

5700 Lindell Blvd. (inside the Missouri History Museum), 314/454-3172, www.mohistory.org
HOURS: Tues. 10 A.M.-8 P.M., Wed.-Mon. 10 A.M.-5 P.M.
Map 6

Named after the greatest real-estate deal in history, the Louisiana Purchase gift shop (inside the Missouri History Museum) offers some of the greatest deals on St. Louis history books that you can find, along with a selection that rivals any bookstore in town. Alongside genealogical research guides, the shop sells St. Louis–themed mugs and tank tops that proclaim, "Well-behaved women seldom make history." This gift store stocks every piece of St. Louis ephemera imaginable. You'll find sculptures, pillows, aprons, and paperweights related to museum exhibits on the Lewis and Clark expedition, Charles Lindbergh, Thomas Jefferson, local aviation, and local brewing. Some of the Louisiana Purchase's most interesting finds are reprints of vintage posters from 19th-century beer advertisements and the 1904 World's Fair.

always in rotation, which makes sense given the neighborhood's ongoing gentrification. A recent visit to this friendly little shop yielded a beautiful Shaker-style headboard inlaid with tiles from a salvaged tin ceiling, shelves made from worn oak window moldings and a couple of antique rockers. The Grove Home Furnishings also carries a large selection of inexpensive gifts, plus great modern shelving units built to spec by a local artisan.

INTAGLIA

1201 Strassner Dr., Brentwood, 314/645-8008, www.intagliahome.com
HOURS: Mon.-Fri. 11 A.M.-7 P.M., Sat. 11 A.M.-6 P.M., Sun. noon-6 P.M.
Map 6

Intaglia's contemporary home furnishings suit an urban landscape well. Most items

O'MALLEY'S IRISH GIFT SHOP
2718 Sutton Blvd., 314/645-8779
HOURS: Mon.-Sat. 10 A.M.-7 P.M., Sun.
noon-6 P.M.
`Map 4`

Should you be struck by the urge to buy a kilt (with matching embroidered hose), O'Malley's is there to meet your needs. A neighborhood fixture in downtown Maplewood, this shop offers plenty of gifts and apparel from the Old Country. Shoppers are likely to encounter the amiable Mr. O'Malley himself; he's always happy to meet new people and show off his latest acquisitions. Many of the unique gifts reflect Mr. O'Malley's offbeat sense of humor—look among the piles of Irish flags and license-plate covers, and you just might find a skull-shaped paperweight engraved with Celtic designs, or a pocketknife emblazoned with a buxom Viking woman in her skivvies.

PHOENIX RISING
6331 Delmar Blvd., University City, 314/862-0609
HOURS: Mon.-Thurs. 11 A.M.-7 P.M., Fri.-Sat.
11 A.M.-8 P.M., Sun. noon-5 P.M.
`Map 6`

When locals need gifts that are sure to delight even the choosiest recipient, they head to Phoenix Rising. This Delmar Loop mainstay sells everything from high-end, artisan-crafted necklaces to cheeky favorites like Dirty Girl soap. There aren't many places in town where you can find beautifully ornate Day of the Dead dioramas, funky journals, *and* books of Bible stories told entirely in Legos. Pack up all of your loot in Envirosax—Phoenix Rising was one of the first St. Louis shops to sell these reusable shopping bags, which fold down small enough to fit in a purse or glove compartment.

URBAN MATERIALS + ACCESSORIES (UMA)
1100 Locust St., 314/241-9990,
www.iloveuma.com
HOURS: Tues.-Sat. 11 A.M.-5 P.M., Sun.
11 A.M.-3 P.M.
`Map 1`

In downtown's growing loft district, UMA is a sort of Modernist dreamland: You'll find beautiful, contemporary design in the shop's furniture (the Oh chair, Chimo wall fireplaces), barware, and eye-catching light fixtures. Sort of like Design Within Reach—but with prices that are *actually within reach* for the ordinary loft-dweller or the suburbanite with cutting-edge taste—UMA is a trendy delight, and the vibe is never cooler-than-thou. This is a great place to make that loft of yours loftier—or to buy the perfect housewarming gift for your friend who's so hip he could use UMA's black toilet paper.

YUCANDU
20 Allen Ave., Webster Groves, 314/963-4400,
www.yucandu.com
HOURS: Mon.-Thurs. 10 A.M.-6 P.M., Fri.-Sat.
10 A.M.-9 P.M.
`Map 7`

This innovative, drop-in craft store in downtown Webster Groves welcomes visitors of all ages with a menu of great projects and two spacious open studios stocked to the hilt with supplies. For only a minimal studio fee (about $3 an hour) and the cost of materials, you can mosaic, scrapbook, and papier-mâché your way to stress-free self-satisfaction. Instructional workshops are available (also on a drop-in basis) for those wary about just digging into a pile of art supplies, and adults are invited to bring a bottle of wine and snacks.

Gourmet Goodies

BERTARELLI CUTLERY INC.
1927 Marconi Ave., 314/664-4005,
www.bertarellicutlery.com
HOURS: Mon.-Fri. 7 A.M.-4:30 P.M., Sat.
11 A.M.-3 P.M.
`Map 5`

The largest cutlery company in St. Louis, Bertarelli provides dozens of area restaurants with expertly sharpened knives. Many at-home cooks love Bertarelli for the inexpensive, high-quality sharpening services available in its quaint store on the Hill. Here, you'll also find an excellent selection of commercial-grade kitchen accessories: Stockpots, aluminum sauté pans, shatter-resistant ceramic serving bowls and antibacterial cutting boards make this friendly place a great stop for the hobbyist chef. Bertarelli is also an authorized dealer of Wüsthof knives and carries a multitude of blade sizes at some of the lowest prices in the city.

EXTRA VIRGIN, AN OLIVE OVATION
143 Carondelet Plaza, Clayton, 314/727-6464,
www.extravirginoo.com
HOURS: Mon.-Sat. 10 A.M.-6 P.M.
`Map 6`

At Extra Virgin, an Olive Ovation, the olive reigns supreme. Visitors can sample from the shop's international selection of more than 40 olive oils at a special tasting bar, and the shelves are brimming with jars of cured olives, tapenades, olive-oil-themed cookbooks—basically, if you're looking for anything olive-related, you're likely to find it here. Olive Ovation is the pet project of a retired clinical pathologist, who is well aware of the humble fruit's outstanding health benefits. She also brings the dedicated precision of lab work to her newfound passion—meaning that, in addition to a host of great gourmet products, Olive Ovation offers a wealth of knowledge.

JOHN VIVIANO & SONS GROCER
5139 Shaw Ave., 314/771-4645,
www.shopviviano.com
HOURS: Mon.-Sat. 8 A.M.-5 P.M.
`Map 5`

Visitors to this historic Italian neighborhood will find a number of old-world Italian grocers, all within a four-block radius of the Hill's nucleus at Shaw and Marconi. If you only have time to visit one, make sure it's John Viviano & Sons. Established in 1949, this beloved neighborhood shop offers imported cheeses and spices alongside terrific homemade sauces, pastas, and olive salads. Nostalgic locals associate Viviano's with the earthy-sweet smell of bulk spices filling the air. Just look for a green awning and follow your nose.

© BROOKE FOSTER

Unleash your inner Food Network star at the Kitchen Conservatory.

KITCHEN CONSERVATORY

8021 Clayton Rd., Clayton, 314/862-2665,
www.kitchenconservatory.com
HOURS: Mon.-Sat. 9:30 A.M.-5 P.M., Sun.
noon-4 P.M.
`Map 6`

Where can you find a gnocchi board, a spaet-zle maker, a tart tamper, a left-handed chef's knife? Where can you find a tagine, a chinois, and the spices to use with them? Where can you find the cookbooks to inspire your gour-met urges? And where, oh where, can you find a "knork"—that's right, the spork's cousin, the knife-fork hybrid—where, that is, but Kitchen Conservatory? Beloved for its daily cooking classes and culinary expertise, this wonderful shop is the sort of place dreamy gourmands should enter at their own risk (lest they leave a few hundred dollars lighter). From old-school canning supplies to Le Creuset cookware, not only do the folks at Kitchen Conservatory carry it, but they can teach you how to use it.

THE WINE & CHEESE PLACE

Four locations, including 7435 Forsyth Blvd.,
Clayton, 314/727-8788,
www.wineandcheeseplace.com
HOURS: Mon.-Sat. 9 A.M.-7 P.M.
`Map 6`

From a splurge-worthy bottle perfect for gracious hosts to an affordable, easy-drinking varietal just right for a picnic, the Wine & Cheese Place has exactly what you seek. Rows and rows of bottles from around the world fill this wine shop, and it all might be too overwhelming to navigate if the staff members weren't so friendly and knowledgeable. And as the store's name indicates, the wine is just the half of it! With cheeses ranging from the familiar to the peculiar, you'll be sure to purchase one that suits your palate and your wine selection—especially since sampling is encouraged here. Plus, the shop offers other snacks and beer as well, making it a most delicious one-stop shop.

Kids' Stores

THE BUILD-A-BEAR WORKSHOP

1440 Saint Louis Galleria, Richmond Heights, 314/725-8282, www.buildabear.com
HOURS: Mon.-Sat. 10 A.M.-9:30 P.M., Sun. 11 A.M.-6 P.M.
Map 6

The Build-A-Bear Workshop in the Saint Louis Galleria appears to be just one of many—but it isn't. There are 370 near-identical Build-A-Bear retailers scattered across the country and the world (Japan, Korea, Denmark, Singapore, Germany, Russia, Thailand, Ireland . . .), but this one is the very first. St. Louisan Maxine Clark founded her customizable-teddy-bear company here in 1997, after resigning from her position as CEO of Payless Shoes. Today, Clark is known around the world as one of the retail industry's great innovators—and as a leading female visionary in a sector often dominated by men.

◖ CITY SPROUTS

6354 Delmar Blvd., University City, 314/726-9611, www.citysprouts.com
HOURS: Mon.-Thurs. 10 A.M.-6 P.M., Fri.-Sat. 10 A.M.-8 P.M., Sun. noon-5 P.M.
Map 6

Opened by the women who own the Phoenix Rising gift shop, City Sprouts takes that shop's joyful, chic aesthetic and applies it to the toddler set. Find precious clothes with hand-stitched details, or amuse yourself (and your friends) with onesies that say things like "I ate my dreidel" or "Someday, I'll egg a house." City Sprouts also sells beautiful children's books, educational toys, multilingual games, nursery decor, and "survival kits" for new parents. The complimentary gift-wrapping service is chic and efficient.

KANGAROO KIDS

10090 Manchester Rd., 314/835-9200, www.kangarookidsonline.com
HOURS: Mon.-Sat. 10 A.M.-7 P.M., Sun. noon-4 P.M.
Map 7

Local parents-on-a-budget absolutely love Kangaroo Kids. The cost of child-rearing adds up quickly, and this Kirkwood shop's selection of gently used, name-brand maternity and children's clothing, toys, books, and equipment is second to none. Parents who bring in items to sell are rewarded either with cash or with store credit. Seasonal items in good condition are purchased at 30–50 percent of their resale value, plus an additional 20 percent in store credit. Kangaroo Kids also sells some new items, including strollers, breast pumps, and the incredibly popular "Slingaroo." These baby slings are handmade locally, and Kangaroo Kids carries them in every color imaginable.

Pet Supplies

GROOMINGDALE'S

3425 Watson Rd., 314/781-6711,
www.groomingdalesstl.com
HOURS: Mon.-Fri. 7:30 A.M.-6 P.M., Sat.
7:30 A.M.-4 P.M.

`Map 4`

Situated behind a massive, neon-pink pawprint marquee, Groomingdale's represents South City's creative streak and proves that St. Louis's pet-care ideals can surpass other places' people-care standards. Offering pet "Playcare" and a full-service pet spa, the folks who invented the now-famous FURminator (a bold tool promising a 90 percent reduction in shedding) will prettify your pooch with special organic treatments for coat, nails, and teeth. And just in case you think little Spot will never be that clean again, Groomingdale's can memorialize that shiny coat in a "Pup-tography" portrait session. They've got plenty of toys and treats to grab on the way home, too.

◗ LOLA AND PENELOPE'S

7742 Forsyth Blvd., Clayton, 314/863-5652,
www.lolaandpenelopes.com
HOURS: Mon.-Fri. 10 A.M.-6 P.M., Sat.
9 A.M.-5 P.M., Sun. noon-4 P.M.

`Map 6`

Walk down any street in Clayton, and you're pretty much guaranteed to find high-end shopping. Lola & Penelope's puts a fun twist on boutique chic—all of the designer clothes, elegant furniture, and gourmet foods are for four-legged friends. Both levels are filled with items for the discerning dog and cat. Visitors will find Chihuahua-sized cardigans, pink Porsche-shaped cat beds, and organic treats. The shop also offers grooming services, including "pawdicures," dental cleanings, and heat massages for older pets. Lola & Penelope's frequently hosts events to benefit abandoned pets, and each year the store honors animals that have behaved heroically.

WOLFGANG'S PET STOP

328 N. Euclid Ave., 314/367-8088,
www.wolfgangspetstop.com
HOURS: Mon. noon-6 P.M., Tues.-Fri.
10 A.M.-6 P.M., Sat. 9 A.M.-5 P.M., Sun. noon-4 P.M.

`Map 2`

Wolfgang's is a delightful place for pet-lovers—and for pets themselves. This shop offers everything from designer collars to couture doggie sweaters to customizable birthday parties and "bark-mitzvahs." Purchase one of these canine soirees, and Wolfgang's will provide a homemade party cake, party favors, gift bags, and games. The on-site pet spa offers a number of grooming options, and Wolfgang's also carries gourmet dog food and a line of orthopedic pet beds. Be sure to give a head-scratch to the eponymous Wolfgang, the beautiful rescued dog who often lolls in front of the shop's entrance.

Shopping Centers

THE BOULEVARD

Brentwood Blvd. at Galleria Pkwy.

Map 6

The Saint Louis Galleria is a mall (and a great one at that), but The Boulevard positions itself as a lifestyle center. When you stroll down The Boulevard's brick-paved avenue—the burbling of fountains in the background, the smells from P.F. Chang's and Maggiano's Little Italy beckoning—you can imagine a lifestyle where you (clad in something spiffy from Ann Taylor Loft) can have your hair done at Mitchell James before heading up to your spacious apartment in this mixed commercial-residential development. There are currently 18 shops and restaurants on The Boulevard, but developers plan to double that soon.

CENTRAL WEST END

Euclid Ave. between Washington Ave. and Forest Park Ave., www.thecwe.com

Map 2

This pedestrian-friendly shopping district is at the heart of one of the city's oldest and most prestigious neighborhoods. The sidewalks along this five-block stretch are canopied by stately trees. Walk down Euclid Avenue (the Central West End's main thoroughfare), and you'll glimpse some of the city's most beautiful homes and gardens.

If you can afford a shopping expedition in the Central West End, by all means go for it. The neighborhood's clothing boutiques are, not surprisingly, upscale—but while some of the prices are astronomical, service is never snobby. Art galleries and high-end furniture showrooms line

McPherson Avenue. On Maryland Plaza, you'll find a Design Within Reach flagship store, an exquisite chocolatier, a ritzy nightclub, and several trendy clothing shops. Salons, spas, and specialty gift stores stretch down Euclid Avenue; the street is also home to two great bookstores and many nice restaurants with see-and-be-seen alfresco seating.

Even if you're not looking to drop lots of cash, the Central West End is the perfect place for an afternoon stroll and leisurely browsing. Prime shopping times include Sunday afternoons, when several of the neighborhood's popular eateries open for a late-morning patio brunch.

CHEROKEE STREET

Cherokee St. between Lemp Ave. and DeMenil Pl.

Map 3

Many locals consider Cherokee Street "antique row." But, in reality, the antique stores occupy only a portion of this seven-block shopping district. In addition to antique and vintage shops, this thriving stretch plays host to several Central American markets, record sellers, restaurants, and bodega-style convenience stores. Make time to walk Cherokee Street from end to end, and you'll encounter more than 50 businesses. The quiet antique row is nestled on Cherokee's eastern stretch; the western side is a lively Latino neighborhood, where visitors will find specialty shops and the finest *taquerías* in all of St. Louis. Be sure to pause for a moment at Shangri-La; this adorable café sits at the street's midway point and offers outstanding homemade strawberry lemonade.

CLAYTON

Between Maryland Ave., Forsyth Blvd., and
Brentwood Blvd.

Map 6

On weekdays, Clayton is a business center,
filled with suited-up folks enjoying power
lunches. But business isn't being con-
ducted just in the conference rooms of the
multistory buildings. Many locally
owned galleries and upscale boutiques
line the walkable streets of this posh
area. Pop into the Duane Reed Gallery to check out the latest art show,
and peruse shops like Elements of
Denim, a designer-jean store, and Byrd,
a boutique that offers style-consulting
services. By night office dwellers emerge
for happy-hour drinks at places the Ritz-
Carlton St. Louis's lobby lounge. Join
them, or find a quiet table at one of many
restaurants for a scrumptious dinner and a
relaxing end to a full day of shopping.

DELMAR LOOP

Delmar Blvd. between Trinity Ave. and Des Peres
Ave., www.ucityloop.com

Map 6

Arguably the most popular entertainment
district in the city, the Loop boasts a variety of restaurants, shops, and live-music
venues. It's also home to several indie-rock
clubs and the city's alternative newspaper;
as such, the area draws a younger, hipper
crowd. Vintage Vinyl, one of St. Louis's
last remaining record stores, calls the Loop
home. The historic Tivoli Theatre is here as
well, as are a number of independent bars
and coffee shops.

The Loop's fashion boutiques, furniture
stores, and gift shops clearly cater to the
youthful demographic. The apartments

north and south of Delmar are home to
hundreds of Washington University students, and Loop businesses lure them in with
trendy fashions and abundant drink specials.
A number of restaurants are here too, including three Thai spots and the ever-popular
Blueberry Hill.

Blueberry Hill has held down the corner of Westgate and Delmar for years.
During that time, the restaurant/rock
club has grown to encompass an entire
block of storefronts. Owner Joe Edwards
spearheaded the reimagining of the once-
dangerous and rundown Delmar Loop.
Today, Blueberry Hill is a tourist flagship,
and everything around it hums with life.

GRAND SOUTH GRAND

South Grand Blvd. between Arsenal St.
and Utah St.

Map 4

The Grand South Grand shopping district may appear a little rough around
the edges, but it's a vibrant neighborhood that appeals to South City residents
and tourists alike. The shops, restaurants, and bars reflect the diversity in
this densely populated neighborhood.
Visitors could easily spend an entire afternoon perusing the street's many
ethnic markets. The most popular and
well-stocked market, Jay's International, sits at its own pedestrian light
in the middle of Grand South Grand's
eight-block stretch. Other landmarks include MoKaBe's, a bustling coffee shop
across the street from Tower Grove Park;
Dunaway Books; and Floored Dance Studio, where interested parties can receive
instruction in everything from tango to
pole-dancing.

OLD WEBSTER
Big Bend Blvd. and Lockwood Ave.

Map 7

There are several worthwhile shopping destinations in the idyllic bedroom community of Webster Groves, and they can be found along Big Bend Boulevard and Lockwood Avenue. The two roads meet in a Y at Euclid Records. This specialty record store shares what was once a DeSoto dealership with Cyrano's, a popular dessert bar. East of here, along Big Bend, visitors will find an upscale fashion boutique as well as long-time resident Music Folk, a folk-instrument shop. West of here, along Lockwood and past a few residential blocks, you'll encounter Old Webster's historic main drag. This stretch is mainly food-oriented, but tucked in amid the casual restaurants are some eclectic gift boutiques, a bookstore, salons and spas, a music store specializing in classical recordings, and a popular high-end grocer.

SAINT LOUIS GALLERIA
Brentwood Blvd. and Clayton Rd.,
314/863-5500, www.saintlouisgalleria.com
HOURS: Mon.-Sat. 10 A.M.-9:30 P.M., Sun.
11 A.M.-6 P.M.

Map 6

This centrally located shopping mall is one of the most popular in the area, thanks to its variety of shops and its accessibility via MetroBus and MetroLink. The Galleria is anchored by Macy's, Dillard's, and a flagship Mark Shale—and has plans for even greater expansion over the next 10 years. On its three levels, the Galleria boasts trendy favorites like Urban Outfitters, the Gap, and Anthropologie, plus a six-theater cinema, a food court, and a few stand-alone restaurants. Visitors tired from a long afternoon of shopping can relax and refuel at outposts of national chains such as California Pizza Kitchen and the Cheesecake Factory. The Galleria recently enacted strict weekend curfew laws—kids age 17 and under must leave the mall before 3 P.M. unless they're accompanied by an adult.

WEST COUNTY MALL
I-270 and Manchester Rd., 314/288-2020,
www.shopwestcountycenter.com
HOURS: Mon.-Sat. 10 A.M.-9:30 P.M., Sun.
11 A.M.-6 P.M.

Map 7

West County Mall completed an extensive renovation in 2002. Today, it is one of the area's premier shopping centers. West County Mall is anchored by Missouri's only Nordstrom (although the Saint Louis Galleria will be getting one soon), a flagship Macy's, and Dick's Sporting Goods. Among its 150 other stores are Brooks Brothers, Clarks, the Apple Store, H&M, and Sephora. In addition to having standard food-court fare, the mall caters to hungry shoppers with a California Pizza Kitchen, an outpost of St. Louis fave J. Buck's, and a see-and-be-seen spot called The Elephant Bar.

Spa, Bath, and Beauty

CASSIE'S FRAGRANCE BOUTIQUE AND SCENT BAR

316 N. Euclid Ave., 314/454-1010,
www.cassiesscents.com

HOURS: Mon.-Thurs. 10:30 A.M.-6 P.M., Fri.-Sat.
10:30 A.M.-8 P.M., Sun. noon-5 P.M.

Map 2

Cassie's is part fragrance shop, part laboratory. Alongside a lovely selection of boutique bath products and handmade soaps, you'll find the scent bar, where you can buy perfume tailored to your exact specifications. The friendly "scent specialists" help patrons mix their own fragrances by combining highly concentrated perfume oils, one drop at a time. The scent can then be purchased as-is or added to lotion or body wash. Locals

© AMY FERGUSON

Looking for an olfactory treat? Sidle up to the scent bar at Cassie's.

flock to Cassie's for the inexpensive, spot-on imitations of such designer fragrances as Marc Jacobs and Burberry Touch.

THE FACE & THE BODY

2515 Brentwood Blvd., Brentwood, 314/726-6112,
www.faceandbodyspa.com

HOURS: Mon.-Fri. 9 A.M.-9 P.M., Sat. 9 A.M.-6 P.M.,
Sun. 10 A.M.-5 P.M.

Map 7

Loyal spa-goers don't just *like* The Face & The Body's house-brand cosmetics and skin products. They love them, adore them, evangelize about them. Founder Peggy Michusson developed the line to complement her services at St. Louis's first full-service day spa. The Face & The Body has grown since its doors opened in 1979, with one location expanding into three and luxurious products selling like hotcakes. Travel-weary tourists looking for true indulgence will find it here. Stop in for a mud wrap, manicure, facial, or massage—or spring for a medical spa treatment, such as laser hair removal or a microdermabrasion session that will leave your skin baby-smooth.

K. HALL DESIGNS

8416 Manchester Rd., Brentwood, 314/961-1990,
www.khalldesigns.com

HOURS: Mon.-Sat. 10 A.M.-6 P.M.

Map 7

The handmade olive oil and shea-butter soaps at K. Hall Designs Apothecary in Brentwood are worth the trip alone. The shop's divinely scented, all-natural home and bath products are made at a small-scale manufacturer less than five miles away, but fans of K. Hall's merchandise hail from all over the globe. This 12-year-old operation distributes its

St. Louis spa-goers swear by The Face & The Body's luxurious treatments.

© BROOKE FOSTER

products to more than 1,200 stores—from New York to Hong Kong—and has been featured in nearly every garden- and food-related publication on the newsstand. Inspired by her own garden, the tranquil, breezy little apothecary on Manchester is owner Kelley Barr's home showcase.

NATURALLY PURE

117 E. Lockwood Rd., Webster Groves, 314/963-7101, www.naturallypuresalon.com
HOURS: Mon. noon–5 P.M., Tues. and Thurs. 8:30 A.M.–8 P.M., Wed. noon–8 P.M., Fri.–Sat. 8:30 A.M.–5 P.M.
Map 7

This cozy converted house, located near Webster Groves' main drag of shops and restaurants, is a favorite getaway for frazzled locals. A full-service Aveda salon, Naturally Pure offers everything from super-soothing scalp massages to eyebrow shaping to exceptionally good haircuts. Stylists here take the time to make you look perfect, so be sure to set aside three hours if you want, say, highlights and a blow-out. Naturally Pure sells the complete line of Aveda cosmetics, plus tons of hair products, facial masques, and body lotions.

Vintage and Antiques

CHERRY BOMB VINTAGE
2303 Cherokee St., 314/762-9722
HOURS: Daily noon-5 P.M.
Map 3

Cherry Bomb Vintage is St. Louis's largest midcentury antique shop. The city's alternative weekly has voted Cherry Bomb "Best Vintage Store" five years running, and it's quite easy to see why. Not only is the selection great, but the location (the heart of the Cherokee Street antique district) is wonderful, and the service is charming and gracious. A visitor could spend hours browsing Cherry Bomb's three jam-packed floors of vintage clothing, accessories, housewares, furniture, jewelry, and books. The market for great vintage in St. Louis hasn't yet been sapped, and out-of-towners are likely to appreciate the veritable gold mine of Mod and kitsch found on every lovingly arranged display.

RAG-O-RAMA
6388 Delmar Blvd., University City, 314/725-2760, www.ragorama.com
HOURS: Mon.-Sat. 11 A.M.-8 P.M., Sun. noon-7 P.M.
Map 6

The stylish mannequins in the windows of this good-size thrift store offer a glimpse of what you'll find inside: funky, eclectic dresses and skirts; jeans and tops for everyday wear; fun costumes; shoes and bags; and tons of jewelry. The racks are always packed with recently recycled wardrobe items and beloved retro-wear for both men and women, and sorting through everything has the feel of a treasure hunt. You might even spot some tags—on items that have never been worn! Prices here aren't as bargain-basement as your average charity-run thrift shop, but the pieces are still easily affordable and worth the hunt.

ROTHSCHILD'S ANTIQUES AND HOME FURNISHINGS
398 N. Euclid Ave., 314/361-4870, www.rothschildsstl.com
HOURS: Mon.-Thurs. 10 A.M.-6 P.M., Fri.-Sat. 10 A.M.-10 P.M., Sun. 11 A.M.-5 P.M.
Map 2

Antiques aficionados say Rothschild's is one of the best antique stores in the country—and the Central West End shop's beautiful collection certainly supports that claim. Owner Pete Rothschild, one of the city's most prominent real-estate developers, began collecting on the local level in the early 1970s; he salvaged interesting odds and ends from the buildings he purchased. Today, Rothschild's showcases rare and wonderful antiques from all over the nation. Everyday finds include such gorgeous pieces as whorled nutmeg-leather wingback chairs and Belgian bluestone-topped cellar tables. Prices can be staggering, but it's always fun to look, and browsing at Rothschild's is the perfect complement to a leisurely Sunday brunch at Duff's Restaurant next door.

TAG (TIMELESS AUTHENTIC GARMENTS)
6314 Delmar Blvd., 314/721-1370, www.tag-stl.com
HOURS: Mon.-Thurs. 11 A.M.-8 P.M., Fri.-Sat. 11 A.M.-9 P.M., Sun. 11 A.M.-6 P.M.
Map 6

This upscale vintage boutique is, appropriately, located in an old record store. The

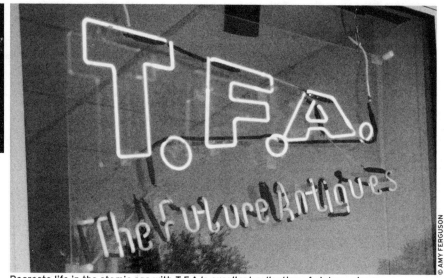

© AMY FERGUSON

Recreate life in the atomic age with T.F.A.'s excellent collection of vintage pieces.

theme here is "what's old is new again," and as with its repurposed location, the shop helps you to rethink vintage and realize that older pieces are still totally wearable. If you're having a difficult time picturing that kind of wardrobe revision, just recall the name of the shop and look at the tags—often you'll find outfit ideas there! The shop carries clothing for men and women (both affordable and designer stuff—think Gucci and Fendi), and don't be surprised if you walk out with something that you wouldn't have ordinarily purchased, but that somehow still feels so very you.

T.F.A.
3229 Morganford Rd., 314/865-1552,
www.tfa50s.com
HOURS: Mon.-Thurs. noon-8 P.M., Fri.-Sat.
10 A.M.-8 P.M., Sun. noon-5 P.M.
Map 4

The Future Antiques, or T.F.A., specializes in midcentury home furnishings: Think Danish Modern, astro-blue vinyl, and the blond-wood decor of 1950s California ranch homes. Fashionable folks looking to recreate life in the atomic age will be impressed by the great selection here. Thanks to its ever-increasing inventory, T.F.A. was recently forced to move to its new, much larger space on Morganford Road.

HOTELS

Because of the sheer number of universities, medical complexes, and conference centers in St. Louis, there are plenty of hotel rooms. Most of the hotels are located in downtown and in the city's central corridor, although there are also delightful bed-and-breakfasts nestled in St. Louis's residential areas. As can be expected in a city of St. Louis's size, the majority of downtown hotels are outposts of pricy chains, but even these have plenty of local touches (not to mention a great location). Travelers looking to indulge themselves will find a healthy number of options, from the astonishing minimalist beauty of the brand-new Four Seasons to the old-world elegance of the Chase Park Plaza. Visitors should know that, because much of the downtown hotel business comes from large, well-funded conventions, there are very few budget options in this area. Tourists looking to spend the night for less than $100 are very unlikely to find such a deal downtown (except in the rare instance of an off-season discount).

The more budget-friendly hotel options are a bit farther from the city center, although there are plenty of affordably priced bed-and-breakfasts. In fact, a stay in a St. Louis B&B promises both a restful night and a glimpse into local history and

© AMY FERGUSON

HOTELS

HIGHLIGHTS

LOOK FOR 【 TO FIND
RECOMMENDED HOTELS.

【 Best Place to Pamper Yourself: The brand-new **Four Seasons St. Louis** is perhaps the most luxurious hotel in the city. Soak in the marble bathtub, stretch out on the chaise longue (while taking in a stellar view of the Arch and the Mississippi River), or head to the seventh floor for a spa treatment (page 153).

【 Best Room with a View: The recently renovated **Hilton St. Louis at the Ballpark** brings new meaning to "field of dreams." Spacious, pretty rooms overlook the city – or, if you're lucky, provide the perfect view of Busch Stadium's infield (page 154).

【 Most Historic Hotel: Built in 1922, the **Chase Park Plaza** is a true St. Louis landmark. But this hotel doesn't rest on its laurels: Rooms are large and luxuriously appointed, on-site dining is first-rate, and visitors will find plenty of entertainment options, including live music and a five-screen movie theater (page 157).

【 Most Chic Bed-and-Breakfast: Forget frilly bedspreads and outdated plumbing fixtures: **Dwell 912** is a bed-and-breakfast for the 21st century. The furniture is sleek and chic, and amenities like wireless Internet and flat-screen televisions will delight the modern traveler (page 158).

【 Most Romantic Accommodations: The stunning **Fleur-de-Lys Mansion** is an object lesson in opulence and romance. Ask for a room with a Jacuzzi – and consider springing for the Ultimate Romantic Getaway Package, which includes a four-course dinner, a carriage ride, and in-room massages (page 160).

【 Best Place to Pretend You're Robin Hood: Reserve the "Treehouse at Sherwood Forest" room at **Cheshire Lodge,** and you'll be sleeping on a vaulted bed beneath an indoor tree canopy. Other quirky room options include "The Captain's Quarters" and "The Raj" (page 161).

【 Best Boutique Hotel: Life is sweet at the Tudor-style **Seven Gables Inn.** Rooms are meticulously decorated, with an eye toward beauty and comfort. Bathrooms are stocked with Aveda products, and gourmet candies from local chocolatier Bissinger's await each night (page 163).

architecture, as most bed-and-breakfasts in town are tucked inside lovely old homes. The budget-conscious traveler who wants to stay close to tourist attractions, restaurants, and entertainment venues will definitely want to look into one of St. Louis' many B&Bs. Those looking for a boutique hotel won't find an abundance of options, but the boutique hotels St. Louis *does* have are great—particularly the Seven Gables Inn in Clayton and the brand-new MoonRise in the Delmar Loop. Hotels in these areas rarely fall in the "budget" category, but their chic ambiance and in-the-middle-of-it-all location makes them worth the price.

PRICE KEY

$ Less than $150 per night
$$ $150-250 per night
$$$ More than $250 per night

HOTELS

Downtown
Map 1

DRURY PLAZA HOTEL $$

2 S. 4th St., 314/231-3003,
www.druryhotels.com

The 10-story Drury Plaza Hotel ($130–160) offers one of the best values downtown. It occupies three beautifully restored 1919 buildings at the corner of 4th and Market, offers great views of the Arch, doesn't charge for its WiFi, and serves a free hot breakfast every morning. Other amenities include a 24-hour business center, exercise room, and indoor pool. Although rooms are run-of-the-mill, they are squeaky clean, and the staff is always friendly. The Drury is only a few blocks from a MetroLink stop, a mile from the Amtrak station, and within walking distance of several important visitor sites, including the Gateway Arch, Busch Stadium, the Old Courthouse, and Union Station.

◖ FOUR SEASONS ST. LOUIS $$$

999 N. 2nd St., 314/881-5800,
www.fourseasons.com/stlouis

Simply one of the most exquisite hotels in the city, Four Seasons St. Louis ($245–450) brings a much-needed update to downtown lodging. The hotel, which adjoins the Lumière Place casino complex, is a work of art. Enter the first-floor foyer, with its stunning minimalist design, and take the elevator to the eighth-floor lobby. There, floor-to-ceiling windows provide one of the best views in the city. Guest rooms offer equally excellent vistas, in addition to plush accommodations and abundant amenities. The marble bathrooms (with glass-enclosed rain showers and LCD televisions) are particularly impressive. Ask about the "hotel credit" when you reserve your room; when the Four Seasons isn't booked to capacity, you can usually get a $50 credit to the spa or to Cielo, the upscale on-site restaurant.

HAMPTON INN $$

333 Washington Ave., 314/621-7900,
www.hamptoninn.hilton.com

Travelers looking for a hotel conveniently located amid the city's many sightseeing destinations will appreciate the clean, comfortable, and affordable accommodations of the Hilton-owned Hampton Inn ($129–159).

© PETER VITALE

Enjoy impressive views from the eighth-floor sky lobby at the Four Seasons St. Louis.

Though the property itself is not much to write home about, the Hampton Inn's location is great. This midpriced hotel is at the eastern end of fashionable Washington Avenue and is within walking distance of several popular downtown destinations, including the Gateway Arch grounds, Busch Stadium, and the Edward Jones Dome. Many of this hotel's 180 reasonably sized suites have views of the Arch, and the nearby Washington Avenue MetroLink stop gives guests convenient access to numerous destinations outside of downtown. Hotel amenities include a complimentary breakfast, indoor pool, and 24-hour business and fitness centers.

HILTON ST. LOUIS AT THE BALLPARK $$

1 S. Broadway, 314/421-1776,
www.hiltonstlouis.com

Find baseball heaven at Hilton St. Louis at the Ballpark ($169–209), which is right next to Busch Stadium. The hotel's proximity to Pujols and the gang make it a popular

"staycation" spot for St. Louis residents, although the halls also hum with convention business. Rooms are large and nicely appointed, with luxe bedding, MP3 player docks, and wireless Internet access. Choose between a city-view or a stadium-view room, but do know the latter can be hard to come by when the Cards are on a winning streak. This Hilton boasts both universally known amenities (a gigantic lobby Starbucks) and local favorites (an outpost of Imo's Pizza).

HOTELUMIÈRE $$

999 N. 2nd St., 314/881-7777,
www.lumiereplace.com

A stone's throw from the Four Seasons, HoteLumière ($129–199) is the more budget-friendly option in the Lumière Place complex. HoteLumière's accommodations aren't nearly as plush as those at the Four Seasons, but the location is good. This is a former Embassy Suites (frequent travelers will recognize that chain's open floorplan in a heartbeat) with a few fun updates, like mod furniture, flat-screen televisions, and a chic bar. Plus, you're just a few steps away from the casino floor and its cadre of restaurants, including the excellent Burger Bar. Service at HotelLumière is not as polished as that at the Four Seasons—but at around 100 bucks less per night, that's more of an observation than a complaint.

HYATT REGENCY $$

1 St. Louis Union Station, 314/231-1234, www.stlouis.hyatt.com

The Hyatt Regency ($129–180), inside historic Union Station, gives guests the opportunity to spend a night in a national landmark. The old-world beauty of this turn-of-the-20th-century train station remains intact, and its Grand Hall serves as the hotel's lobby. Outstanding features include the hall's stately marble arches, its towering barrel-vaulted ceiling, and period furnishings, although the visual impact here is mostly reserved for common spaces. Rooms offer a few deluxe accoutrements (comfy pillowtop mattresses, Egyptian cotton sheets, super-fast in-room Internet connections), and some have nice garden views, but are nothing to write home about. Hotel amenities include a 24-hour business center, fitness center, and outdoor pool. Guests can have a drink or casual meal at the adjoining shopping center (waaay touristy) or go upscale at the Station Grille, the Hyatt's on-site steakhouse.

OMNI MAJESTIC $$

1019 Pine St., 314/436-2355, www.omnihotels.com

Omni hotels are almost always a great bet, and the Omni Majestic ($139–239) is a particularly bright feather in that chain's cap. This boutique hotel, constructed in 1913, is full of old-world beauty. Mahogany furnishings lend an air of drawing-room elegance, and the service—from the front-desk staff to the caterers to the porters—is outstanding. A perennial favorite with St. Louis couples seeking nice accommodations for their wedding guests, the Omni offers large rooms and suites at reasonable prices. The charming hotel bar is several steps up from most others in the area, and the grand piano in the lobby is a lovely touch.

RENAISSANCE GRAND $$

800 Washington Ave., 314/418-5600, www.marriott.com

Because of its proximity to the city's convention center and downtown commerce district, the Renaissance Grand ($209–250) is a very popular choice with business travelers. The service is pleasant and efficient, and the rooms—while nothing extraordinary—are comfortable. Bathrooms are lavish and spa-like. While common spaces are sometimes an afterthought in midrange hotels, the sitting areas and lobby at the Renaissance are beautifully appointed. Request a top-floor room, and you'll be rewarded with panoramic city views and easy access to the rooftop pool. This hotel is also home to a Starbucks outpost and three restaurants, including the venerable An American Place. Before you book a reservation, be sure to visit the Renaissance Grand's website for great "weekend getaway" packages.

THE ROBERTS MAYFAIR $$

806 St. Charles St., 314/421-2500, www.wyndham.com

Situated at the corner of 8th Street and St. Charles Street, just one block south of bustling Washington Avenue, the elegant

HOTELS

Roberts Mayfair ($139–170) brings a bit of old-world charm to St. Louis's burgeoning downtown. Stained-glass windows, marble floors, and wooden handrails give this historic hotel a romantic ambiance and make it a truly charming place to stay. The Mayfair's state-of-the-art amenities are impressive as well, and include premium 42-inch plasma flat-screen TVs, Aeron chairs, down pillows, thick terry towels, and spacious spa-like bathrooms stocked with Bath and Body Works products. Guests will love the fresh, bright, modern feel of these rooms (and the comfort of the crisp luxury linens). The hotel also boasts free WiFi in every room, a fully equipped workout facility, and sparkling rooftop swimming pool. The Roberts Brothers, who own the gorgeous Roberts Orpheum and a large amount of real estate on the city's north side, bring elegance to all of their projects—and the Mayfair is no exception.

SHERATON ST. LOUIS CITY CENTER $$

400 S. 14th St., 314/231-5007,
www.starwoodhotel.com

Breathe easy at the Sheraton St. Louis City Center ($139–199), a completely smoke-free hotel. This quiet property is a good bet for business travelers, although its proximity to the Edward Jones Dome and Scottrade Center also make it popular with football and hockey fans. The digs aren't particularly fancy, but service is friendly, amenities are thoughtful, and rates are reasonable. Swim laps in the huge heated pool, or stretch out with a book on the sundeck. The Sheraton St. Louis isn't known for its restaurants (a recently shuttered hockey-themed restaurant was particularly ill-conceived), so avoid the dark hotel dining room and head instead to a downtown eatery.

WESTIN ST. LOUIS $$

811 Spruce St., 314/621-2000,
www.starwoodhotel.com

The Westin ($169–209) is one of the city's newest luxury hotels, enjoying a premier location in the center of downtown. It is directly across the street from Busch Stadium and within walking distance of several important St. Louis sights, including the Gateway Arch, the Old Courthouse, and Washington Avenue. The plush, spa-inspired rooms have a clean, Modernist design and pamper guests with fluffy towels and super-high-thread-count bedding. The marble bathrooms, with glass-enclosed showers and separate soaking tubs, are particularly nice. Enormous arched windows in many rooms offer outstanding views of the city skyline. The hotel's many amenities include a full-service spa, health center, and late-night lounge and grill. Potential guests should make particular note of the Westin's proximity to the baseball stadium: On game nights, this place can be a zoo.

Midtown and Central West End   Map 2

CENTRAL WEST END
BED & BREAKFAST 💲💲

4045 Washington Blvd., 314/535-7900,
www.cwebedbreakfast.com

Depending on your viewpoint, the Central West End Bed & Breakfast ($125–600) represents either the pinnacle of luxury or the nadir of kitsch. Either way, guests with an adventurous spirit will get a kick out of this gotta-see-it-to-believe-it inn. Each of the historic home's eight themed suites (Asia, Kenya, Beach, etc.) boasts features that B&B buffs don't exactly see every day. We're talking about baby grand pianos, waterfalls, heart-shaped whirlpool tubs, live doves (yep), and a "beach" made of real sand. Other amenities include an in-house masseuse, Rolls-Royce car service, a daily four-course breakfast, and complimentary wine. This unique bed-and-breakfast is west of Midtown's Grand Center and six blocks from the heart of the Central West End.

🌙 CHASE PARK PLAZA 💲💲💲

212 N. Kingshighway Blvd., 314/633-3000,
www.chaseparkplaza.com

This stately four-star hotel is both a civic treasure and a historic landmark. When the Chase Park Plaza ($269–389) opened its doors in the 1920s, it welcomed the crème de la crème of celebrity society. For years, the Chase was *the* destination for upscale business and leisure travelers. The hotel hosted the Rat Pack, Bob Hope, and every visiting United States president from 1920 to 1980. The Chase fell into disrepair toward the end of the 20th century, but a $100 million renovation restored the

©AMY FERGUSON

HOTELS

Get a glimpse into St. Louis's history at the legendary Chase Park Plaza.

legendary hotel to its former glory, and there are enough luxurious amenities to make this hotel a destination in itself. Popular with wealthy socialites and brides on an unlimited budget, the Starlight Lounge and Khorassan Ballroom are state-of-the-art event facilities. The hotel is also home to a quaint five-screen cinema, a bistro and lounge, a beautiful pool and patio, and a full-service salon and spa.

MARRIOTT RESIDENCE INN 💲💲

525 S. Jefferson Ave., 314/289-7500,
www.marriott.com

The brand-new Residence Inn ($154–175) near downtown St. Louis is conveniently located off US-40/64, at the Jefferson exit, and is a five-minute drive from several important tourist sites including Forest Park, the Missouri Botanical Garden, the Arch, and Busch Stadium. The beautiful and historic Lafayette Square neighborhood is just around the corner, as are the neighborhoods of South City and Soulard. The Residence Inn is in a centrally located (though particularly unattractive) corridor of the city and is a good choice for travelers who place a premium on convenience. Amenities include a fitness center, a lounge, an indoor pool, free continental breakfast, and private galley kitchens with a coffeemaker, toaster, microwave, refrigerator, and utensils. The Residence Inn offers guests a complimentary cocktail hour and light evening meal Monday through Friday.

THE PARKWAY HOTEL ❺

4550 Forest Park Ave., 314/256-7777,
www.theparkwayhotel.com

The Parkway Hotel ($117–126) is, to paraphrase Ernest Hemingway, a clean, well-lighted place. You won't find mod chaise longues or commissioned art here, but you *will* find comfortable rooms and a helpful staff. The hotel's proximity to the Barnes-Jewish Hospital and St. Louis Children's Hospital complex make it a logical choice for visiting surgeons and for families with loved ones undergoing medical procedures. The Parkway is also quite close to a MetroLink station, making it a good choice for visitors traveling without a car. Avoid the adjacent Applebee's and walk a few blocks into the Central West End, where the options are far more interesting. Special rates for AAA members, AARP members, and government employees are available.

Soulard and Lafayette Square   Map 3

❰ DWELL 912 ❺❺

912 Hickory St., 314/599-3100,
www.dwell912.com

Stay at Dwell 912 ($150–175), and you can almost pretend that it's your own fabulous apartment in the heart of the city. This private two-story guesthouse, nestled in historic LaSalle Park, is just a half mile from the must-visit neighborhoods of Soulard and Lafayette Square. Dwell 912 sleeps up to four people on its second floor and is ideal for extended stays. This urban oasis is styled like a five-star boutique hotel—but without the boutique-hotel price. Amenities include 600-thread-count linens, an oversized Egyptian bath, a wood-burning fireplace, and such aesthetic delights as

13-foot ceilings and original modern art. On the first floor, you'll find an art library, a gorgeous lounge-style sitting area (with HDTV and free WiFi), and a kitchen stocked with gourmet treats and breakfast items. If you book four nights or more, you'll receive a $25-per-night discount.

LEMP MANSION
RESTAURANT & INN ❺❺

3322 DeMenil Pl., 314/664-8024,
www.lempmansion.com

Travelers looking for a night's stay unlike any other will certainly find it at the Lemp Mansion Restaurant & Inn ($115–195). This historic home once belonged to the powerful and suicide-prone Lemp family, a clan of beer barons whose trajectory went from incredible success to heartbreaking tragedy. The Lemp Mansion and Inn is a beautiful example of historical preservation, and guests who like a few ghost stories with their stay will certainly be delighted. Each of the inn's suites is decorated with period furnishings, fixtures, and artwork—much of it original to the house—and is named after a departed member of the Lemp family. Three of the suites have private baths, and two connected suites on the third floor boast Jacuzzi tubs. The amenities are thoughtful, but it's the fascinating history of the place that draws visitors here year after year.

NAPOLEON'S RETREAT ❸❸
1815 Lafayette Ave., 314/772-6979, www.napoleonsretreat.com
Located just outside of downtown in the historic Lafayette Square neighborhood, Napoleon's Retreat ($99–175) entices visitors with its charm and history. Built in 1880, this French Second Empire Victorian home was chosen by *Better Homes and Gardens* and *Architecture Magazine* as one of the "Prettiest Painted Places" in America. Jeff Archulata is the B&B's amicable innkeeper,

and his thoughtful hospitality draws guests back again and again. After a restful night's sleep, indulge in a breakfast of fresh fruit, juice, and gourmet teas. Savor the quiche, Napoleon French toast, and Belgian waffles, then head for Lafayette Park. Weekend reservations at Napoleon's Retreat require a minimum of two nights' stay.

PARK AVENUE MANSION BED & BREAKFAST ❸❸
2007 Park Ave., 314/588-9004, www.parkavenuemansion.com
Picture-perfect suites make the Park Avenue Mansion Bed & Breakfast ($89–225) a favorite with locals celebrating special occasions. Gracious hosts Kathy and Michael Petetit prepare a gourmet breakfast every morning, and guests dine in the tranquil English garden whenever weather permits. Every room here is unique and has its own bathroom, complete with whirlpool bath. A gourmet coffee, tea, and snack bar is open in the kitchen around the clock, and a candlelit dinner in Park Avenue's elegant dining room is available upon request. Front rooms offer a view of Lafayette Park, and downtown is only a mile and a half away. A minimum of two nights' stay is required.

HOTELS

South City

Map 4

HOTELS

CASA MAGNOLIA BED AND BREAKFAST $

4171 Magnolia Ave., 314/664-8702,
www.casamagnoliabandb.com

Travelers looking for a home away from home will truly appreciate Casa Magnolia ($110). This carefully restored 1906 Shaw Park home enjoys an outstanding view of Tower Grove Park and is around the corner from the Missouri Botanical Garden. Every beautifully appointed room is unique. The house showcases warm wooden furnishings and the owners' impressive antique collection. Each of the three guest rooms has its own bathroom, and guests share a second-floor study with a library and fireplace. Breakfast is prepared every morning by Casa Magnolia's gracious hosts, Lillabet and Jordi. The hot meal is served every morning between 7:30 and 8 A.M. and can be enjoyed poolside during summer months.

C FLEUR-DE-LYS MANSION $$

3500 Russell Blvd., 314/773-3500,
www.thefleurdelys.com

The beautiful accommodations within this historic South City mansion are as gracious as its hosts. Jan and Dave Seifert welcome every guest personally, and their much-loved Fleur-de-Lys Mansion ($150–295) at Russell and Grand has been voted one of the city's top bed-and-breakfasts by countless

© RAY MARKLIN

The Fleur-de-Lys Mansion brings four-star opulence to this traditional B&B.

local and national polls. Each of this home's four spacious, carefully appointed suites is unique and offers views of the gardens below, or Reservoir Park across the street. A gourmet breakfast is available to guests every morning, and a four-course dinner can be served in the elegant dining room on any night, upon special request. The Fleur-de-Lys also offers a handful of special weekend packages that change regularly. Carriage rides and in-room massages are often available, too.

Dogtown and the Hill   Map 5

DRURY INN & SUITES 💲💲

2111 Sulphur Ave., 314/646-0770,
wwwc.druryhotels.com

The convenient central location of the Drury Inn & Suites near Forest Park ($109–129) makes this brand-new economy lodge one of the best bargains in the area. Located just off the Hampton Avenue ramp at I-44, Drury is a five-minute drive from Forest Park, the Missouri Botanical Garden, and the city's historic South City and Southampton neighborhoods. Downtown is a mere 10-minute drive from here, as are the suburban enclaves of Maplewood and Webster Groves. Though this standard chain hotel is anything but fancy, rooms here are quiet and kept immaculately clean, and the hotel's menu of amenities covers all the basics, from a lounge and restaurant (the locally owned Italian restaurant Bartolino's Osteria) to a workout room and free daily breakfast. (And there's a certain local pride surrounding the Drury chain, since it started in southeast Missouri.) Ask about the Drury's St. Louis Weekend Fun packages. Special discounts are available to those in town for sightseeing and sports events.

RED ROOF INN ST. LOUIS-HAMPTON 💲

5823 Wilson St., 314/645-0101,
www.redroof.com

What the Hampton Red Roof Inn lacks in panache, it makes up for in cost and convenience. The clean, simply furnished rooms here rent for around $74 a night, and access to the motel's WiFi network is available for only $5 extra a night. Most of the rooms also have a small walk-out patio, a great little attribute not often found on the St. Louis hospitality scene. In addition to great rates and the outdoor space, the motel's location couldn't be any better. The Red Roof Inn is just off I-44, at the Hampton Avenue exit, and is less than a 10-minute drive from downtown.

Delmar Loop and University City   Map 6

🄲 CHESHIRE LODGE 💲💲

6300 Clayton Rd., 314/647-7300,
www.cheshirelodge.net

Experience British hospitality at the Cheshire Lodge ($100–175), an old(e)-English themed hotel that has been in operation for more than 40 years. This hotel offers 100 decently appointed rooms, six themed fantasy suites, and a brand-new courtyard and pool. Kitsch-loving visitors will get a kick out of the lobby's decor, which includes a stuffed, snarling grizzly mounted on its hind legs, model ships, British phone booths, and other odds and ends. Guests can enjoy a simple pub meal or late-night libation at the adjacent Fox and the Hound Tavern—a popular meeting spot for locals—but the cozy guests-only lounge off the lobby has a fireplace and is the perfect place for a winter nightcap. The hotel is very conveniently located: It's near the Skinker Boulevard exit off US-40/64, just beyond the world's largest Amoco sign.

HOTELS

The themed suites at the Cheshire Lodge make it *the* place for whimsical pampering.

CROWNE PLAZA ST. LOUIS-CLAYTON 💲💲

7750 Carondelet Ave., Clayton, 314/726-5400, www.cpclayton.com

The St. Louis Crowne Plaza ($90–210) offers great rates, plus the centralized convenience of a downtown Clayton location. This executive-class hotel resides in the heart of the Clayton business district and is just three blocks from a MetroLink stop. The Crowne Plaza caters to the corporate set with abundant conference rooms, a business center, a 24-hour fitness room, a restaurant, and same-day dry-cleaning service, but it's kid-friendly, too. Spacious adjoined suites, an indoor/outdoor swimming pool, a free arcade, and dog-friendly rooms are among Crowne Plaza's family-oriented offerings. Luxury features in each room, from the two-bedroom executive suite to the single-room double, include Italian marble showers, Simmons pillow-top mattresses, and plush bathrobes. Hungry guests should bypass the just-okay on-site grill and head instead for one of Clayton's great restaurants.

MOONRISE HOTEL 💲💲💲

6177 Delmar Blvd., 314/721-1111, www.moonrisehotel.com

A standout among St. Louis's new crop of high-concept boutique hotels, the Moon-Rise ($189–409) fills a too-long-vacant niche in one of the city's most popular entertainment districts. This plush, sophisticated hotel is located on the Delmar Loop, just steps from The Pageant. Slated for a May 2009 opening, the MoonRise will be the first hotel in this area in years. Envisioned and bankrolled by Loop entrepreneur Joe Edwards, this boutique hotel puts visitors within shouting distance of a MetroLink stop, not to mention the neighborhood's myriad restaurants and shops. LCD flat-screen televisions, luxury bedding, and Aveda bath products are standard in every one of the hotel's unique moon-themed suites (and the all-important WiFi is free). Nice in-room St. Louis touches include locally roasted Kaldi's premium coffee and Bissinger's chocolates. Guests are also welcome to take advantage of MoonRise's bike-rental service and a complimentary shuttle to Clayton, the Central West End, and Midtown.

MARRIOTT RESIDENCE INN 🟢🟢

1100 McMorrow Ave., Brentwood, 314/862-1900, www.marriott.com

Sure, it's part of a big chain, but the Marriott Residence Inn does offer home-like accommodations. This is a good option for businesspeople, or for families who want to save a bit of money by preparing a few meals in their hotel room. Every suite at this Brentwood hotel comes equipped with a full kitchen, comfortable work and seating areas, satellite TV, free WiFi, a daily newspaper, and complimentary parking arrangements. This Residence Inn boasts close proximity to some of the city's finest shopping destinations, including downtown Clayton and the Saint Louis Galleria. Guest amenities available upon request include on-site laundry, an inexpensive grocery-shopping service, and dinner delivery from a handful of area restaurants. A complimentary hot breakfast is served every day off the lobby.

RITZ-CARLTON ST. LOUIS 🟢🟢🟢

100 Carondelet Plaza, Clayton, 314/863-6300, www.ritzcarlton.com

The Ritz-Carlton St. Louis ($299–499) lives up to the implicit promises made by its brand name. This downtown Clayton hotel represents the height of luxury and elegance— and, if you can pull yourself away from your beautiful room and the snazzy piano lounge, you'll find you're within walking distance of dozens of restaurants and shops. Every room includes a broad private balcony, offering lovely views of the city below. The hotel houses three restaurants, one of which serves the most sumptuous Sunday brunch in the area. The Ritz-Carlton is a good option for guests traveling sans car; it is directly across from a MetroLink stop.

🌙 SEVEN GABLES INN 🟢🟢🟢

26 N. Meramec Ave., Clayton, 314/863-8400, www.sevengablesinn.com

Seven Gables Inn ($129–309) is a 32-room boutique hotel in the middle of downtown Clayton. Guests spending the night here will revel in the attention to detail. There are always freshly baked cookies in the lobby, Bissinger's chocolates accompany the turn-down service, and a copy of Nathaniel Hawthorne's *The House of Seven Gables* comes standard with every room. Staying here is a little like visiting your hip grandmother, and you can't beat the Seven Gables' location and extras. This cozy Tudor-style chalet is only two blocks from the Clayton MetroLink stop, has its own restaurant (American eclectic), provides free WiFi,

HOTELS

offers a complimentary continental breakfast, and serves free wine and cheese on the weekends. A 15 percent discount is available to those booking online.

SHERATON CLAYTON PLAZA HOTEL $$

7730 Bonhomme Ave., Clayton, 314/863-0400, www.starwoodhotels.com

The suburban location of the Sheraton Plaza Hotel in Clayton ($205–370) puts guests within blocks of this ritzy borough's busy downtown—and shopaholics should note that it's just a mile away from the Saint Louis Galleria and only five miles northeast of the super-spendy Plaza Frontenac. Every room here recently underwent complete renovation and features updated yet classic decor. There aren't many surprising twists here (with few exceptions, a Sheraton is a Sheraton is a Sheraton), but service is great and rooms are comfy. Among the Sheraton Plaza Hotel's many convenient amenities are a full-service salon, a car-rental service, a business center, a lounge, and a heated pool and sundeck. Those who travel with their pets should know that furry critters are welcome here, for just a small deposit.

SPRINGHILL SUITES $

1231 Strassner Dr., Brentwood, 314/647-8400, www.marriott.com

The spacious, South Beach–style rooms of the Marriott-owned Springhill Suites ($89–139) boast a clean, modern decor and abundant amenities at some of the area's most reasonable rates. Visitors will love this stylish hotel's close proximity to Lambert International Airport, the St. Louis Galleria, and downtown Clayton. Springhill is off of Brentwood Boulevard, one block west of I-170, and three minutes from the Clayton business district. In addition to the hotel's great location and friendly, eager-to-please staff, complimentary services include a daily continental breakfast, in-room coffee, a coin-operated laundry center, and valet dry-cleaning. The views aren't much, but you just can't beat the price or the location.

EXCURSIONS FROM ST. LOUIS

St. Louis is great in a lot of ways: low cost of living, strong diversity, world-class universities and health care, ample cultural experiences, wonderful restaurants. Still, sometimes even the most proud St. Louisans just want to see their city in the rear-view mirror. Fortunately, there are several great day- and weekend-trip options that are as convenient as they are affordable. Three of the most popular options—the collegiate streets of Columbia, the rolling hills of Missouri wine country, and the family-friendly shores of Lake of the Ozarks—are also three of the closest.

Columbia is the quintessential college town. About 90 minutes from downtown St. Louis, this collegiate burg offers many cultural events, great dining, fun boutique shopping, and—of course—the chance to see the Mizzou Tigers on the hardwood and the gridiron. Hotel options are limited in downtown Columbia, but there are a number of affordable lodging places just off the main drag. Proximity to downtown Columbia is key, as the town's many restaurants and shops are concentrated in these 43 square blocks.

Many St. Louisans own timeshares at Lake of the Ozarks, as this in-state vacation destination offers plenty of recreational

© LAKE OF THE OZARKS CONVENTION & VISITORS BUREAU

EXCURSIONS

HIGHLIGHTS

LOOK FOR 【 TO FIND RECOMMENDED
SIGHTS, ACTIVITIES, DINING, AND LODGING.

【 **Best Folk-Art Collection:** Lauded by arts-and-crafts publications nationwide, **Bluestem Missouri Crafts** in downtown Columbia is a can't-miss stop. The gallery-caliber work and artful displays make Bluestem a great place to browse, and the prices are so reasonable that visitors can afford to take something home (page 170).

【 **Best Place to Feel Like a Student Again:** The **University of Missouri** campus is pretty much the Platonic ideal of a university. Stroll along the broad lawns, taking in the lovely Peace Park and the affecting Memorial Union. Wear a Mizzou sweatshirt and you'll fit right in (page 171).

【 **Best Underground Attraction:** While some caverns are little more than cheesy tourist traps, **Bridal Cave** near Lake of the Ozarks is a truly stunning sight. This series of subterranean rooms got its name from the delicate "veils" of stalactites – and from the Osage Indian marriage ceremonies that were once performed here (page 175).

【 **Best Golf Excursion:** There are plenty of nice golf courses in the St. Louis area, but **Osage National Golf Resort** is a true golf getaway. The course, which was designed by no less a golfer than Arnold Palmer, is both challenging and gorgeous. Thirsty players can repair to the bar inside the 20,000-square-foot clubhouse (page 176).

【 **Most Picturesque Winery:** When St. Louisans think about Missouri wine country, they usually conjure up images of **Hermannhof Winery.** This idyllic German-style vineyard is the perfect place to relax, to picnic, and to (of course!) drink wine (page 180).

【 **Best Wine Innovators:** The winemakers at **Sugar Creek Winery and Vineyards** do things a bit differently. Rather than bottling the same varietals that are available at other wineries, they take those varietals and create bold and bright blends. The results are nothing short of delicious (page 182).

【 **Best Place to Commune with Nature:** The **Katy Trail** just might be Missouri's most beautiful hike-and-bike path. Run or ride along the trail, and you'll get a perfect view of the Missouri River below. Lush greenery and the occasional darting eagle complete the tableau (page 182).

options (including boating, golfing, hiking, and waterskiing). Visitors looking for a quiet weekend at the lake are wise not to go at the peak of summer, when many of the boats turn into floating keg parties. Most of the time, though, the Lake of the Ozarks is a pleasant getaway.

In the wonderfully temperate fall and spring months, many St. Louisans head to Missouri wine country for a mini-retreat. This area is also well worth the trip for out-of-towners; the vistas are gorgeous, and the wines are affordable and often quite good. Antique buffs will find browsing bliss in the antique shops of Hermann and Augusta.

PLANNING YOUR TIME

Although Columbia, Missouri wine country, and Lake of the Ozarks are all just a pleasant drive or train ride away, visitors should take caution while planning their time. If you have just three or four days to explore St. Louis, you'll find plenty to do in the city itself and may want to save day trips and weekend excursions for a later visit. Missouri wine country's bed-and-breakfasts are lovely, but the area can also be enjoyed in an afternoon. Consider arriving in Hermann or Augusta around lunchtime, savoring a light meal at one of the area restaurants, and then heading to a winery for a tour and tasting. You can be back in St. Louis by supper. Columbia is less than two hours away and, as such, could feasibly be explored in a day. The only downside to that strategy is that—as is true of most college towns—the main thoroughfare really comes alive at night. Lake of the Ozarks is a little over three hours away, so making the roundtrip in a single day would be rather exhausting and impractical. Plan on staying at least one night at the lake, to give yourself time to enjoy the steak-and-seafood restaurants, the fun bars, the great golf, *and* the lovely hiking and biking trails.

EXCURSIONS

EXCURSIONS FROM ST. LOUIS

EXCURSIONS

EXCURSIONS

Columbia

Spend even a few days in St. Louis, and you will see a great many "Mizzou" bumper stickers, T-shirts, and ball caps. As home to the University of Missouri's flagship campus, Columbia holds a special place in the hearts of countless St. Louisans and offers visitors the vitality of any great college town: buzzing coffeehouses, funky boutiques, dusty used bookstores, and live music almost every night. The annual True/False documentary film festival draws filmmakers and movie buffs from around the world. And, of course, sports are a huge draw, with the university's football team having recently emerged from years of futility to become a national-title contender.

As hard as it might be to imagine when you see the throngs of students walking through downtown and packing the (smoke-free) bars, Columbia is more than just a college town. Its best restaurants match up course-for-course with St. Louis's standouts, and the nearby parks and trails offer a sense of escape from the urban bustle. Families will want to plan trips around outdoor recreation: There are few kid-specific attractions, though 2008 did see the opening of the YouZeum, an interactive science center.

SIGHTS
◖ Bluestem Missouri Crafts

Named "Top Retailer of American Crafts" by *Niche* magazine, Bluestem Missouri Crafts' downtown location (13 S. 9th St., 573/442-0211, www.bluestemmissouricrafts .com, Mon.–Wed. 10 A.M.–6 P.M., Thurs.

Downtown Columbia is a hotbed of great restaurants, fun bars, and collegial cheer.

COURTESY OF COLUMBIA CVB

EXCURSIONS

10 A.M.–8 P.M., Fri.–Sat. 10 A.M.–6 P.M., Sun. noon–5 P.M.) features the work of more than 300 artists and craftspeople from Missouri and neighboring states. Here you can browse jewelry, ceramics, quilts, paper vases, and glass art; the selection is limited only by the artists' imaginations. The staff is handy with information about the artists, and custom gift-wrapping is offered. You can preview and order much of Bluestem's inventory on its website, but work this unique really should be seen in person.

Columbia Art League

The Columbia Art League (CAL) (207 S. 9th St., 573/443-8838, http://cal.missouri .org, Tues.–Fri. 11:30 A.M.–5:30 P.M., Sat. 11 A.M.–5 P.M.) is both an exhibition space and an ambassador of the arts. Exhibitions run for six weeks on average. Recent shows have featured "The Horse in Fine Art" and the work of art professors from Missouri colleges and universities, and each year CAL hosts several juried competitions. CAL also offers classes for kids and adults, including weekend workshops that visitors could include on a trip. Each June CAL hosts the Art in the Park Festival at Stephens Lake Park, with more than 100 artists, live music, and interactive activities.

Columbia Cosmopolitan Recreation Area

Covering 533 acres, the Columbia Cosmopolitan Recreation Area (1615 Business Loop 70 West, 573/874-7460)—more commonly known as Cosmo Park—is the largest park in Columbia. There are fields for football, soccer, and softball as well as a golf course, tennis courts, and a roller-hockey rink. Kids might enjoy the skate park and the track for remote-control cars. The 1.75-mile Cosmo Nature Trail winds through wetlands and, if you're lucky, might include the sight of dam-building beavers. Each summer Cosmo Park hosts the Show-Me State Games. This Olympics-inspired competition gathers amateur athletes in nearly three dozen events, from the triathlon to paintball, over three consecutive weekends in July and August.

◖ University of Missouri

The University of Missouri—the first public university west of the Mississippi—sprawls over 1,358 acres in the heart of Columbia. No visit to the campus is complete without a stop in front of the Columns, the only part of Academic Hall to survive an 1892 fire. Other notable spots include the Memorial Union, a Gothic structure intended as a memorial to alumni killed in World War I, and the lovely Peace Park (once the locus of student protests against the Vietnam War, and now a popular gathering spot). The university's athletic facilities are south of the main academic campus. The Missouri Tigers play on Faurot Field at Memorial Stadium, while the men's and women's basketball teams call the new 15,000-seat Mizzou arena home. The campus is an easy walk from downtown Columbia. With many of Mizzou's 28,000 students living on campus or nearby, the entire city can often seem like university property.

YouZeum

While Columbia's cultural diversity and world-class university system make it a great place to raise kids, there really aren't many kid-specific activities. That is, there

EXCURSIONS

weren't—until the YouZeum (608 E. Cherry St., 573/886-2006, www.youzeum .org, Wed.–Fri. 10 A.M.–5 P.M., Sat. 10 A.M.–6 P.M., Sun. 1–5 P.M., ages 14 and older $8, ages 4–13 $5, age 3 and under free) opened in 2008. This totally hands-on museum (motto: "It's all about you!") teaches lessons about human health and bodily systems through fun, interactive activities. Kids can play on the virtual obstacle course (which teaches about things like reaction time and coordination), do "interviews" as the on-air anchors of "YouNewz," and learn about the human body with the 3D film *All Systems Go!* The YouZeum is housed in Columbia's historic Federal Building.

RESTAURANTS

Booches Billiard Hall (110 S. 9th St., 573/874-9519, entrées less than $10) is a 125-year-old treasure: a bar and pool hall that happens to serve some of the best burgers not just in Columbia, but in the whole country. The burgers are rather small—most diners order more than one—and each is served without fanfare on a sheet of wax paper. Not in the mood for a burger? Come back to Booches another time. The kitchen (a grill behind the bar) doesn't turn out much else, not even French fries. Booches is cash-only, and you can buy a T-shirt proclaiming its famous policy: "Closed on Sundays. See you in church."

Stories abound of University of Missouri alumni having frozen pizza from **⟨ Shakespeare's Pizza** (225 S. 9th St., 573/449-2454, www.shakespeares.com, daily 11 A.M.–close, entrées less than $10) shipped halfway around the globe. It's *that* good. The dough is made from scratch each day, the cheese is aged provolone, and the

pepperoni is hand-sliced nice and thick. The restaurant itself is the Platonic ideal of the college hangout: dim, loud, and drowning in pitchers of beer. Drinks are served in plastic souvenir cups—most St. Louisans own at least one. Shakespeare's is open "past your bedtime," making it a perfect end to a night on the town.

Step inside **⟨ Sycamore** (800 E. Broadway, 573/874-8090, www.sycamore restaurant.com, Mon.–Fri. 11 A.M.–2 P.M. and Mon.–Sat. 5–10 P.M., bar Mon.–Thurs. 5–11 P.M. and Fri.–Sat. 5 P.M.–midnight, entrées $18), and you could suddenly be in a city two or three times Columbia's size. This large, high-ceilinged restaurant has a cosmopolitan feel, from the beautiful bar to the open kitchen situated on a mezzanine above the dining room. The menu features contemporary American bistro fare, with a focus on local produce and meat. Pork dishes are a sure bet. Or you can build a meal out of several of the fantastic appetizers, like the thick-cut fries dusted with Parmeggiano-Reggiano cheese or the homemade gnocchi. The lunch menu offers salads, soups, and sandwiches at very reasonable prices.

The name is literal: You enter the **Wine Cellar & Bistro** (505 Cherry St., 573/442-7281, www.winecellarbistro.com, Mon.–Fri. 11 A.M.–2 P.M. and Mon.–Sat. 5–10 P.M., entrées $25) at ground level and then descend into the casually elegant dining room. The atmosphere is perfect for either a romantic dinner or a relaxed get-together with friends. Owner and executive chef Craig Cyr's menu reflects his traditional technique and his interest in exotic ingredients and unexpected flavor combinations: lamb, duck, wild-boar, and seafood dishes as satisfying as they are dazzling. Cyr's wife, Sarah, is in

EXPERIENCE THE DISTRICT

Every college town worth its salt needs a bustling arts-and-culture hub, and The District gives Columbia plenty of cool cachet. Shops, clubs, coffeehouses, galleries, cafés, and bars are packed into a wonderfully walkable 43 square blocks. (The District's website claims the area has 5,900 parking spaces, and while that's probably technically true, parking in Columbia is rarely convenient or free.)

Feel like a college kid again at the **Cherry Street Artisan** (111 S. 9th St., 573/817-3274), a huge, hip space that doubles as an eatery and a performance venue. Or get your caffeine fix at **Lakota Coffee Company** (24 S. 9th St., 573/874-2852), a lodge-inspired coffeehouse with abundant laptop space and the best espresso in town. Grab a groovy, earth-friendly bite at **Main Squeeze Natural Foods Café** (28 S. 9th St., 573/817-5616); the vegetarian fare here is so good that even carnivores are won over (seriously).

Shops in The District range from wink-wink incense-and-lava-lamp stores to high-end boutiques – there are hours' worth of browsing here. **Britches** (130 S. 9th, 573/499-1401) carries *au courant* clothes that don't tip into super-trendy territory (think good denim and lines by stalwarts like Kenneth Cole). The clothes at **Elly's Couture** (914 E. Broadway, 573/499-4401) are a bit more trend-hugging, but the cruise-cute pieces

from Lacoste are hard to resist. Feel the collegiate love by stopping in **Tiger Spirit** (111 S. 9th St., 573/449-0608), where Mizzou memorabilia fills every bit of the shop's 2,400-square-foot space. Other great specialty shops in The District include stationery heaven **Pen Point Paperie** (913 E. Broadway, 573/449-6956); the superbly stocked **Top Ten Wines** (207 S. 9th St., 573/442-2207), which is worth a visit just to chat with the incredibly knowledgeable staff; and **A la Campagne** (918 E. Broadway, 573/815-9464), an antiques shop that is always chic and never fussy.

Of course, a college's cultural district must also be graded by its nightlife, and The District passes (with honors). At Columbia's cultural core is the **Blue Note** (17 N. 9th St., 573/874-1944), a live-music venue that books the best of the best. Performances here tend toward indie-rock (TV on the Radio, Ani DiFranco, Sonic Youth) and alt-country (Wilco, Avett Brothers, Old 97s), but the Note also lets folks in for live broadcasts of political speeches and Mizzou sporting events. Great nightlife continues at college-student faves like **Harpo's** (29 S. 10th St., 573/443-5418) and **Quinton's** (124 S. 9th St., 573/815-1047). Looking for something a little less *Animal House*? Consider a nightcap at **Sycamore** (800 E. Broadway, 573/874-8090), where the bar stays open till midnight on weekends.

EXCURSIONS

charge of the wine list, which *Wine Spectator* magazine has honored with its Award of Excellence. Beer connoisseurs will want to check out the restrooms, which are decorated with old beer cans.

HOTELS

Location, location, location: **The Regency Downtown Premier Hotel** (1111 E. Broadway, 573/443-2090, www.regency downtown.com, $79–149) is the only hotel located within downtown Columbia. The hotel has 100 guest rooms, and during special events these fill quickly. Rooms include data ports and cable TV with HBO. There is an outdoor pool, and hotel guests have access to the Gold's Gym down the block. The hotel restaurant serves lunch and dinner, but you will probably want to explore the many restaurants within walking distance before you settle on this. A free continental breakfast is available every morning. It is no insult to say that the hotel's best amenity is its free parking, a rarity in downtown Columbia.

The 100-year-old **⦗** **Taylor House** (716 W. Broadway, 573/256-5567, www.taylor -house.com, call for room rates) looks as good as new thanks to a recent two-year, $1.3-million restoration that turned it into the Taylor House Inn bed-and-breakfast. The house, now included in the National Register of Historic Places, offers five guest rooms. The Preston Tucker Room and the Letter Room each provide king-size beds and separate bathrooms; the Preston Tucker Room has a shower and a claw-foot tub, while the Letter Room contains a shower and a Jacuzzi tub. The other three rooms have queen-size beds, private water closets, and, charmingly, bathtubs in the main room. All five rooms

feature gorgeous fixtures and furniture. On the ground floor are several elegant sitting rooms as well as the kitchen and the dining room, where breakfast is served. Free wireless Internet access is available throughout the house, which is a short drive or leisurely walk from downtown Columbia.

PRACTICALITIES
Tourist Office

The **Columbia Convention and Visitors Bureau** is located at 300 South Providence Road.

Media

The *Columbia Missourian* (www.columbia missourian.com) and the *Columbia Tribune* (www.columbiatribune.com) are the area's two daily newspapers.

Getting There

The drive from downtown St. Louis to downtown Columbia is straightforward. From St. Louis, take I-70 west for approximately two hours to Exit 128. Turn left at North College Avenue and then right onto East Broadway, and you'll be on downtown Columbia's major thoroughfare. You can ride Greyhound (www.greyhound.com) from St. Louis to Columbia; buses depart in the early morning and early evening from the Downtown station. An even cheaper option is the MegaBus (www.megabus.com/ us). The Chicago–Kansas City line makes a daily stop in Columbia. Round-trip tickets are around $30 per person.

Getting Around

Downtown Columbia and the University of Missouri campus are wonderfully walkable. Parking is another matter, especially when the university is in session. Make sure to have change and cash on hand to feed meters and pay for garage spots. The Columbia Area Transit Line provides bus service throughout the area, but outside of downtown a car is useful.

Lake of the Ozarks

A weekend at the Lake of the Ozarks means different things to different people. Some St. Louisans have many fond memories of childhood summers spent on the lake's sandy shores. Others think of it as a business-conference destination, thanks to plentiful golf courses and convention-center-huge hotel ballrooms. Still others will wink knowingly at a mention of Lake of the Ozarks—they're undoubtedly thinking of the secluded area called Party Cove, which *The New York Times* dubbed a "floating bacchanal."

The reasons for going to Lake of the Ozarks are varied, but the fact is that people flock there in droves. The body of water itself—one of the largest man-made lakes in the nation—is great for boaters and water-skiers. (Swimmers, on the other hand, should be advised that this isn't exactly the cleanest place around.) The glittering lake and hilly topography make the region a truly lovely place, particularly once you get off the main tourist drag and away from the bars and tchotchke shops. The higher-end restaurants serve good steaks and seafood in heaping portions, and the resorts offer a variety of spa treatments. Lake of the Ozarks prides itself on being a family-friendly destination, and with the exception of Party Cove and a few other boozy hangouts, it truly is. Water parks, swimming pools, and miniature golf courses abound.

SIGHTS
◖ Bridal Cave

More than 2,000 couples have wed in Bridal Cave (526 Bridal Cave Rd., Camdenton, 573/346-2676, www.bridalcave .com), which is full of veil-like stalactites and was once the site of Osage Indian marriage ceremonies. Even if you're not interested in a subterranean wedding, the Bridal Cave is worth seeing. The cool temperatures make it a nice escape from southwest Missouri summers, and the rock formations are truly lovely. The Bridal Cave contains more onyx formations than any other cavern. "Soda-straw" formations and enormous columns fill each room of the Bridal Cave. Guided tours, which leave every few minutes and last about an hour, are the best way to see and learn about the cave. Admission is $15 for visitors age 13 and up, and $7 for the 12-and-under set.

Lake Ozark State Park

At 17,626 acres, the beautiful Lake Ozark State Park (304 Hwy. 134, Kaiser, 573/348-2694, www.mostateparks.com/lakeozark) is the largest park in Missouri. This is a great place to escape the touristy noise of the lake's bars and resorts, as the emphasis here is truly on nature. Hikers and bicyclists can take advantage of the park's 12 trails, which wind along 85 miles of shoreline and through old-growth hickory forests. Many families opt to camp here rather than stay at a resort, and there are nearly 250 campsites (some are super-primitive, while others offer electricity hookups). The park's two public beaches are prime spots for fishing, swimming, and boating. Boaters should pick up an informational booklet about the Lake of the Ozarks Aquatic Trail, a buoy-marked boat trail that highlights significant spots.

GOLF
Old Kinderhook

The stunning Old Kinderhook golf course (20 Eagle Ridge Rd., Camdenton, 573/346-4444, www.oldkinderhook.com), designed by Tom Weiskopf, offers a golfing experience that capitalizes on the natural land features of southwest Missouri. The course welcomes players of all skill levels, and you don't have to be a birdie-shooting superstar to appreciate the waterfalls and flowering trees that dot Old Kinderhook's landscape. Amenities here include a clubhouse and pro shop, a health and fitness area, and meeting rooms. Both fine and casual dining are offered. Play 18 holes for $75 Monday through Thursday; on Friday, Saturday, and Sunday, the fee is $89.

◖ Osage National Golf Resort

Golfers from throughout the Midwest make it a point to play at Osage National Golf Resort (400 Osage Hills Rd., Lake Ozark, 573/365-1950, www.osagenational.com). Living legend Arnold Palmer designed the course in 1992, and the bentgrass greens and zoysia fairways provide an experience as lovely as it is challenging. Because of the popularity of this course, it's recommended that prospective golfers reserve a tee time no less than 48 hours in advance.

© LAKE OF THE OZARKS CONVENTION & VISITORS BUREAU

Find a perfectly picturesque golf getaway at Lake of the Ozarks.

Eighteen holes will cost you $75 Monday through Thursday, and $89 Friday through Sunday. The 20,000-foot clubhouse houses the Eagle View Bar & Grille, a restaurant that offers everything from onion rings to blue-point mussels.

RESTAURANTS

Dinner at the ◖ **Blue Heron** (Business Hwy. 54 and Horseshoe Bend Pkwy., Lake Ozark, 573/365-4646, www.blueheron pottedsteer.com, Tues.–Sat. 5:30–10 P.M., cocktail lounge 5–10 P.M., entrées $25) is a treat. Everything about the place is over-sized and opulent, from the gilded dining room to the house specialty—a huge deep-fried lobster tail served atop shoestring potatoes. If you're looking to indulge while at Lake of the Ozarks, this is the place to do it. Other restaurants tout their own deep-fried lobster, but the Blue Heron did it first and does it best. The lengthy menu is meat-centric, with generous cuts served in classical preparations. There are also quite a few European options (schnitzel, Dover sole meunière), no doubt thanks to owner Joseph Boer's Dutch heritage. A first-generation American, the delightful, avuncular Boer circulates through the dining room every night, offering after-dinner cordials to everyone (although pretty women seem to get first dibs).

J. Bruner's (5166 Hwy. 54, Osage Beach, 573/348-2966, www.jbruners.com, 5–9 P.M. daily, cocktail lounge Sun.–Thurs. 4:30–10 P.M., Fri.–Sat. 4:30–11 P.M., entrées $25) recipe for success is a straight-forward one: Serve luxurious food in an un-pretentious setting. Cultivate a strong wine list, offer weekend specials, and throw in a few unexpected twists—like a selection of adults-only ice-cream drinks. J. Bruner's hasn't changed much in its nearly three decades of operation, and for its many faithful patrons that's a *good* thing. It's worth making sure your trip to the lake falls on a Friday or Saturday, as those are the nights that J. Bruner's offers its out-standing prime rib.

Whether you've built up an appetite waterskiing or just need a big meal to soak up last night's margaritas, **J.J. Twig's Pizza & Pub** (1815 Bagnell Dam Blvd., Lake Ozark, 573/365-9911, www.jjtwigs.com, daily 11 A.M.–midnight, entrées $10) has you covered. This family-run pizza place serves up the best pies in town and specializes in "double-deckers": hubcap-sized pizzas stacked with two layers of crust, cheese, and toppings. Other options, such as lasagna and chicken parmesan, are serviceable but not nearly as good as the pizza. In 2007, another J.J. Twig's opened in a St. Louis suburb, delighting the many St. Louisans who make a pilgrimage to Twig's every time they visit the lake.

Some area restaurants deserve the following backhanded compliment: "Pretty good—for Lake of the Ozarks." Not so with ◖ **On the Rise Bakery** (5439 Hwy. 54, Osage Beach, 573/348-4224, www.ontherisebakery.com, Wed.–Sun. 7 A.M.–3 P.M., entrées $10), which could be plunked down in the middle of St. Louis or Chicago and still be one of the best spots in town. Helmed by Culinary Institute of America graduate Mike Castle and his wife Cheryl, On the Rise represents a welcome departure from typical lake fare. You won't find deep-fried seafood or neon-hued shooters here. Instead, you'll be served delicious freshly baked breads and pastries, in

EXCURSIONS

addition to Kobe burgers, wood-fired pizza, and lobster pot pie. Wine is available; wet T-shirt contests are not.

HOTELS

The **◖ Lodge of Four Seasons** (Horseshoe Bend Pkwy., Lake Ozark, 573/365-3000 or 888/265-5500, www.4seasonsresort.com, rooms start at $139, condos at $209) is one of the Lake's spiffiest overnight options. There are 350 guest rooms at the Lodge of Four Seasons, and furnished condominiums are also available. Many rooms feature lake views, natural-rock walls and gas fireplaces. Nightly turndown service is available. The Lodge of Four Seasons caters more to the adult set than to kiddos, so don't expect lots of kid-friendly options. That's a plus for people who just want to relax, and the on-site Spa Shiki offers a full menu of luxurious treatments. There are several restaurants on the property, and—as is true at most Lake of the Ozarks eateries—the fare is almost hilariously over-the-top. Think batter-fried turkey, chicken Oscar, and a massive lamb porterhouse. Healthier options are available, of course, but for most folks the lake is all about indulgence.

The sprawling **Tan-Tar-A Resort** (State Road KK, Osage Beach, 573/348-3131, www.tan-tar-a.com, $151–173; call for special packages and conference rates) is a favorite destination for family reunions and business conferences. The rolling golf course is perfect for on-the-green client meetings, and Tan-Tar-A offers plenty of kid-friendly options (including multiple swimming pools and a water park). Choose between a standard hotel room in the main complex, or reserve a small house in the "Estates" section of the resort. The main hotel complex is within walking distance of Tan-Tar-A's shops and restaurants; guests staying in the Estates must drive a few miles. The rooms themselves are nothing special (think early-'90s decor and spartan bathrooms), but they're clean and, for the most part, quiet. The on-site Black Bear Lodge offers a great full breakfast, and there's also a food court (with a Burger King and Sbarro) for late-night snacking. Avoid Wind Rose, Tan-Tar-A's "fine dining" option, and head to Blue Heron or J. Bruner's instead.

PRACTICALITIES
Tourist Office

The Lake of the Ozarks Convention and Visitor Bureau is at 5816 Highway 54 in Osage Beach.

Media

The *Lake Sun Leader* (www.lakesunleader .com) is the area's daily newspaper.

Getting There and Around

The drive from St. Louis to Lake of the Ozarks is a very pretty one. From the city, take I-44 west to Exit 195 toward St. James. Make a right at MO-68, and then make another right at US-63. Then, take a left at MO-42. This route, also known as West 5th Street, is beautifully bucolic. The gentle hills of MO-42 lead up to US-54. Take a left at US-54, drive for about 10 minutes, and you'll be in the heart of Lake of the Ozarks. Do know that neither trains nor buses make the St. Louis-to-Lake of the Ozarks trip, so you will need to rent a car if you would like to visit the lake.

The best way to get around Lake of the Ozarks is by car. There's very little in the way of public transportation.

Missouri Wine Country

Missouri's wine country is a cherished getaway for St. Louisans looking to escape the noise and stress of city life. The rolling hills and bluffs of this picturesque region are less than an hour from the city, making a wine-country jaunt the ideal day trip. Visitors wishing to spend a weekend in this pastoral paradise certainly can, as there are many quaint and affordable bed-and-breakfasts. Augusta and Hermann, the small towns nestled among the wineries, boast a handful of lovely inns. There are also plenty of restaurants and antiques shops.

Visitors to Augusta and Hermann will find old-world charm in spades. Hermann centers around a Main Street that's straight out of a Norman Rockefeller print, but be advised that there's little in the way of grocery-shopping or entertainment (outside of drinking wine, of course). But it's precisely this lack of hubbub that makes Hermann so appealing; pack a picnic and capitalize on the opportunity to enjoy true serenity. The views here are outstanding, and sweeping vistas can be enjoyed from many vantage points throughout the region.

The wine-making operations here are still young (which explains why some people do a double-take at the mention of "Missouri wine"). The area was established as a wine region in the 1850s, but progress was halted by Prohibition and then stymied by economic depression for a full 40 years after that. Despite this late start, Missouri winemakers have made some notable achievements. The zinfandel-style reds

EXCURSIONS

© TONY KOOYUMJIAN

Augusta Winery

made from the region's own Norton grapes have earned acclaim in international competitions. The Missouri vignole, a lovely dry white with notes of gardenias and peach pits, has been garnering praise as well. Winemakers throughout the region are friendly, knowledgeable, and unfailingly generous— tastings are free at all wineries.

WINERIES
Augusta Winery

Augusta (5601 High St., Augusta, 888/667-9463, www.augustawinery.com, Mon.–Fri. 10 A.M.–5:30 P.M., Sat. 10 A.M.–6 P.M., Sun. noon–6 P.M.) may not have the old-world elegance of other area wineries, but it offers some fantastic wines at the lowest per-bottle price in the region. There's not much more to the place than a small tasting room, bottling facilities, and a narrow patio, but the tasting counter is always packed. The award-winning wines start at $7 per bottle and peak around $20 (Augusta's luscious pinot noir–style chambourcin is a real bargain at just $12 a bottle). Visitors may notice some similarities between the wines sold here and those sold at the Montelle Winery, and with good reason: Augusta's owner purchased Montelle in 1987 and oversees both operations.

ⓒ Hermannhof Winery

As its name suggests, the Hermannhof Winery (330 E. 1st. St., Hermann, 800/393-0100, www.hermannhof.com, Mon.–Sat. 10 A.M.–5 P.M., Sun. 11 A.M.–5 P.M.) is in the historic small town of Hermann and has a German lineage. The winery's cozy red-brick manor, Bavarian-style guest houses, and stone cellars were built in the 1850s, and are a testament to the

craftsmanship of Hermannhof's founders. Picnickers can sit beneath the grape arbor near the main house or snag a shady spot on the winery's rolling lawn. Beneath this lawn are 10 stone cellars, which produce 15,000 cases of wine each year. Hermannhof's casks are made from white oak harvested in France and Missouri, and the winery is a two-time winner of the Brown-Foreman trophy for "Best New World White," but buyers should always taste first. Vintages vary greatly in quality, and at upwards of $25 a bottle, you don't want to get a bum year. In addition to a host of reds, whites, and sparkling wines, Hermannhof sells a selection of cheeses and locally made German-style sausages.

Montelle Winery

Montelle Winery (201 Montelle Dr., Augusta, 636/228-4464, www.montelle.com, Mon.–Fri. 10 A.M.–5:30 P.M., Sat. 10 A.M.–6 P.M., Sun. 11 A.M.–6 P.M.), off of Highway 94, offers some of the area's absolute best views. Visitors can see all the way to the Missouri River from the winery's expansive, multi-level deck. Coolers and picnic baskets are prohibited beyond the parking lot, but the gift shop sells a nice selection of domestic cheeses, sausages, sandwiches, and pizzas. Fruit and sandwich trays can be ordered in advance, and a three-course dinner is offered on weekend evenings (just be sure to reserve a spot at least 48 hours prior to arrival). Montelle was opened in 1970 by Clayton Byers, one of the pioneers responsible for revitalizing the entire Missouri wine region. In addition to making some great vignoles and a number of fruit wines, Montelle distills grappa and a brandy made from Golden Delicious apples. These,

© MONTELLE WINERY

view from the Montelle Winery

too, are available for tasting—although at a small additional charge.

Mount Pleasant

Mount Pleasant (5634 High St., 636/482-9463, Augusta, www.mountpleasant.com, daily 11 A.M.–5:30 P.M.) is the oldest operating winery in Augusta and the most popular winery in the region. Manicured grounds and stone paths weave their way through an assemblage of quaint cottages, which house a tasting room, banquet facilities, a market, and a grill. Drinking at Mount Pleasant is no bargain, as visitors must pay restaurant-markup prices to enjoy a bottle of house wine on the grotto-like patio. Don't even try to buy a bottle at the retail counter and drink it on the patio, as that is strictly prohibited. The rule seems a bit unfair, but the view from the bluffs is worth the extra bucks. Grapes grown at Mount Pleasant include cabernet, merlot, and chardonnay, and the winery's ports have won several awards in recent years. Tours of the winery's cellar and bottling facility are offered 1–3 P.M. on Fridays and Saturdays (April–October).

St. James Winery

St. James Winery (540 Sidney St., 800/280-9463, St. James, www.stjameswinery .com, Mon.–Sat. 8 A.M.–7 P.M., Sun. 11 A.M.–7 P.M.) is in the Ozark Highlands, which makes it a little out of the way for visitors doing a tour of Missouri's wine country. It's off of Highway 44, between the towns of Cuba and Rolla, and is about an hour's drive from Hermann. An early Italian settlement left behind a strong Italian heritage and an equally strong wine-making tradition. St. James Winery's "School House"-label wines are named for the one-room schoolhouse built by the town's original settlers. Complimentary wine tastings and tours are offered daily, and the expansive gift shop boasts an array of gourmet gift items, baskets, and juices. Most of the wines produced here are on the light-bodied side, and the catawba-grape dessert wine is one of St. James's best sellers.

Sugar Creek Winery and Vineyards

Sugar Creek Winery's tasting room (125 Boone Country Ln., Defiance, 636/987-2400, www.sugarcreekwines.com, Mon.–Sat. 10 A.M.–5:30 P.M., Sun. noon–5:30 P.M.) is nestled inside a charming turn-of-the-20th-century Victorian home. On cold days, visitors are invited to enjoy the hospitality of the home's cozy parlor. When the weather turns warm, wine-drinkers head to the terrace patio, which overlooks the vineyards and the Katy Trail below. Sugar Creek produces a handful of estate wines but is most well-known for its unique blends of the four popular Missouri varietals grown on the premises: chambourcin, chardonel, cynthiana, and vidal. French and American hybrid grapes are grown here and blended to coax out each varietal's best qualities and brightest notes. The results have been praised by some of the industry's toughest critics. On weekends between April and October, the winery hosts live music, and picnic baskets are welcome.

SIGHTS
The Deutschheim State Historic Site

This park and historic village (109 W. 2nd St., Hermann, 573/486-2200, www.lib.iupui.edu/kade/deutschheim.html, Mar.–Dec. daily 8 A.M.–4 P.M., Jan.–Feb. Wed.–Sun. 8 A.M.–4 P.M., free) is dedicated to the preservation of Missouri's rich German heritage. An on-site gallery explores the lives of early German immigrants, who came to Missouri by the thousands between 1820 and 1850. Visitors can also check out a half-timbered barn, a print shop, a faithful re-creation of an 1830s kitchen garden, and two typical 19th-century German-style homes. The park is open during all seasons and hosts some great festivals throughout the year. Among these is Hermann's poplar Kristlekindt, an outdoor winter festival and market that celebrates the Christmas season. Guided tours of the Deutschheim State Historic Site are available daily and depart from the park's main office at 10 A.M., 12:30 P.M., and 2:30 P.M.

Katy Trail

This 225-mile recreational trail, encompassed by Katy Trail State Park and built on the bed of a former railroad track, is one of the longest of its kind in the nation. The Katy Trail hugs the Missouri River and leads hikers and cyclists through some of the state's most beautiful rural corners. Trailheads are located in St. Charles and in the tiny town of Clinton. The trail is made of crushed limestone, and bike-friendly bridges allow one to cross the Missouri River into Hermann, Washington, or Jefferson City for lunch or a night's respite. The park's outstanding website (www.bikekatytrail.com) offers downloadable maps, trail FAQs, up-to-date information on trail conditions, and links to several Katy Trail trip-planning services. To get to St. Charles from St. Louis, take I-70 west to the Fifth Street exit. Make a slight right on Boone's Lick Road. Follow Boone's

Lick until it turns into Riverside Road. Trail-head parking lots are on the right.

RESTAURANTS

A welcoming Augusta restaurant, **(Ashley's Rose Restaurant and Lone Eagle Pub** (5567 Walnut St., Augusta, 636/482-4108, Tues.–Sun. 11 A.M.–7 P.M., Fri.–Sat. 11 A.M.–9 P.M., entrées $18) resides in an early-20th-century frame building known as "the white house" and sports a quirky aviation theme. It is cozy (seats about 60 people) and has a fully stocked bar. The menu features about 20 entrées and is fairly straightforward in its aims. Ashley's grills a great steak and offers a popular weekly wiener schnitzel special with homemade sweet-and-sour red cabbage and potato pancakes. The restaurant also offers a handful of nice regional wines and runs some additional specials that change with the season. Come early on the weekend—this tiny place fills up fast.

Augusta Brewing Company and Beer Garden (5521 Water St., Augusta, 636/482-2337, www.augustabrewing .com, Sun.–Thurs. 11 A.M.–7 P.M., Fri.–Sat. 11 A.M.–9 P.M., entrées $12) is a popular stop for cyclists on the Katy Trail; the restaurant's shady beer garden is just 30 steps from it. Fare here is American pub food with a few traditional German beer haus items thrown in, like the freshly baked Bavarian pretzel served with Tannhauser mustard and a beer brat smothered in house-made sauerkraut. Several locally produced wines are offered in addition to the microbrewery's own handcrafted ales, wheats, and lagers, and the menu recommends several great pairings. In addition to a friendly atmosphere and beautiful surroundings, the restaurant also has a great summer schedule of country and bluegrass music.

A cozy little family restaurant in historic Hermann, **The Cottage Restaurant and Gallery** (1185 Highway H, Hermann, 573/486-4300, www.goodfoodfineart .com, Wed.–Sat. 11 A.M.–2 P.M., Fri.–Sat. 5–8 P.M., entrées $15) is a perennial favorite. The food here isn't fancy, but it's very well-prepared—don't miss the golden-brown fried chicken, served with a heaping mound of home-style mashed potatoes. (Also on the Do Not Miss list: homemade pie.) Outdoor seating is available on The Cottage's lovely patio, which overlooks 22 acres of forest. Want to take a painting home with your leftovers? All of the art decorating the walls is for sale, and some of it's great. Besides, the restaurant's motto is "Fried Chicken, Fine Art"—and there's just something undeniably appealing about that.

Beloved by locals, the established **Europa Restaurant** (1100 Washington St., Hermann, 573/486-4333, hours vary, entrées $18) offers an eclectic menu of traditional French, Spanish, Italian, German, and Mediterranean dishes. The focus of Europa's self-taught chefs changes with the season, and all dishes are prepared from scratch. An extensive wine, beer, and spirits list is annotated with recommended food pairings. Prices are low, and portions tend toward the ridiculously large side. While the food is good, the best thing about Europa might be its wonderful atmosphere. Meals are served in a meticulously restored 19th-century Victorian home.

HOTELS

The hosts of the **(H.S. Clay House and Guest Cottage** (219 Public St., Augusta,

314/504-4203, www.hsclayhouse.com, $150–270) bring 50-plus years of hotel-hospitality experience to this B&B. Each spacious suite here offers luxurious amenities on par with a four-star hotel. Covered porches, private balconies, whirlpool tubs, fireplaces, and flat-screen TVs with surround sound are only a few of the inn's great features. Outdoor amenities include an 18,000-square-foot double-tiered deck, swimming pool, and hot tub. The careful clutter and lush landscaped grounds of this whimsical place draw guests back again and again. Hosts Leigh and Alan Buerhe are happy to arrange a romantic gourmet dinner for two in the home's elegant dining room, or to recommend a local restaurant. And guests are sent off every morning on the right foot: A gourmet breakfast served in the first-floor common space features handmade specialties like shirred eggs, sage sausage, and custard French toast.

The inviting suites of **The Iron Horse Inn** (207 E. 4th St., Hermann, 573/486-9152, www.theironhorseinn.net, $115–150) exude warmth and comfort—all within walking distance of Hermann's historic Main Street. Each suite in this beautifully restored 1901 Victorian Queen Anne home is completely self-contained (a plus for those not keen on sharing the bathroom with strangers). Visitors here will love the combination old-fashioned elegance with modern amenities. Some of the suites offer whirlpool baths big enough for two, while others have lovely claw-foot tubs—and every suite is furnished with heirloom antiques. Rhianna, the Iron Horse's innkeeper, is perhaps the most gracious host in the area. She is happy to give shop and restaurant recommendations to newcomers, and will also make dinner reservations for guests upon their request. In addition to its proximity to Main Street, the Iron Horse is near the riverfront and the Amtrak station. A $15 per-night discount is applied to any stay of more than one night.

The School House Bed and Breakfast in Rocheport (504 3rd St., 573/698-2022, www.schoolhousebb.com, $135–230) is a little off the beaten path—about an hour's drive west of Hermann—but well worth a side trip. This unique inn is an expertly converted, turn-of-the-20th-century schoolhouse, and it offers some great modern amenities. The school's original oak floors and 13-foot ceilings accentuate every addition, including private luxury baths complete with whirlpool tubs, fireplaces, antique furnishings, and luxury down bedding. Abundant windows flood every room with great morning light, and during the warm-weather months guests usually begin their day with gourmet coffee in the School House's serene garden. This bed-and-breakfast has been featured in numerous national publications, including *Midwest Living* and *Southern Living*. It is two blocks from the Katy Trail and a mile from Les Bourgeois Winery. Travelers should check the website for last-minute deals, particularly in the off-season.

PRACTICALITIES
Tourist Office

Information about Missouri wine country can be found on the Missouri Division of Tourism's website (www.visitmo.com). The Hermann Chamber of Commerce (207A Schiller St., 573/486-2313) maintains a web presence at www.hermannmo.com. You'll find the Augusta Chamber of

Commerce (5601 High St., 636/228-4005) on the web at www.augusta-missouri.com/chamber-commerce.

Media

Keep up-to-date on Hermann happenings with the town's weekly newspaper, the *Hermann Advertiser Courier*. Augusta distributes a bimonthly community newspaper, the *Augusta Neighborhood News*.

Getting There and Around

Highway 94 is the route to take. This scenic two-lane stretch south of US-40/64 is nicknamed the Weinstrasse, or "Wine Street." There are four family wineries along this road and eight more within a 10-mile radius. Simply take US-40/64 to I-94 and travel south. Numerous signs are posted to point visitors in the right direction.

It is recommended that travelers rent a car and drive, but train service is available as well. **Amtrak** provides train service to Hermann from the historic Kirkwood station and back again, via the *Kansas City Mule* and *A. Ann Rutledge*. The fare is approximately $20 each way. Visit www.amtrak.com for a complete timetable.

Cyclists should check out the Katy Trail (www.katytrail.org), as a 30-mile stretch of this bike route runs directly alongside the Weinstrasse.

EXCURSIONS

BACKGROUND

The Setting

GEOGRAPHY AND CLIMATE

St. Louis is located near the geographical center of the United States and stands at the confluence of the Missouri and Mississippi Rivers. Together with the Meramec River, these major waterways constitute the city's most outstanding geographical (and ecological) feature and border the city on nearly every side. The Mississippi River forms much of St. Louis's eastern border, the Missouri forms its northern boundary, and the Meramec River runs along its southern edge. Together, these rivers' broad floodplains have shaped St. Louis's gently rolling topography—and, despite plenty of human intervention, they continue to affect it today. In 1993, a "500-year" flood devastated the area, and in 2008 the waters rose once again, swelling the Meramec River to three times its normal size.

Not surprisingly, St. Louis is built upon the material of riverbeds. Beneath the city's surface is a thick crust of limestone and dolomite, corkscrewed with sinkholes and

©GATEWAY ARCH RIVERFRONT

caves. St. Louis's 62 square miles of zoysia lawn, pavement, and parkscapes hide a vast network of naturally occurring limestone caverns, as well as the seam of two major tectonic plates. The New Madrid Fault Line is a hair's breadth from the city proper and has been threatening St. Louis with a devastating, nonelective remodeling for the past century. In 1811, one of the largest earthquakes in recorded history toppled chimneys and reversed the flow of the Mississippi River. Residents have felt occasional rumblings ever since—including a spring 2008 quake that measured 5.2 on the Richter scale—and experts predict that an earthquake of even greater magnitude will occur before the year 2040.

The climate of this otherwise landlocked region is characterized by four full seasons and lengthy periods of high heat and humidity. Spring weather arrives as early as March, and July typically brings the year's highest temperatures. On average, St. Louisans suffer temperatures of 100-plus degrees five days out of every year—but, on the plus side, growing seasons are long and winters are relatively mild. Winter temperatures hover around 30 degrees Fahrenheit, while summer temps average 80 degrees. St. Louis receives an average of 23 inches of snow per year and more than 46 inches of rain.

The collision of the humid Gulf Stream and cool Canadian air masses helps keep St. Louis's median temperature at approximately 55 degrees—and also causes frequent shifts in weather conditions. Throughout the spring and summer months, severe thunderstorms strafe the city with damaging straight-line winds and (sometimes) golf ball–sized hail. They also whip up an occasional tornado, although it's been 50 years since one caused

significant damage here. The thunderstorms can cause travel delays, as can the fairly frequent ice storms that occur throughout the winter months. No matter the season, visitors to St. Louis should check the forecast and come prepared.

ENVIRONMENTAL ISSUES

While St. Louisans often joke about the area's unpredictable weather, the air quality here is no laughing matter. During the summer months, the region is blanketed by warm, heavy air that creates a less-than-ideal environment for allergy sufferers. People who believe themselves to be allergy-free are sometimes proven wrong when they move to St. Louis—thanks to abundant allergens like the yellow-green pollen that dusts windshields beginning in May.

In terms of air pollution, the region's record is fairly clean. St. Louis was the first city in the nation to enforce a set of laws meant to reduce air pollution. During the 1940s, in an effort to reduce the smog created by coal-burning, St. Louis launched one of the most effective clean-air campaigns to date. Today, the St. Louis Regional Clean Air Council continues this breathe-easy mission by monitoring the city's air quality and enforcing measures to reduce harmful vehicle emissions. The organization posts its findings daily via special billboards throughout the area, as well as on its website at www .cleanair-stlouis.com.

The city is also adopting LEED (Leadership in Energy and Environmental Design) standards for much of its new construction. The membership of the Missouri LEED chapter is growing quickly, and the United States Green Building Council has certified a dozen projects throughout the area. Of particular note is the Alberici Group head-quarters, a beautiful wind-powered, sun-lit office building not far from Lambert-St.

Louis International Airport. For more information on the Missouri chapter of LEED, visit http://chapters.usgbc.org/stlouis/.

History

THE FOUNDING OF ST. LOUIS

St. Louis has acquired quite a few nicknames over the years. "Mound City" is a nod to the area's first inhabitants, ancient tribes who shaped the river valley's topography with elaborate patterns of mounded earth. "Gateway City," St. Louis's more common nickname, refers both to its middle-of-the-country location and to its history; St. Louis was a trailhead during the great western migration. The city's full name is Saint Louis, a moniker bestowed by French settlers in honor of their king, Louis IX.

The French heritage here is strong, and it's particularly evident in the architecture of the city's oldest neighborhoods. In 1673, French explorers Louis Joliet and Jacques Marquette surveyed the Mississippi River Valley, the geographical feature from which St. Louis would rise. Five years later, Robert La Salle claimed the entirety of the river's banks for France and named the territory Louisiana (in honor of King Louis XIV). In the years that followed, the French government established settlements throughout this territory, but it wasn't until 1763 that France decided to make St. Louis the first stop on a north–south trade route.

The following February, French settler Auguste Chouteau laid out the city's New Orleans–inspired grid pattern. St. Louis's life as a successful river city had

begun. Trade along this important river route flourished over the next 150 years, thanks in no small part to the introduction of the steamboat. Great infusions of wealth pushed the city's boundaries west (the Paris Treaty of 1763 had granted the territory east of the Mississippi to Britain). In 1780, as the American Revolution ground on, the British attacked St. Louis and were soundly defeated by combined French and Spanish forces. In 1804, the United States obtained the area as part of the Louisiana Purchase, and St. Louis was incorporated as an American city soon after.

By the middle of the 19th century, St. Louis's thriving economy had transitioned from trade to manufacturing. The city's burgeoning industry was driven largely by incoming German and Irish immigrants, who took full advantage of St. Louis's proximity to the Mississippi River. This proximity, in conjunction with the ever-expanding railroads, gave manufacturers easy access to raw materials and affordable means for shipping. By the time the Civil War began, northern St. Louis had emerged as a major provider of furniture, machinery, lumber, coal, and livestock. The flourishing garment district along historic Washington Avenue supplied the nation with much of its first ready-to-wear apparel. In Midtown, manufacturers began producing some of the country's first Brass Era automobiles.

POPULATION DECLINE

It was at the height of this manufacturing era that St. Louis would see its largest population spike. By 1956, the city's population had reached nearly 900,000—but it began to decline soon after. By the mid-1980s, the city proper had lost 50 percent of its population. In fact, between 1957 and 2006, St. Louis experienced the sharpest population decline of any American city. There are many theories about this rapid loss, but the easiest theory to defend is also the most general: St. Louis simply could not adapt quickly enough to compete in a changing market. As more efficient means of transportation turned steamboats into antiquities, businesses began to leave the area in pursuit of better opportunities.

ST. LOUIS TODAY: BACK IN BUSINESS

Today, St. Louis is experiencing a re-emergence—thanks to another industry altogether. Leading biotech firms and world-class medical facilities are filling in the once-abandoned warehouse district between Forest Park Southeast and the Central West End. Bioengineering giant Monsanto continues to prosper in suburban St. Louis. Pfizer, the world's largest pharmaceutical company, operates one of its major U.S. research complexes in West St. Louis County. In conjunction with the Washington University School of Medicine, the Saint Louis University School of Medicine, and the St. Louis College of Pharmacy, Pfizer has helped establish St. Louis as a respected center of medical technology. Optimists

© BROOKE FOSTER

Dozens of small businesses have built lasting success in the once-residential Lafayette Square.

project that a "Silicon Valley of biotechnology" will someday stand in the place of departed stalwarts like TWA, McDonnell Douglas, and Chrysler.

In the meantime, local government and the St. Louis Regional Chamber and Growth Association (RCGA) are developing incentive programs meant to encourage business development and preservation—particularly in the city proper, where population loss has taken its greatest toll. In 1998, Missouri adopted a tax credit for the redevelopment of historic buildings, which made large-scale development more financially feasible. The incentive attracted dozens of developers from all over the nation; as a result, areas such as downtown's Washington Avenue have been redeveloped into mixed-use residential and retail districts. The city's redevelopment strategy received international recognition in 2007, when it was given the World Leadership Award for Urban Renewal. St. Louis also receives frequent accolades for its implementation of LEED's strict, eco-friendly development standards.

Government and Economy

Despite the common (mis)perception that the Midwest is politically conservative and primarily Republican, St. Louis is domi-nated by the Democratic Party—and has been for years. The city has not had a Republican mayor since 1949, nor have St.

© BROOKE FOSTER

Many of St. Louis's stately homes − including this one near the Compton Hill Reservoir − have survived despite the city's economic uncertainties.

© AUGUST JENNEWEIN

The multimillion-dollar Touhill Performing Arts Center brings top acts to the UMSL campus.

Louisans elected a Republican to a major city office since the 1970s. Twenty-seven of the city's twenty-eight aldermen are Democrats. St. Louis's mayoral office has set some important precedents, including an exceptionally even distribution of executive powers among nine elected city officials. The often-overlooked offices of comptroller, treasurer, and collector of revenue have significant influence here, as do the city's aldermen.

EDUCATION

St. Louis is home to several dozen colleges and universities, both public and private. Washington University and Saint Louis University enjoy the greatest renown on both local and national levels. Other major area institutions include Fontbonne University, Webster University (home to a terrific fine-arts program), the University of Missouri-St.

Louis, and Southern Illinois University-Edwardsville. The University of Missouri's flagship campus is located two hours west in Columbia, while the University of Illinois is three hours northeast.

Washington University is a significant economic force. The university reported $1.6 billion in expenditures in 2007, including over $900 million in payroll, and ongoing construction on the campus has created more than 3,000 jobs. A study commissioned in 2002 found that the university's overall economic impact on the region is $2.2 billion. In 2006 Saint Louis University, a Jesuit institution located in Midtown, boasted an operating revenue of $563 million and an endowment of $825 million. The university's new Chaifetz Arena is home to the school's popular Division I men's basketball team and also hosts national touring acts.

HEALTH CARE

St. Louis benefits from some of the nation's best and most affordable health care. Its impact on the local economy is substantial. The 13 hospitals of the BJC HealthCare network boast more than 26,000 employees and an annual net revenue of $2.8 billion, and BJC estimates that its contribution to the region's economy is $1.8 billion per year. BJC's flagship facility, Barnes-Jewish Hospital, is consistently ranked among the nation's top hospitals by *U.S. News & World Report*

and is also home to Washington University's renowned medical school. Both *U.S. News & World Report* and *Child* magazine have named BJC's St. Louis Children's Hospital one of the country's top pediatric facilities.

SSM Health Care employs 11,200 at seven hospitals, including St. Mary's Health Center and Cardinal Glennon Children's Medical Center. Several SSM facilities are teaching hospitals affiliated with Saint Louis University School of Medicine, as is Saint Louis University Hospital.

People and Culture

At the beginning of the 20th century, the population of St. Louis City was well over half a million and climbing. One-fifth of this population was foreign-born, and nearly half of it was German, but the demographics and population of the area have changed drastically in the past 100 years.

When considering St. Louis's census statistics, it's important to note that the populations of the city and the county are surveyed separately—and have been since St. Louis City separated from the larger St. Louis County in 1880. Today, a majority of St. Louisans live in the suburbs rather than in the city proper. Although the 2006 population of St. Louis City was just 347,181, the population of St. Louis County was 1,016,315. The massive migration to the suburbs began shortly after World War II, when the population boom created an outsized demand for housing. By 1950 there were 856,796 people living in St. Louis proper. By 2000, the number had dwindled dramatically, to 348,189. It was during those five decades that St. Louis

experienced the largest population decrease of any American city. Today, the numbers aren't exactly up, but the population decline has slowed down significantly.

St. Louisans are keenly aware of their city's history. They take pride in its rapid ascension as one of America's great early cities, and they smart at its mid-20th-century decline. As is true in most "second cities"—large metropolitan areas that aren't as wealthy or as culturally diverse as places like New York or San Francisco—St. Louisans subject their city to some good-natured teasing. For the most part, though, civic pride is strong. That pride can morph into occasional snobbery, as evidenced by native St. Louisans' favorite breaking-the-ice question: "So, where did you go to high school?" (St. Louis high schools vary widely in quality, reputation, and cost, so sometimes the inquisitor is actually asking a loaded question about socioeconomic standing.) The high-school question is only asked by one St. Louisan of another, though, so out-of-towners need not worry. St. Louisans are gracious and friendly, and almost always eager to share advice with visitors.

IMMIGRANT GROUPS

Many residents and urban planners are optimistic about St. Louis City's future, and a thriving immigrant culture plays a big part in that revival. Planners predict that the city will soon see a population surge, thanks to residential development downtown and to the unexpected revival in South City's once-beleaguered Bevo Mill neighborhood. In the 1990s, Bevo Mill's surplus of inexpensive housing (coupled with St. Louis's overall low cost of living) attracted more than 15,000 Bosnian refugees. The Bosnian community here is one of the largest in the United States; only Chicago has a bigger Bosnian population.

According to 2006 statistics gathered by the United States Census Bureau, St. Louis City and County are home to more than 28,300 Latinos and more than 38,400 people of Asian descent. There is also a strong Ethiopian and Eritrean community, and many Indian and Pakistani families live in both the city and in West St. Louis County.

AFRICAN AMERICAN CULTURE

In the city, African American and Caucasian populations are about equal. In the county, however, African Americans compose just a fifth of the population—which is disheartening evidence of the "white flight" that took place in St. Louis City in the mid-20th century. St. Louis owes much of its success and its cultural strength to the African American community. Scott Joplin, Maya Angelou, and Chuck Berry are just a few of the internationally known luminaries who hail from St. Louis, and St. Louis's historical role in the Dred Scott case makes it a crucial birthplace of the civil-rights struggle.

Although some areas of the city are well-integrated—particularly the neighborhoods surrounding Tower Grove Park and South Grand—St. Louis is plagued by de facto segregation. The city's north side is almost entirely African American, and while some neighborhoods are thriving, others suffer. Many in the community—both African American and Caucasian—feel that the mayor's office does little to support and strengthen north-side neighborhoods, and many of the once-beautiful buildings have fallen prey to speculators who blight entire areas with no real intention to develop.

Despite these obstacles, St. Louis's African American community is a significant force in the city's cultural development and business growth. Groups like the St. Louis Black Leadership Roundtable—a nonprofit composed of African American politicians, attorneys, journalists, law-enforcement officers, and educators—work to build voter awareness, to support the growth of black-owned businesses, and to "advocate for an improved climate of justice and fairness." Another force for change is the *St. Louis American,* the city's outstanding African American newspaper.

The Arts

ARTS, CRAFTS, AND FOLK TRADITIONS

Any city with a history as rich as St. Louis's is bound to have a strong folk-art tradition. Whether they're preserving centuries-old practices or putting new twists on the form, St. Louis's folk artists are a talented and dedicated bunch. Visitors to the city have many opportunities to see the tradition for themselves.

Many of St. Louis's most talented artisans create, display, and sell their work at the **Craft Alliance** (www.craftalliance.org). Since its establishment in 1964, this cooperative has helped artists make a living—and has educated a whole city in the process. The bright, funky Craft Alliance building in the Delmar Loop hosts classes for all ages and skill levels, and the retail shop features beautiful wares made by local hands. Unlike studios that only feature work in a specific medium, the alliance is broad in its definition of the word "craft." Glass, metal, fiber, clay, and wood crafts are all created and sold here. Craft Alliance funds itself through tuition, sales, and membership fees, and local groups such as the Regional Arts Commission often give grants to help the Alliance continue its excellent educational mission.

Despite its rather catch-all name, the **St. Louis Artists' Guild** (www.stlouisartistsguild.org) focuses primarily on classic and modern folk art—and does an outstanding job of it. Exhibits here vary from found-object collections to stunning metal sculptures to fascinating displays of "tattoo paintings." Particularly excellent are the frequent book-arts shows, which gather talent from all around the nation. The guild also houses the only non-university printmaking studio in the area, and visitors are welcome to rent space in the studio for just $6 an hour. Local artists frequently teach classes at the artists' guild, and children's work is displayed in the Monsanto Children's Gallery.

The **Portfolio Gallery** (www.portfolio-stl.com), on the northern edge of Midtown, features work in both the fine- and folk-art tradition. The gallery's mission is to preserve and foster the work of local African American artists, and talents on display here include watercolor painter Henry Dixon and the great portrait artist C'babi Bayoc. Founded by sculptor Robert A. Powell, the Portfolio Gallery has been a vibrant part of the St. Louis art scene for nearly 20 years.

On the south side of town, **Skif International** (www.skifo.com) is creating some of the most exciting, earth-friendly textiles around. While most of Skif's artwork is of the wearable variety, its beauty is just as impressive as its functionality. The owners of this folk-arty collaborative are part of a growing movement in St. Louis, one that takes the DIY ethos seriously and creates amazing art as a result. Dozens of like-minded artisans get together at the bi-annual **Rock n Roll Craft Show** (www.rocknrollcraftshow.com), a roving bazaar stocked with every cool handmade item imaginable. Many, many St. Louis shops carry items made by local craftspeople—and it's that kind of community support that makes the city's folk-art scene so continually viable.

LITERATURE

Although St. Louis's literary importance sometimes flies under the radar—even in the consciousness of the city's own residents—the literary history here is rich. Many of America's most important authors, poets, and playwrights have called the Gateway City home, and St. Louis is the subject of and setting for dozens of works.

Much of St. Louis's literary history survives in its very buildings. The childhood home of T. S. Eliot (*The Wasteland, The Love Song of J. Alfred Prufrock*) is at the corner of Westminster Place and Euclid Avenue in the Central West End. Eliot claimed that the Missouri and Mississippi Rivers made a deeper impression upon him than any other part of the world. Another award-winning poet, Sara Teasdale, fondly referred to the city throughout her body of work and even named a poem in its honor: *Sunset (St. Louis)*.

Novelists and playwrights also found inspiration in St. Louis. Kate Chopin (*The Awakening*) spent her young married life here before moving to New Orleans. Chopin is buried at Cavalry Cemetery in North St. Louis, as is Tennessee Williams (*The Glass Menagerie, A Streetcar Named Desire*). Maya Angelou, American poet laureate and bestselling author of *I Know Why the Caged Bird Sings*, spent many childhood summers visiting her mother in St. Louis; several of her stories are based on time spent in the city.

Young literary lights also focus on St. Louis. Gifted postmodern novelist Jonathan Franzen, who grew up in Webster Groves, set his ambitious political thriller *The Twenty-Seventh City* in St. Louis and lived in the Central West End while composing the novel. Mystery writer Ridley

ST. LOUIS'S FAMOUS FACES

On the whole, St. Louisans are welcoming and down to earth – but don't let that humble facade fool you. This river city has produced dozens of famous people, from major-league sluggers to matinee idols. If the St. Louis Walk of Fame included all of the area's celebs, it would likely stretch for a few more miles. Following are people who were born in St. Louis or lived here for a significant part of their lives.

Actors and other Hollywood types: Kate Capshaw, Phyllis Diller, Redd Foxx, Bob Gale (cowriter of *Back to the Future*), John Goodman, Betty Grable, Robert Guillaume, Jon Hamm (*Mad Men*'s Don Draper), Kevin Kline, Vincent Price

Artists and writers: Maya Angelou, William S. Burroughs, Kate Chopin, Charles Eames, Stanley Elkin, Jonathan Franzen, William H. Gass, Al Hirschfeld, A. E. Hotchner, Marianne Moore, Gyo Obata, Irma Rombauer, Ernest Trova, Mona Van Duyn, Tennessee Williams

Athletes and broadcasters: Cool Papa Bell, Yogi Berra, Jack Buck, Joe Buck, Harry Caray, Jimmy Connors, Bob Costas, Dwight F. Davis, Joe Garagiola, Jackie Joyner-Kersee, Sonny Liston, Stan Musial, "Cowboy" Bob Orton, Ozzie Smith, Rusty Wallace, Dick Weber

Singers and musicians: Josephine Baker, Fontella Bass, Chuck Berry, Grace Bumbry, T-Bone Burnett, Miles Davis, Grant Green, Julius Hemphill, Johnnie Johnson, Scott Joplin, Albert King, Oliver Lake, Nelly, David Sanborn, Clark Terry, Ike and Tina Turner

Pearson (*The Body of David Hayes, No Witnesses*) divides his time between St. Louis and Sun Valley, Idaho. Talented young author (and *New York Times* bestseller) Curtis Sittenfeld (*Prep, American Wife*) also currently lives in St. Louis.

Thanks to its rich history and still-thriving community of up-and-coming authors, the city's literary tradition continues to this day. Also key to St. Louis's literary success are its great universities and network of notable literary publications. The imitable William Gass (*Omensetter's Luck, The Tunnel*) resides here and for years was a professor of humanities at Washington University. Wash. U.'s program for English graduate studies is one of the top in the country. The faculty has included novelist Stanley Elkin, 1988 United States Poet Laureate Howard Nemerov, and the remarkable husband-and-wife poets Donald Finkel and Constance Urdang. Today, the faculty roster boasts some of the academic scene's most promising newcomers.

The English department at Webster University, in the suburban enclave of Webster Groves, is a hidden gem. Although MFAs in writing are not yet offered here, the undergraduate department has snapped up a sharp staff of Ivy League–educated instructors from all over the country, and the program's reputation in the community is growing. Excellent literary publications dedicated to preserving the area's written heritage include the University of Missouri's *Missouri Review* (www.missourireview.org) and the local quarterly *River Styx* (www.riverstyx.org).

MUSIC

Despite its struggles with population decline and limited visibility in the professional music world, St. Louis's contribution to American music has been immense. There is simply no way to overstate music's impact on St. Louis—and St. Louis's music's impact on the nation. The Gateway City has served as a musical incubator, fostering both young artists and young movements. Many St. Louis musicians have been very successful, even revolutionary.

St. Louisan Scott Joplin chartered a movement. He is widely considered the father of ragtime, and he composed the most famous example of that genre: "Maple Leaf Rag." Visitors can tour the modest 19th-century walkup where Joplin wrote many of his legendary songs. The visionary Miles Davis—who was born across the river in Alton, Illinois, and spent much of his life in East St. Louis—changed the face of jazz. Josephine Baker, the extraordinary chanteuse and civil-rights proponent, was born here and got her start with the St. Louis Cabaret.

As the city approached its population peak in the mid-20th century, it was contributing more than its fair share to the emerging rock and soul genres. Recording studios popped up all over the city. Chuck Berry, one of rock's most influential forefathers, grew up in north St. Louis. In the 1950s, he recorded the now-legendary songs "Johnny B. Goode" and "Maybelline." After decades of history-making collaboration, Berry returned to his hometown, and to this day he plays monthly shows at Blueberry Hill in the Delmar Loop.

Many blues giants have also called the St. Louis area home. The St. Louis blues—a unique, piano-driven sound with roots in ragtime and Delta blues—can be heard almost any night of the week at beloved joints like B.B.'s Jazz, Blues, & Soups and Beale on

Broadway. Sadly, many of the genre's most talented musicians have passed on in recent years, owing to advanced age and limited health care. Their torch is carried, though, by incredible blues prodigies like the teen-aged Marquise Knox.

Funk and soul were also nurtured in St. Louis. In 1959, Ike Turner met Anna Mae Bullock (known to millions by her adopted stage name, Tina Turner) in a St. Louis nightclub. The pair became the Ike & Tina Turner Revue and turned out hit after hit, including the barn-burning "Proud Mary." While Ike's poor treatment of Tina often overshadowed the music itself, the Turners' impact upon soul and R&B music cannot be underestimated.

In recent years, St. Louis and its surrounding suburbs have produced many successful musicians. After studying at the University of Columbia, Grammy-winning musician Sheryl Crow taught elementary-school music classes in the St. Louis exurb of Fenton. Story of the Year, a post-grunge outfit currently signed to the major label Epitaph, formed in St. Louis. Musicians from the local twang scene are responsible for some of alt-country's most respected bands, including Wilco, Son Volt, and the Bottle Rockets. Members of the successful glam rock-psychobilly band 7 Shot Screamers grew up in Fenton (and tour with the legendary Exene Cervenka under the *nom du stage* The Original Sinners). Members of the funk-reggae-rock hybrid The Urge attended high school together nearby, as did the Grammy-winning hip-hop artists Nelly, Chingy, and Murphy Lee.

FILM

The most iconic St. Louis film is, of course, *Meet Me in St. Louis*—the classic 1944

Judy Garland film that added ditties like "The Trolley Song" and "Have Yourself a Merry Little Christmas" to the American show-tune canon. With the 1904 World's Fair as its backdrop, *Meet Me in St. Louis* made its title city look at once progressive, romantic, and whimsical (never mind the fact that most of it was shot on a Culver City back lot).

Films released after St. Louis's early-20th-century heyday provide a more realistic, if not always Chamber of Commerce–approved, glimpse into the city. *The Great St. Louis Bank Robbery,* a Steve McQueen vehicle released in 1959, capitalized on St. Louis's late-'50s noir appeal (the bank in question is Southwest Bank, a gorgeous building that's still in business at the corner of Kingshighway Boulevard and Southwest Avenue).

In 1981, action-adventure director John Carpenter filmed much of *Escape from New York* in St. Louis. This decision was the ultimate in backhanded compliments: Carpenter chose St. Louis because much of its downtown looked like a bombed-out, apocalyptic New York. (Fortunately for downtown boosters, Carpenter would be out of luck today.) Crucial scenes were filmed at the Old Chain of Rocks Bridge, the Civil Courts Building, and Union Station. *National Lampoon's Vacation* (1983) took another swipe at St. Louis: The Griswolds' car breaks down in St. Louis and, in a scene that now seems cringe-inducingly racist, a cadre of young African American kids strip the vehicle.

One of the more interesting St. Louis film stories revolves around *White Palace,* the steamy Susan Sarandon-James Spader movie that came out in 1990. The original name was *White Castle*, a real Midwest burger chain mentioned in the novel upon which the movie is based. The folks at White Castle corporate refused to lend their name to the racy flick, so Universal Pictures shot the film at a downtown St. Louis diner. The diner was renamed "White Palace" for the duration of filming—but when the owners asked to keep the name, Universal Pictures said no. The restaurant changed its name to "White Knight" and slings steak-and-egg platters to this day.

A few recent movies have been better for civic pride. *The Game of Their Lives*, released in 2005, is based on the true story of the 1950 United States soccer team that beat England in a crucial World Cup–qualifying match. Because many of the team members grew up on the Hill, St. Louis's predominantly Italian neighborhood, much of the film was shot here. Merchants and restaurant owners willingly altered their facades to lend a true 1950s feel to the film, turning one of St. Louis's most charming neighborhoods into a picture-perfect backdrop. That same year, St. Louis had another (brief) star turn in *Fever Pitch*, the Jimmy Fallon-Drew Barrymore romantic comedy about an over-the-top Red Sox fan.

ESSENTIALS

Getting There

Coast-dwellers may consider St. Louis "flyover country," but it's precisely that on-the-way-to-everywhere status that makes the city so accessible. Lambert-St. Louis International Airport is short on creature comforts but quite navigable. Visitors can also arrive in and depart from St. Louis via train, bus, or automobile; several major highways (including I-70, I-55, I-64, and I-44) run right through the city.

BY AIR

Located 15 miles from downtown, **Lambert-St. Louis International Airport** (314/890-1370 or 314/241-5820, www.lambert-stlouis.com) was once one of the busiest hubs in the nation. Before it stopped offering direct international flights, this airport welcomed more than 20 million passengers and 460,000 flights each year. These numbers have dwindled significantly in the past decade, but Lambert still hosts a few major air carriers, including American Airlines (www.americanairlines.com), Continental (www.continental.com), Delta (www.delta.com), and Northwest (www.nwa.com) in the Main Terminal and

Southwest (www.southwest.com) and USA 3000 (www.usa3000.com) in the East Terminal. While Lambert's dining options are limited at best, the airport recently inked a $16 million expansion contract with its concessions provider. By 2011, the renovations will be complete on the airport's existing restaurants, and eight new eateries will be added—including upscale spots and airport outposts of local favorites. For now, however, Lambert's conveniences are sufficient if not impressive. One particularly welcome amenity is the business center (with computer docking stations, printers, copiers, and fax machines) on the lower level of the Main Terminal. An interfaith chapel is located next to the Main Terminal's baggage claim. This chapel, which is staffed by a chaplain seven days a week, offers a Catholic mass on weekends.

Lambert-St. Louis International opened in the 1930s. The Main Terminal's striking domed structure, considered a forerunner in modern airport design, was built in the mid-'50s to the specifications of architect Minoru Yamasaki. While passing through the airport, you may want to visit the legendary *Spirit of St. Louis*—the single-engine monoplane that Charles Lindbergh piloted across the Atlantic Ocean. *Spirit* is suspended above Lambert's central security checkpoint. Also of note is the five-panel installation *Black Americans in Flight*. This series of paintings, located near the baggage-claim area, pays tribute to African American aeronautic heroes from 1917 to the present.

To and From the Airport

Visitors looking for cheap transportation to and from the airport will likely be most pleased with **MetroLink,** the city's efficient light-rail system. The station is a five-minute walk from the Arrivals gate, and trains depart every 25 minutes. You can catch a ride on MetroLink between 4:30 A.M. and 11:10 P.M. Monday through Friday, and between 5 A.M. and 11 P.M. Saturday and Sunday. One-ride tickets are $2 ($1 for students and seniors), and all-day passes are $4.50. Alternatively, a two-hour pass is available for $3.50 and comes with a free transfer at the Central West End/ DeBaliviere station. From this point, you can transfer to trains headed to multiple destinations, including downtown and Grand Boulevard.

Cabs queue up right outside the Main and East Terminals' baggage claims, but be aware that the ride is a rather expensive one. The fare from Lambert-St. Louis to downtown is rarely less than $40, and the cab companies tack on an additional $3 "airport use fee." The popular SuperShuttle service does not operate at Lambert, but many area hotels offer a similar service for a nominal charge (or for free). Limousines and private cars are also available.

Long- and short-term parking options are abundant at Lambert, and prices vary fairly widely. One of the cheapest options—just $6 a day for remote parking in an uncovered lot—is available through **SuperPark** (314/890-2800, www.superparkinglot.com). For $12 per day, SuperPark offers parking in a lot that is much closer to the Main Terminal. SuperPark's garage-parking option gets you the closest and costs $20 per day. **The Parking Spot** (314/426-4510 or 314/428-5146, www.theparkingspot.com) offers remote covered parking (valet service is also available) and a free, nonstop shuttle to the airport. Daily rates range $11.50–17.50, and the website always features a coupon. Prices at **FastTrack Airport Parking** (314/428-4204, www.fasttrack.com) range from $8.95 per day (for outdoor self-parking) to $14.95 per day (for covered valet parking). Like The Parking Spot, FastTrack operates a 24-hour shuttle to the airport. Customers who book their parking reservation on FastTrack's website receive a 10 percent discount.

Car Rental

Travelers arriving at Lambert-St. Louis International Airport have their pick of rental-car agencies. Outside the baggage claim, you'll find representatives from eight of the major companies, including **Hertz** (800/654-3131, www.hertz.com), **Budget** (800/527-0700, www.budget.com), and St. Louis–based **Enterprise** (800/261-7331, www.enterprise.com).

BY CAR

Many major highways run right through St. Louis, making the city very accessible to road warriors. Those traveling on **I-44** will want to take Exit 208 (Park Avenue), which will deposit them in downtown St. Louis. Travelers on **I-55** can reach downtown by connecting with **I-64/U.S. 40** (signs for St. Louis/U.S. 40 W/I-64 W) and then exiting at 40A (Ninth Street). From I-70, take exit 250B to merge onto North Memorial Drive.

BY TRAIN

At the turn of the 20th century, visitors to St. Louis arrived in style, as locomotives chugged into elegant Union Station. Today, the structurally stunning Union Station houses chain restaurants and a lackluster mall, and those who choose to travel by train will arrive in and depart from St. Louis's downtown **Amtrak station** (550 S. 16th St., 314/331-3309, www.amtrak.com); take one step inside, and you'll understand why locals have nicknamed the place "Amshack." Still, the fares are reasonable, and the trains themselves are pleasant. Popular destinations include Kansas City ($25, 5.5 hours) and Chicago ($23 to $42, 5.5 hours), for which there are several departures daily. The ride to Chicago is particularly lovely, as it wends through tiny Illinois towns and verdant countryside. The volunteer-run, historic train station in Kirkwood is far more charming than the downtown depot, but daily train service is limited to day-trip jaunts to places like Alton, Illinois, and Washington, Missouri.

BY BUS

You won't find an operational train service at Union Station, but you *will* find the pickup point for **Megabus** (877/462-6342 or www.megabus.com). A Scottish concept that came to the U.S. fairly recently, Megabus offers nonstop service to and from Chicago, twice a day, for fares as low as *one dollar*. Other destinations in its affordable inter-city network include Kansas City, Columbia, and Bloomington-Normal. (Do note that tickets must be purchased online in advance.)

Located downtown, **Greyhound** (1450 N. 13th St., 314/231-4485, www.greyhound.com) offers a much more complete, though less expedient, service. Here, visitors will find buses headed for most major cities, as well as popular Midwestern destinations such as Columbia and Kansas City. Route and ticket information are available at Greyhound's website.

Getting Around

PUBLIC TRANSPORTATION

Getting around St. Louis is inexpensive and fairly convenient thanks to **Metro**, the area's transit authority. Metro operates both the bus and the MetroLink (the region's light-rail system), and together these can take you practically anywhere—for cheap. Metro passes allow travelers to transfer from bus to light rail as needed, and every light-rail station is conveniently near a bus stop. A one-ride ticket aboard either the bus or MetroLink is $2, while a two-hour, multi-use pass (useful for short return trips and transfers) is $2.25. For visitors planning to do most of their sight-seeing via public transportation, a one-day pass is probably the best deal: For just $4.50, the pass allows unlimited, all-day use of both the bus and the light-rail system. If you are staying in St. Louis for more than a couple of days, consider a weekly (seven-day) pass, which is available for $20. The majority of MetroLink stations (with the exception of the downtown stops) offer free or inexpensive public parking, making light rail a great alternative for drivers looking to save money and fuel.

At www.metrolinkstlouis.org, travelers can view route maps, plan their trips, check bus and MetroLink time tables, and purchase passes in advance with a credit card.

The MetroLink has two lines that meet in the West End, at the Forest Park/ DeBaliviere station. From this point, one can travel as far east as Fairview Heights, Illinois, and as far west as Shrewsbury. MetroLink trains also run to such inner suburbs as Maplewood. Points of interest made easily accessible by the MetroLink include tourist favorites such as the Gateway Arch and Busch Stadium, shopping destinations like the Galleria and Brentwood Promenade, and the Delmar Loop and Washington Avenue entertainment districts. The recently established 93 Midtown bus route connects the downtown area to some of the city's most popular tourist destinations. Via the 93 Midtown, visitors can disembark at the Anheuser-Busch Brewery, the City Museum, Grand Center, Cathedral Basilica, the Missouri Botanical Garden, and the historic Hill neighborhood.

© AMY FERGUSON

MetroLink, St. Louis's efficient light-rail system, is quickly expanding to meet commuters' needs.

DRIVING

Unfortunately—in light of rapidly ascending fuel prices—a car is the most convenient way to get around St. Louis. There are some perks to assuage your driving headache, though. In all but Clayton and the downtown area, parking is readily available and frequently free. Traffic congestion is minimal outside of peak drive times, and a car offers the convenience of not having to abide by the Metro time table (buses often run in excess of 30 minutes apart). Be forewarned, though, that newcomers often find St. Louis's long, name-shifting streets confusing. A good street guide is highly recommended; the *Rand McNally St. Louis Street Guide* is particularly useful.

TAXIS

St. Louis is not a cab-hailing sort of town. Visitors seeking a taxi will have to call for one; restaurants and bars always keep a few companies' numbers on hand. Locals don't frequently use taxis, so the only place cabs converge en masse is at the airport. Popular taxi companies servicing the area include **Laclede Cab** (314/652-3456) and **Metropolitan Cab** (314/773-1000). For journeys outside of St. Louis proper, a traveler's best bet is **St. Louis County Cab** (314/991-5300). A complete listing of taxi companies can be found at http://stlouis .missouri.org/transportation/cabs.html.

BICYCLING

St. Louis was recently declared one of the nation's most dangerous cities for cyclists, but nonprofit groups such as **Bike St. Louis** and **TrailNet** are working to turn the tide. Visit their useful websites (www .bikestlouis.org and www.trailnet.org) for guides to the city's existing bike lanes, tips for mapping out trips, and downloadable maps. By

© BROOKE FOSTER

Bike St. Louis's clearly marked routes are a dream come true for two-wheeled tourists.

2009, Bike St. Louis, the city's largest public-interest group, expects to have established more than 77 miles of dedicated bike and shared-traffic lanes. On a regional level, the **Great Rivers Greenway District** is working to establish a Missouri-wide system of interconnected parks and trails. Information on their progress can be found at www.greatrivers.info.

DISABLED ACCESS

All Metro buses are equipped with wheelchair lifts and universal wheelchair tie-down systems. Metro also offers small, similarly outfitted vans for door-to-door service, but interested parties must prove they meet eligibility requirements by applying for a Call-A-Ride Plus ID. The process usually takes a week, and reservations for rides need to be made at least 24 hours in advance. For more information, call 314/982-1510 or visit www.metrostlouis.org.

Tips for Travelers

WEATHER

The weather in St. Louis can be very unpredictable, particularly as the seasons shift from winter to spring. Those planning a March or April visit are advised (only half-jokingly) to bring shorts, tank tops, long underwear, and galoshes. If locals overhear visitors complaining about the weather, they'll likely advise the out-of-towners to "just wait a few hours." Often, this advice is spot on.

The growing season here is long, which explains the many farms and orchards that dot the landscape just outside St. Louis. Still, the area fully experiences all meteorological extremes. St. Louis receives an average of 43 inches of rain per year and has an average of 164 cloudy days. Visitors with a strong distaste for heat and humidity will likely be uncomfortable in July and August, when temperatures can break 100 degrees. Winters aren't quite as harsh here as in other Midwestern burgs, although the mercury can dip into the single digits. Spring brings a lot of rain (often accompanied by a lot of thunder), but it also ushers in the city's most beautiful days, along with temperatures around 70 degrees. Autumn in eastern Missouri is absolutely dazzling, as golden light falls across the numerous bright-red trees. Check out weather updates and related travel tips at www.weather .com, or read the local forecast at www .stltoday.com.

HOURS

True to its Midwestern roots, St. Louis is a city that goes to bed rather early. Only a handful of bars—mostly concentrated downtown and in South City—stay open until 3 A.M., with the majority closing at 1 A.M. (or even earlier, if business is slow). South Grand Boulevard can become particularly chaotic on weekend nights, as revelers migrate en masse from the 1 A.M. bars to the 3 A.M. bars. Cops patrol the area on foot and in squad cars, but visitors who dislike drunken shouting (and the occasional fight) may want to call it a night after 1 A.M.

Most St. Louis restaurants also close up shop fairly early. Some places do offer limited late-night menus, but be advised that dinner service typically ends by 10 P.M. on weeknights and 11 P.M. on weekends. In St. Louis, it's usually best to eat dinner before any other evening activities—by midnight, your choices narrow to fast food joints and 24-hour diners.

The financial and business center of downtown St. Louis shuts its doors around 6 P.M., but visitors will find plenty of dining and entertainment options on Washington Avenue, downtown's vibrant main drag. Drinking and dancing last till 3 A.M. at most Wash. Ave. hotspots, and even many of the boutiques stay open till 9 or 10 P.M. on weekend nights.

TIPPING

The tipping standard for full-service dining in St. Louis is 15–20 percent of the total bill, including alcohol. Today, many in the service industry consider 15 percent to be insulting, but rude or inattentive servers shouldn't expect much more. Good servers average about 18 percent over the course of an evening by being knowledgeable and courteous. (Remember, too, that tips make up the bulk of a waitperson's income; servers in Missouri currently earn $3.25 per hour.) Bartenders are tipped between $1 and $2 per drink, or 20 percent of the tab. At many St. Louis bars, particularly the popular ones, your generous tips will be rewarded with faster service. Sommeliers are generally tipped 15 percent of wine sales. Standard gratuity for takeout and delivery is 10 percent. At nicer restaurants, where preparing a takeout order is an exception to the usual routine, you may want to tip closer to 15 percent.

Practically every popular restaurant downtown and in Clayton offers valet service. Because this service is often complimentary, it's nice to be a bit generous with the tip (between $3 and $4 is standard). Coat-check attendants typically receive $1 per checked item. If you travel by taxi, tip your driver 10–15 percent of the total fare.

Hair stylists and salon technicians (such as manicurists) are usually tipped 15 percent, as are masseurs. Feel free to tip above that, though, for particularly good service—or if the salon or spa is high-end. In hotels, tipping expectations vary significantly. Consider leaving between $2 and $10 per day for the housekeeping staff, depending on the quality of the hotel and the work required to put your room back in order. Room-service attendants typically receive 10–15 percent of the total bill, and bell-desk employees are often given $2–3 per bag. It's perfectly fine to ask a hotel's concierge about tipping procedures—and, in all tipping situations, it's nice to err on the side of generosity.

SMOKING

Thanks to its lax smoking laws (and abundance of fried foods and beer), St. Louis has long held a reputation for being one of America's most unhealthy cities. For the past several years, individual businesses have been leading the smoke-free charge. Many bars, restaurants, and hotels ban smoking on their premises (visit www.breatheasymo.org for a complete list). Local government has long discussed a citywide smoking ban and an increase on cigarette taxation, but initial attempts at enacting such legislation were voted down in 2006. For now, the city requires that all businesses post signs stating their smoking policies, and proponents of the ban have gone back to the drawing board.

Health and Safety

CRIME

When Morgan Quitno Press announced that St. Louis was one of the most dangerous cities in the nation, St. Louisans responded with a mixture of anger and disbelief. From South City to Webster Groves, from Richmond Heights to Dogtown, the St. Louis area is imbued with strong civic pride. Many residents have spent their entire lives here. They went to school here, raised families here—and they can't imagine living anywhere else. On many of St. Louis's tree-lined avenues, nothing bad *ever* seems to happen. Still, the statistics (particularly in relation to property crimes and nuisance crimes) tell a slightly different story. As would be true in any large city, visitors are advised to exercise caution, particularly when exploring unfamiliar places on foot.

The revitalization of St. Louis's urban core is an ongoing success story, and most neighborhoods are perfectly safe by day. Still, there are areas that should be avoided altogether. The once-thriving outdoor mall across from Crown Candy Kitchen in North City fell victim to neglect and abandonment, and now exists in a seemingly permanent state of deterioration. Entire neighborhoods of condemned and dilapidated homes in this area (just north of downtown's Washington Avenue) have met the same fate, and the result is both eerie and sad. Areas that are reasonably safe during the day but require extra vigilance at night include the northernmost edge of the Central West End, the quiet fringes of Soulard and downtown, the area surrounding South Broadway, and the neighborhoods due east of Grand Boulevard.

The best rule to apply is that of common sense: If an area appears dangerous or abandoned, tourists should avoid it. As in any large city, visitors should be equal parts adventurous and vigilant. At night, stick to well-lit, pedestrian-friendly areas. Explore less-familiar areas during the day and with a friend or two, and don't be shy about asking the locals for advice. Most St. Louisans love to talk about their city and are more than happy to help tourists.

HOSPITALS AND PHARMACIES

BJC HealthCare (www.bjc.org) operates several major hospitals in the area, including **Barnes-Jewish Hospital** and **St. Louis Children's Hospital** in the Central West End. BJC also operates health-care centers in the suburbs, including **Missouri Baptist Medical Center** in West County, the **Christian Memorial Hospital** in St. Charles County, and **Progress West Healthcare Center** in O'Fallon.

St. Louis is fortunate to have world-class health care, particularly in the area of pediatrics. Both St. Louis Children's Hospital and **Cardinal Glennon Children's Medical Center** (on Grand Boulevard) continually rank among the best children's hospitals in the country. Cardinal Glennon is operated by SSM Health Care (www.ssmhc .com), which also runs **St. Joseph Hospital** in Kirkwood, **DePaul Health Center** in Bridgeton, and **St. Mary's Health Center** in Richmond Heights. Hospitals outside of the huge BJC and SSM systems include **St. Luke's Hospital** in Chesterfield (www .stlukes-stl.com), **St. John's Mercy Medical Center** on New Ballas Road (www.stjohns

mercy.org), and **St. Anthony's Medical Center** (www.stanthonysmedcenter.com), which maintains urgent-care facilities in the suburbs of Arnold, Fenton, and Lemay. The Saint Louis University Medical School operates the **Saint Louis University Hospital** (www.sluhospital.com) and its neighboring state-of-the-art cancer center.

Popular insurance providers in St. Louis include **Aetna, AFLAC, Blue Cross Blue Shield,** and **United Healthcare.** The national drugstore chain **Walgreens** operates locations all over the area, and most locations offer a 24-hour pharmacy. **Rite Aid** and **CVS** also operate pharmacies in the area. For a complete listing of Walgreens, Rite Aid, and CVS pharmacies, as well as the many independently owned pharmacies in the area, visit www.yellowpages.com.

EMERGENCY SERVICES

To call the police, or in the case of a fire or a medical emergency, dial 911. (Call 314/231-1212 for nonemergency services.) If you experience a power outage or other electrical emergency in St. Louis, dial 314/342-1000. Direct any calls about gas emergencies to 314/342-0800 (if this number is busy, dial 314/621-6960). The Poison Center can be reached at 314/772-5200. To report a water or sewer emergency in St. Louis, dial 314/768-6260. The toll-free number for the St. Louis Regional CrimeStoppers is 866/371-8477.

Information and Services

MEDIA AND COMMUNICATION
Phones and Area Codes

The area code for the City of St. Louis and its innermost suburbs is 314. In May 1999, many towns in West St. Louis County transitioned from 314 to 636. The 636 area code serves eastern-central Missouri, including the West County suburbs of Chesterfield, Ballwin, and Wildwood; the cities of Union and Troy; and all of St. Charles County and Jefferson County. The 618 area code serves the Metro East, a swath of Illinois considered part of the Greater St. Louis region. Towns using the 618 area code include Belleville, Alton, and Granite City. It is not necessary to dial an area code when calling from within that code's region.

Internet Services

Visitors can go online at all branches of the **St. Louis Public Library** (314/241-2288, www.slpl.org). Internet access is free at each branch, although a temporary library card is required and can be obtained by showing a state-issued driver's license or valid passport. Wireless access is available at numerous cafés, bars, and restaurants around town; an up-to-date list of WiFi hotspots can be found at www.wififreespot.com/mo.html (just scroll down to the St. Louis section). Some of the most popular places—think strong signals, lots of electrical outlets, and staff who won't rush you away from your table—include all **Saint Louis Bread Co.** locations (www.panerabread.com), all three outposts of **Companion** bakery (www.companionstl.com), and all **Kaldi's Coffee House** locations. Most major hotels also offer free high-speed wireless, and the entire city center of Clayton is a wireless hot spot.

© BROOKE FOSTER

Wow your friends with this bit of trivia: St. Louis is home to the world's largest Amoco sign.

Mail and Messenger Services

Visitors will have little trouble finding a convenient post office, as the **United States Postal Service** operates branches in nearly every St. Louis neighborhood. To find a specific location, visit www.usps.com or call 800/275-8777. For international shipping or overnight delivery, consider using **UPS** (800/742-5877, www.ups.com), **FedEx** (800/463-3333, www.fedex.com), or **DHL** (800/225-5345, www.dhl-usa.com). All three of these companies have St. Louis stores and drop boxes; visit the websites to find the nearest location. Post office boxes may be rented at **The UPS Store** (4579 Laclede Ave., 314/361-5505, www.theupsstore.com) or **Pak Mail** (12545 Olive Blvd., 314/469-6116, www.pakmail.com). The majority of Pak Mail locations are in St. Louis County and the Metro East, while The UPS Store has locations all throughout the city and county. Copying, faxing, packing, and shipping services are available at The UPS Store as well as at **FedEx-Kinko's** (800/254-6567, http://fedex.kinkos.com).

Bike messengers are fairly uncommon in St. Louis, but there are several courier companies that deliver by car. Your choices include **Access Courier** (314/962-8000, www.accesscourier.com), **Ontime Express** (314/729-7878, www.ontimeexpress.net), and **JS Logistics** (800/814-2634, www.jslogistics.com).

Magazines and Newspapers

The *St. Louis Post-Dispatch* is the city's only major daily, although the area once boasted several. The *Globe-Democrat,* St. Louis's last competing daily, was shuttered in 1986 after more than 130 years in operation. The *St. Louis Sun,* founded in 1989 by the publishing company responsible for the still-thriving *St. Louis Suburban Journals,* folded in less than a year. A good source for local news and weather, the *Post-Dispatch* is hanging in there—and adapting to 21st-century journalism at its website, www.stltoday.com.

Despite the *Post-Dispatch*'s tenacity, however, there is some discontent in the newsroom. Once celebrated for its liberal, humanist leanings and top-notch editorial staff, the daily lost some of its cachet after a hotly contested 2005 buyout. The *Post-Dispatch* was founded by Joseph Pulitzer in 1878 and, for more than a century, enjoyed the auspicious reputation associated with the good Pulitzer name. Today, the paper is owned by the publicly traded media company Lee Enterprises, one of the largest newspaper conglomerates in the nation. Many old-guard staff members were laid off or accepted buyouts, and the *Post-Dispatch* is frequently criticized for its heavy reliance on wire-service stories and guest editorials. Additional massive layoffs in 2007 and 2008 did little to quell people's fears about this rapidly declining dynasty.

St. Louis also has a number of weeklies. The **St. Louis Suburban Journal** (http://suburbanjournals.stltoday.com) is the umbrella company for 40 publications in the region, including 31 community newspapers (such as the *South County Journal, West County Journal,* the *Kirkwood-Webster Journal,* and the magazine-style *Ladue News*). The **St. Louis Business Journal,** published each Friday, offers comprehensive coverage of the region's business news. On Thursdays, St. Louis's alternative weekly, the **Riverfront Times** (www.riverfronttimes.com), hits the streets. The *Riverfront Times* features in-depth reporting and the most exhaustive arts and entertainment coverage in the area. Owned by national conglomerate Village Voice Media, the *Riverfront Times* has social commentary and extensive music listings that make it particularly popular with twenty- and thirtysomethings. The paper is free and can be found at bars, restaurants, shops, and clubs all over the city.

Strong reporting and excellent opinion columns are par for the course in the **St. Louis American** (www.stlouisamerican.com), the city's African American weekly. Established in 1928, the *American* covers news, politics, entertainment, and more. Other African American weeklies include the **St. Louis Argus** (www.stlouisargus.com) and the **St. Louis Sentinel** (www.stlouissentinel.com). **Limelight,** the region's African American monthly, addresses current issues with insight and historical perspective.

Visitors to St. Louis should seek out a copy of the **Evening Whirl** (www.myspace.com/thewhirl1938). The 70-year-old *Whirl,* which reports on local crime using delightfully over-the-top purple prose, has earned an enormous cult following. At the hands of *Whirl* scribes, local politicians earn 1930s-gangster-style nicknames, and crimes are recounted in cartoonishly lurid detail.

Red Latina (www.redlatinastl.com) serves the city's Hispanic community, and the **Jewish Light** (www.stljewishlight.com) focuses on issues of importance to Jewish St. Louisans. **The Vital Voice** (www.thevitalvoice.com) is a biweekly paper serving the lesbian, gay, bisexual, and transgendered communities throughout the city and the state.

Over the past two decades, regionally focused magazines have flourished in St. Louis. **Sauce,** a tabloid-sized monthly, covers the city's dynamic restaurant scene and includes the sort of food and travel writing made popular by *Saveur* and *Bon Appétit*. You can pick up *Sauce* (it's free) at most restaurants and specialty food shops in the region. And be sure to peruse the excellent website, www.saucemagazine.com; it's an invaluable tool when making St. Louis dining plans. *Alive Magazine* (www.alivemag.com) is a luxury lifestyle publication. Available for free at many area locations, *Alive* focuses on the trends and desires of St. Louis's young and upwardly mobile. *St. Louis Magazine* (www.stlmag.com) is a subscription-based monthly with plenty of great information and increasingly substantive reporting. Beautiful photography and an exhaustive events calendar make *St. Louis Magazine* perfect for visitors.

St. Louis has a strong cultural history, and several small-scale art and literary magazines operate here. The poetry quarterly **River Styx,** published since the early 1970s, was one of the first journals to print such poets as Czeslaw Milosz, Yusef Komunyakaa, Howard Nemerov, and Derek Walcott. In nearby Columbia, **The Missouri Review** (www.missourireview.com) continues to enjoy its stellar national reputation; the *Review* publishes fiction, poetry, plays, essays, and author interviews. The award-winning **Boulevard** (www.richardburgin.net) is based at Saint Louis University and has printed works by such luminaries as Joyce Carol Oates, John Updike, Charles Simic, and Philip Levine. **Mesh** covers the latest happenings at the Contemporary Art Museum St. Louis and is available with a one-year museum membership. **52nd City** (www.52ndcity.com), a relative newcomer on the art-mag block,

is a collaborative venture between local artists and writers. Each issue of the quarterly is accompanied by a launch party that brings together young, creative St. Louisans.

Radio and TV

St. Louis carries affiliates of every major television network. **KETC** (www.ketc.org), the city's PBS station, has been providing educational and community-focused programming to residents for more than 50 years. **STLTV** (http://stlouis.missouri.org/citygov/stltv/index.htm) is the city's oldest community television station; it often broadcasts programs about cultural and entertainment options in St. Louis.

KDHX, the not-for-profit media organization that provides St. Louis's excellent community radio, also operates public-access stations on channels 21 and 22.

St. Louis has many radio stations; a complete listing and links to each station's site can be found at www.ontheradio.net/metro/Saint_Louis_MO.aspx. A combined listing of television and radio stations is available at www.macrosign.com/stlouis/tv.htm. Some of the more popular area stations include **KDHX 88.1 FM** (noncommercial community radio, with both talk and music programming), **KMOX 1120 AM** (news and talk), **KFNS 590 AM** (sports news), **KFUO 99.1 FM** (classical), **WSIE 88.7 FM** (jazz), **KTRS 550 AM** (sports—all Cardinals games are broadcast here), **KWMU 90.7 FM** (St. Louis's NPR affiliate) **KSHE 94.7 FM** (classic rock), **WHHL 104.1 FM** (hip-hop), **KPNT The Point 105.7 FM** (alternative rock), **KWUR 90.3 FM** (college eclectic), and **KFTK 97.1 FM** (news and talk).

PUBLIC LIBRARIES

The St. Louis Public Library is a full-service public library that, with the help of 15 satellite branches throughout the city, provides invaluable information to a diverse array of residents and visitors. The SLPL educates its community not just through an enormous catalog of books, music, videos, and databases, but also through free events, exhibits, and programs. Educational offerings are abundant and eclectic; the SLPL hosts seminars on such topics as traditional Japanese flower arranging, classic motorcycle design, and local bass fishing.

Central Library (1301 Olive St., 314/241-2288), SLPL's main branch, is one of the city's great architectural treasures. Designed by renowned architect Cass Gilbert and dedicated in 1912, the Italian Renaissance-inspired building features beautiful stained-glass windows, Tennessee marble, elaborate hand-carved moldings, painted ceilings, and glass floors. Today, this busy hub houses several special research divisions within its walls, including a fine-arts library, pop library, rare-books library, and books-on-tape library. The genealogy department here is one of the best in the country; this library-within-a-library is staffed with specialists working to trace and preserve the history of St. Louis through the lineages of its families.

Many of the genealogy department's resources are now available online at library's main website (www.slpl.org), alongside its extensive catalog and an "electronic city hall" that provides access to local government information. Those interested in doing business in St. Louis will find this meticulously organized history of current and past legislation particularly useful. Also of great use is the St. Louis Area Studies Center, which brings together pamphlets, periodicals, and other clippings on the history of the city.

All of the SLPL's satellite locations offer an up-to-date selection of books, CDs, and films. Nearly every neighborhood boasts a library branch. The **Schlafly** (225 N. Euclid Ave., 314/367-4120) location in the heart of the Central West End and the **Buder** (4401 Hampton Ave., 314/352-2900) location in South City offer beautiful, brand-new facilities and convenient parking. The **Carpenter** (3309 S. Grand Blvd., 314/772-6586) branch is just a five-minute walk from South Grand's busy main drag, and the elegant old-world building underwent a complete renovation in 2007. Visit www.slpl.org for a complete list of library locations and events.

MAJOR BANKS

St. Louis is home to several locally owned banks, and many St. Louisans choose to keep their accounts and investments at these institutions. One of the best-known is Southwest Bank (visitors might recognize the branch at Kingshighway and Southwest from the Steve McQueen vehicle *The Great St. Louis Bank Robbery*). Travelers need not worry about finding a branch of their home institution; US Bank, Regions Bank, Bank of America, Commerce Bank, and other financial institutions maintain offices and ATMs here. If you use an ATM that belongs to a bank other than your own, be prepared to pay $2–5 in fees. (Fees are particularly steep at the airport and in entertainment districts.)

PLACES OF WORSHIP

Today, St. Louis is home to nearly 400,000 people from diverse religious and ethnic backgrounds. Nearly all of the world's religions are represented here, but from the time of its founding in the 1700s, the city has been predominantly Christian. Many consider St. Louis a "Catholic town," thanks to its deep French roots, its strong communities of Irish-Catholic and Italian-Catholic immigrants, and its excellent Jesuit schools.

In 1827, the widely read German travel writer Godfried Duden published an account in which he compared the Mississippi and Missouri River Valleys to Germany's famous Rhine River Valley. Inspired by what he saw, Duden urged his countrymen to settle where the two great rivers met, and many German Catholics did. As America received its first large wave of immigrants in the 1840s, hundreds of thousands came to St. Louis. Cities such as Boston, New York, and Philadelphia were considered "tolerant" of Catholics, whereas St. Louis truly welcomed them. Within a few decades—thanks to the large number of Catholic immigrants—St. Louis's population had doubled.

Today, there are more than 339 parishes in the St. Louis Archdiocese, including the **Cathedral Basilica** (4431 Lindell Blvd., 314/373-8200, www.cathedralstl.org), **Saint Pius V** in South City (3310 Grand Blvd., 314/772-1525, www.stpiusv.org), and **Little Flower Church** in Richmond Heights (1264 Arch Terrace, 314/645-1445, www.little -flower-parish.org). For a complete directory, visit the archdiocese's website at www.archstl.org.

Godfried Duden's exhortation evidently made an impact on Germany's Lutherans, as well. The **Missouri Synod Lutheran Church**—a denomination that split off from the Catholic church during Martin Luther's reformation—thrives here. The Synod's headquarters, Concordia Lutheran Seminary, and Concordia Publishing House are all located in St. Louis, as are dozens of Lutheran congregations. To view the complete list of these churches, including the city's oldest (Trinity Lutheran Church in Soulard, 1805 S. 8th St., 314/231-4092, www.historic trinity.org) and largest (Concordia Lutheran Church in Kirkwood, 505 S. Kirkwood Rd., 314/822-7772), visit www.lcms.org.

The St. Louis area is also home to a large Jewish population. At the turn of the 20th century, the Jewish Federation of St. Louis formed to help meet the needs of new immigrants. Now, more than 100 years later, the Jewish community continues to expand in both size and influence. One of the city's largest and most culturally active temples is the progressive **Central Reform Congregation** (5020 Waterman Blvd., 314/361-1564, www.centralreform.org). Information about other congregations (as well as an events calendar and a wealth of community news) can be found at the Jewish Federation's website, www.jewish instlouis.org. The **Jewish Community Center** in Creve Coeur (2 Millstone Campus Dr., 314/432-5700, www.jccstl.com) provides educational, recreational, and cultural programming—including consistently excellent theatrical productions—to people of all faiths.

The African Methodist Episcopal (A.M.E.) Church is a vital spiritual and cultural wellspring for many of St. Louis's African American residents. The A.M.E. church is the nation's oldest historically black denomination, and congregants are known for their faith-based altruism within the community. St. Louis congregations include **Ward Chapel** (2840 Locust St.,

314/652-1990) and the **St. James African Methodist Episcopal Church** (314/371-0687, www.stjamesstl.org).

St. Louis has a relatively small but active Muslim population; the heart of St. Louis's Islamic community is the **West County Islamic Center** in Manchester (517 Weidman Rd., 636/394-7878, www.islamic foundationstlouis.org). This important and architecturally stunning complex is home to the large **Daar-ul-Islam mosque** and the **Al-Salam Day School.** Other Muslim congregations include the **Masjid Al-Mu'minun** (1434 N. Grand Blvd., 314/531-5414) and the **Masjid Qooba** (1925 Allen Ave., 314/771-3548), a South City mosque that provides assistance to Muslim refugees.

Those interested in an ecumenical, humanist service should visit the **Ethical Society** (9001 Clayton Rd., 314/991-0955, www.ethicalstl.org). This outstanding community resource offers lectures and seminars by noted educators, scientists, and social reformers. The society's motto, "Deed Before Creed," emphasizes its desire to put good works before doctrine.

Hindus in St. Louis are well served by the **Hindu Temple** in Ballwin (725 Weidman Rd., 636/230-3300, www.hindutemple stlouis.org), which offers a full complement of services and activities. Many Buddhists congregate at the **Thai Buddhist Temple** in Florissant (890 Lindsay Ln., 314/839-3115, www.stlthaitemple.org), and a **Baha'i information center** was recently established in the heart of Webster Groves (30 W. Lockwood Ave., 314/963-1415).

RELOCATION

Thinking about making the Gateway City your permanent home? You can begin your research before you even arrive in St. Louis. You'll find a compendium of relocation resources via the city government's community information network (http://stlouis.missouri .org/housing/resources/index.html). The site offers information about everything from car registration to child care, from finding a doctor to finding a job. Newcomers may also be interested in the exhaustive collection of links compiled by the **St. Louis Rehabbers Club** (www.rehabbersclub.org/newbies .html). The St. Louis page at About.com (http://stlouis.about.com) offers moving-service advice, cost-of-living statistics, and a list of real-estate and employment agencies. While the About.com page can be useful, do know that, unlike the two aforementioned sites, it is supported by advertisers and may present biased information.

To learn more about the city's real estate and neighborhoods, visit **STL Agent** (www .stlagent.com), a great home-buyer's resource that offers guided tours designed to introduce new residents to St. Louis's diverse properties. STL Agent even sends out free "relocation packages" by mail—just be prepared for a sales pitch or two.

Finding a Job

The *St. Louis Post-Dispatch,* like any other large daily paper, offers job listings. The paper keeps its print classified section fairly small, so job seekers will fare better by visiting www.stltoday.com, where the *Post-Dispatch* lists hundreds of jobs.

Those seeking service-industry jobs would do well to peruse the *Riverfront Times* (www.riverfronttimes.com), St. Louis's alternative weekly paper. Like the *Post-Dispatch,* the *Riverfront Times* lists the bulk of its positions online. Job hunters can also find valuable information through St. Louis Employment Links (www.stlouis employmentlinks.com), a compendium of local recruiters, staffing, and employment agencies. Many St. Louis employers use Craigslist—particularly when seeking applicants for creative jobs such as marketing, writing, or graphic design. Local government positions are posted at http://stlcin.missouri .org/OnlineJob/jobs.cfm.

In addition to conducting research, jobseekers should consider joining professional organizations with ties to their field. The Internet-based St. Louis Ad Club (www .adclubstlouis.org), for example, is a great resource for researching and networking in the city's advertising industry. The St. Louis Metropolitan Medical Society (www.slmms .org) is a well-regarded Web community for those in the medical field—the city's largest, fastest-growing employment sector. Find other useful networking groups (as well as labor organizations) by performing a search at stlouis.citysearch.com.

Some favorite employers in the St. Louis area include Anheuser-Busch (lauded for the long-term employment it offers workers and for its great benefits packages), SBC (for its excellent benefits, which also extend to employees' domestic partners), Ameren, AG Edwards, BJC HealthCare, and Washington University.

Housing

Roommate matching services (such as www .roommates.com and www.roomiematch .com) offer thousands of listings, but the hits for St. Louis are relatively few. Newcomers seeking a roommate are likely to have better luck on Craigslist—or by checking out the bulletin boards at colleges and coffee shops.

If the national roommate-search sites don't really provide an accurate picture of St. Louis, then the same must be said for the advertiser-run apartment sites. Visits to sites such as www.apartments.com and www.stlaptfinder.com will yield many listings for complexes—but, in reality, the nicest and most affordable apartments in St. Louis are often in two- and four-family flats. You'll find these spacious abodes throughout the city, and many are privately owned and leased for less than their market value. Do a search on Craigslist (most apartment listings are accompanied by pictures), and then set up appointments. You may also want to take a walking tour of areas that appeal to you. Landlords with property in some of the more desirable city neighborhoods, such as Shaw and Tower Grove, simply advertise with a sign.

Apartment-seekers who know little about St. Louis or just want some extra advice will appreciate the one-on-one attention provided by Stl-Apartments.com (www .stl-apartments.com). This locally run service matches renters with apartments and makes every effort to find housing that suits a person's needs and preferences. Best of all, the service is free. **Red Brick** (314/361-7067, www.redbrickmanagement.com) and **Front Door LLC** (314/446-4501, www.frontdoorstl .com) are St. Louis's largest propertymanagement companies, and both broker nice, updated apartments in the city's most desirable areas. Comprehensive apartment listings can be found in the *Apartment Guide,* which is published quarterly and distributed at local retailers.

Those interested in exploring the St. Louis real-estate market certainly should. The city is known for its abundant, affordable housing stock and beautifully distinct neighborhoods. Newcomers who want to work with a real-estate agency should begin at the St. Louis Association of Realtors' website (www.stlrealtors.com). Here, you'll find a complete listing of local agents and agencies, as well as an abundance of useful sales statistics. Favorite agencies include locally owned **Coldwell Banker Gundaker** (www.cbgundaker.com) and **Janet McAfee Inc.** (314/997-4800, www.janetmcafee.com). Both are popular agencies with strong reputations, sound financial relationships, and numerous properties throughout the region.

Information about grants, housing tax credits, and assistance programs meant for home buyers can be found at the city's housing and development site (www.hud.gov). The St. Louis Rehabber's Club (www.rehabbersclub.org) is also an outstanding resource for potential home buyers—this nonprofit offers the perspective of some of the city's most preservation-minded homeowners and developers.

RESOURCES

Suggested Reading

HISTORY AND GENERAL INFORMATION

Gordon, Colin. *Mapping Decline: St. Louis and the Fate of the American City.* University of Pennsylvania Press, 2008. Gordon's brand-new book is both a thorough explanation of St. Louis' modern history and a harsh indictment of its politics. This story of urban decline isn't exactly fodder for the Visitors & Convention Bureau, but it is a brilliant and vital work nonetheless. Gordon's use of maps is quite effective.

Hernon, Peter and Terry Ganey. *Under the Influence: The Unauthorized Story of the Anheuser-Busch Dynasty.* Avon Books, 1992. This is a wonderfully compelling (if at times breathless) history of the Busch family. *Under the Influence* has something for history buffs, true-crime junkies, and mystery lovers alike. A great read that serves as a nice companion piece to broader histories of St. Louis.

McNulty, Elizabeth. *St. Louis Then and Now.* Thunder Bay Press, 2000. This beautiful coffee-table book reveals St. Louis's history through its iconic structures. *St. Louis Then and Now* might be of particular interest to visitors who take a Downtown architecture tour; the photos reveal the former lives of Downtown's many rehabbed lofts and condos.

Primm, James Neal. *Lion of the Valley: St. Louis, Missouri, 1764–1980.* University of Missouri Press, 1982. Primm's exhaustive history of St. Louis is one of the best resources available. Visitors seeking to truly understand the city's complicated past are wise to pick up *Lion of the Valley.* The clear writing and abundant photos make this a must-have book for urban historians and tourists alike. If you only read one book about St. Louis's rich history, make it this one.

LITERATURE AND FICTION

Angelou, Maya. *I Know Why the Caged Bird Sings.* Random House, 1969. St. Louis native Maya Angelou is the author of some of the most beautiful, lyrical prose in the American canon. Maya's autobiographical *I Know Why the Caged Bird Sings* tells the story of her difficult upbringing in Arkansas and St. Louis.

Elkin, Stanley. *George Mills.* E.P. Dutton, 1982. For years Elkin taught at Washington University in St. Louis. Elkin's poignant, acerbic, and downright funny observations are on display in *George Mills,* which traces the lives of people named George Mills throughout human history—including a furniture mover from St. Louis.

Franzen, Jonathan. *The Twenty-Seventh City.* Farrar, Straus & Giroux, 1988. While not as critically acclaimed as his National Book Award-winning *The Corrections,* Jonathan Franzen's *The Twenty-Seventh City* is a fun, fascinating look at the seedy side of St. Louis politics. Webster Groves native Franzen writes about the Midwest with a mixture of affection and derision, and *Twenty-Seventh City* shows the stark contrast between abandoned city neighborhoods and the affluent enclaves of St. Louis County.

Hamilton, Laurell K. The *Anita Blake: Vampire Hunter* series. Jove Books. Hamilton's long-running *Anita Blake* series (she's currently on the 17th installment) is a hit with supernatural-thriller fans. Each of the books is set in a parallel St. Louis, where the streets are besieged by vampires and werewolves.

Pearson, Ridley. *Cut and Run*. Hyperion, 2006. Affable St. Louis author Ridley Pearson has found incredible success with his crime novels—but not many take place in the River City. Enter *Cut and Run,* which focuses on a U.S. marshal from St. Louis. The storyline is standard crime thriller, but Pearson's smart literary style elevates the writing. A quick airplane read for visitors making the journey to St. Louis.

Williams, Tennessee. *The Glass Menagerie.* Premiered in 1944. Available in paperback from New Directions Publishing Corporation, 1999. Williams' legendary, autobiographical play is the perfect companion piece for a trip to St. Louis's Central West End and old Gaslight Square areas.

Internet Resources

GENERAL INFORMATION

About.com: St. Louis
www.stlouis.about.com

This St. Louis-centric page is a fairly new addition to About.com's compendium of local expertise. While it doesn't contain as much information as About.com's more well-established city pages, it *does* have some nice insider info about visiting St. Louis on the cheap and finding fun things to do with the family. The frequently updated front page is a great place to find up-to-the-minute event listings.

City of St. Louis Community Information Network
http://stlouis.missouri.org

The city's official website is perhaps more useful to residents than to visitors. Still, there is some great background reading to be found here. Of particular note is the History & Heritage section, which is rich with urban-planning and genealogy documents.

Explore St. Louis
www.explorestlouis.com

Explore St. Louis is the official site of the St. Louis Convention & Visitors Commission. The site received a total revamping in the past year or so, and now it is both well designed and super helpful. This is a great place to find hotel information, restaurant listings, kid-friendly events, and more. The site also provides information for business travelers and devotes a page to LGBT visitors.

International Institute of St. Louis
www.iistl.org

This is the website for an absolutely vital St. Louis institution. The International Institute provides invaluable support for the city's immigrant communities, offering everything from English classes to job-placement services. Visitors will find information on events and volunteering opportunities, as well as plenty of background information on the institute itself.

St. Louis Guide
www.stlouis.com

The layout of this St. Louis tourist site practically screams "Visit our sponsors!" But there are still plenty of good listings here, and the site does a nice job of collecting and organizing dozens of helpful links. It is recommended that you double-check restaurant opinions on a more objective website, such as www.saucemagazine.com.

St. Louis Indymedia
www.stlimc.org

St. Louis Indymedia is a progressive site covering local and regional news. All information is filtered through a liberal lens, and news items tend to focus on key human-rights and environmental issues. This is a great resource for visitors looking for insight into St. Louis's underground sociopolitical culture. The Indymedia group formed in protest to the World Trade Organization (WTO).

STL Punk
www.stlpunk.com

This punk-scene stalwart promises a website overhaul "coming soon." But even if it doesn't have all the bells and whistles of some sites, STL Punk is a great place for information on everything from concerts to punk-rock boutiques and tattoo parlors. It's also a sounding board for up-and-coming rockers, who can post their songs to the site and solicit comments from listeners.

Toasted Rav
www.toastedrav.com

Toasted Rav (named after that legendary St. Louis appetizer, toasted ravioli) is a fabulous new site that's full of reviews, forums, advice, and photos. Created by (and directed toward) younger residents and visitors, Toasted Rav is the perfect place to find a nightclub recommendation or to get the scoop on a trendy new boutique.

EVENT LISTINGS

The Partnership for Downtown St. Louis Events Calendar
www.downtownstl.org/EventsCalendar_21.aspx

The Partnership for Downtown St. Louis provides a nice, straightforward presentation of local events. Because the Partnership focuses on the ongoing revitalization of downtown, most of the listed events take place near the city center. This makes the website a worthwhile stop for visitors staying downtown.

Riverfront Times Events Calendar
www.riverfronttimes.com/events

This is one of the best places to find local goings-on. The *Riverfront Times,* the city's alt-weekly, organizes events in an easily navigable fashion. You'll find mainstream listings here, but also plenty of under-the-radar events. Many of the listings also include snappy editorials from the *RFT* staff.

St. Louis Post-Dispatch Events Calendar
www.stltoday.com/calendar

St. Louis's daily newspaper produces this online events calendar. The events featured here are mainstream activities—think art exhibits, symphony concerts and kid-friendly festivals.

ST. LOUIS BLOGS

St. Louis's blog culture seems to grow richer and more expansive with each passing week. There are thousands of St. Louis–area bloggers. The very best shed new light on the Gateway City, either by digging deeper than some of the area's journalists or by offering excellent commentary.

ArchPundit
www.blogsaintlouis.com

The eponymous blogger ArchPundit does a nice job rounding up local, regional, and state politics. ArchPundit's left-leaning, Democratic perspective makes the blog particularly popular in St. Louis—widely considered a blue island in a red state.

Built St. Louis
www.builtstlouis.net/arch.html

Built St. Louis is a beautiful, passionately written blog that makes a fine case for the future of urban St. Louis. This blog tracks the history of some of the city's most important buildings. It also issues warnings about buildings that are about to fall to the wrecking ball—either because of neglect or because of the city government's seemingly endless obsession with eminent domain.

The Ecology of Absence
http://ecoabsence.blogspot.com

The Ecology of Absence focuses on the tragedies and triumphs of the city's north side. Blogger Michael Allen posts beautiful photos and well-researched information about many of the area's historic buildings.

52nd City
http://blog.52ndcity.com

The blog's name is a tongue-in-cheek reference to St. Louis's standing among the nation's cities, but the blog itself is full of love for STL. Written by and for a young, hip group of St. Louisans, 52nd City often offers great insight about local politics. Plus, the site is frequently updated to include events—making 52nd City a valuable resource for visitors.

Urban Review STL
www.urbanreviewstl.com

Steve Patterson's Urban Review STL is a must-read for local politicians and journalists. Patterson takes to the street (an avid cyclist, he's usually on two wheels) to expose urban blight and make recommendations for a healthier, more livable city. Patterson's devotion to the city is inspiring—and if he ever sounds pissed off, it's likely very justified.

Viva El Birdos
www.vivaelbirdos.com

Even for non-rabid Cardinals fans, Viva El Birdos is a fantastic read. Site founder L. Boros has assembled a gifted team of sports writers, and the site's good sense of humor recalls sports-blog powerhouse Deadspin. com. Sabermetrics fans will find plenty to geek out about.

Index

Restaurants Index

Nightlife Index

Shops Index

Hotels Index

www.moon.com

DESTINATIONS | ACTIVITIES | BLOGS | MAPS | BOOKS

MOON.COM is all new, and ready to help plan your next trip! Filled with fresh trip ideas and strategies, author interviews, informative blogs, a detailed map library, and descriptions of all the Moon guidebooks, Moon.com is all you need to get out and explore the world—or even places in your own backyard. As always, when you travel with Moon, expect an experience that is uncommon and truly unique.

MAP SYMBOLS

Expressway	**C**	Highlight	✗	Airfield	♨	Golf Course
Primary Road	○	City/Town	✈	Airport	**P**	Parking Area
Secondary Road	◉	State Capital	▲	Mountain	⏢	Archaeological Site
Unpaved Road	⊛	National Capital	✦	Unique Natural Feature	⌂	Church
Trail	★	Point of Interest			⛽	Gas Station
Ferry	•	Accommodation	☂	Waterfall		Glacier
Railroad	▼	Restaurant/Bar	▲	Park		Mangrove
Pedestrian Walkway	▪	Other Location	▯	Trailhead		Reef
Stairs	Λ	Campground	🍇	Winery		Swamp

CONVERSION TABLES

°C = (°F - 32) / 1.8
°F = (°C x 1.8) + 32
1 inch = 2.54 centimeters (cm)
1 foot = 0.304 meters (m)
1 yard = 0.914 meters
1 mile = 1.6093 kilometers (km)
1 km = 0.6214 miles
1 fathom = 1.8288 m
1 chain = 20.1168 m
1 furlong = 201.168 m
1 acre = 0.4047 hectares
1 sq km = 100 hectares
1 sq mile = 2.59 square km
1 ounce = 28.35 grams
1 pound = 0.4536 kilograms
1 short ton = 0.90718 metric ton
1 short ton = 2,000 pounds
1 long ton = 1.016 metric tons
1 long ton = 2,240 pounds
1 metric ton = 1,000 kilograms
1 quart = 0.94635 liters
1 US gallon = 3.7854 liters
1 Imperial gallon = 4.5459 liters
1 nautical mile = 1.852 km

MOON ST. LOUIS

Avalon Travel
a member of the Perseus Books Group
1700 Fourth Street
Berkeley, CA 94710, USA
www.moon.com

Editor: Elizabeth Hollis Hansen
Series Manager: Erin Raber
Copy Editor: Deana Shields
Graphics Coordinator: Kathryn Osgood
Production Coordinators: Darren Alessi,
    Nicole Schultz
Cover Designer: Kathryn Osgood
Map Editor: Albert Angulo
Cartographers: Chris Markiewicz,
    Lohnes & Wright, Jon Twena

ISBN: 978-1-59880-174-3
ISSN: 1947-5810

Printing History
1st Edition – June 2009
5 4 3 2 1

Text © 2009 by Brooke S. Foster.
Maps © 2009 by Avalon Travel.
All rights reserved.

Front cover photo: Missouri, St. Louis, Gateway Arch, low angle view © Randy Wells/getty
Title page photo: Missouri Botanical Garden © Missouri Botanical Garden

Interior color photos Page 2 left Shaw Nature Reserve © Missouri Botanical Garden, middle Gateway Arch © National Park Service, Jefferson National Expansion Memorial, right Left Bank © Amy Ferguson; Page 19 thumbnail, butterfly © Missouri Botanical Garden; bottom, City Museum's "MonstroCity" © City Museum; Page 20 © Holly Gitlin; Page 21 top © Missouri Botanical Garden; bottom © Brooke Foster; Page 22 © National Park Service, Jefferson National Expansion Memorial; Page 23 © Amy Ferguson; Page 24 © Ray Meibaum, Saint Louis Zoo

Printed in the United States by RR Donnelley

KEEPING CURRENT

If you have a favorite gem you'd like to see included in the next edition, or see anything that needs updating, clarification, or correction, please drop us a line. Send your comments via email to feedback@moon.com, or use the address above.